The Beauty and Glory
of Christ

The Beauty and Glory
of Christ

Edited by
Joel R. Beeke

Reformation Heritage Books
Grand Rapids, Michigan

Published by
Reformation Heritage Books
2965 Leonard St. NE
Grand Rapids, MI 49525
616-977-0889 / Fax 616-285-3246
e-mail: orders@heritagebooks.org
website: www.heritagebooks.org

Printed in the United States of America
11 12 13 14 15 16/10 9 8 7 6 5 4 3 2 1

Library of Congress Cataloging-in-Publication Data

The beauty and glory of Christ / edited by Joel R. Beeke.
    p. cm.
 Includes bibliographical references.
 ISBN 978-1-60178-142-0 (hardcover : alk. paper) 1. Jesus Christ—Person and offices. I. Beeke, Joel R., 1952-
 BT203.B433 2011
 232'.8—dc23
                          2011019620

For additional Reformed literature, both new and used, request a free book list from Reformation Heritage Books at the above address.

With heartfelt appreciation for

Henk Kleyn

lover of Christ, His beauty and glory;
loved for his large servant-heart by all the faculty, staff, and students
of Puritan Reformed Theological Seminary; and
the most loyal and best Director of Admissions and Registrar
a seminary could wish for

Contents

Preface   ix

Christ's Beauty Prophesied and Typified
1. The Beauty of God's Servant — *David Murray*   3
2. The Song of David's Son — *Iain D. Campbell*   15
3. "He Is Altogether Lovely" — *Iain D. Campbell*   29

Christ's Glory from Bethlehem to Golgotha
4. The Glory of Christ's Victorious
    Incarnation — *Richard D. Phillips*   45
5. The Glory of Christ's Parables — *Gerald M. Bilkes*   59
6. Jesus: Master of Storms — *David Carmichael*   75
7. Jesus: Master of Stress — *David Carmichael*   87
8. The Glory of Christ's Victorious Death — *Albert N. Martin* . . . 101

Christ in Historical Theology and Everyday Life
9. Glorying in the Imputed Righteousness
    of Christ — *Richard D. Phillips* 121
10. Thomas Goodwin on Christ's Beautiful Heart — *Joel R. Beeke* . . 135
11. "The True Knowledge of Jesus Christ and Him Crucified":
    Christology in Marrow Theology — *William VanDoodewaard* 155
12. Christology: Calvin, Kuyper, and Politics — *Ray Pennings* 169
13. The Daily Challenge of Christ-Centered Living — *Ray Pennings* 187

Christ's Glorious Exaltation
14. The Glory of Christ's Victorious Resurrection — *Albert N. Martin* 205
15. The Investiture of the Lamb — *James Grier* 221
16. Hallelujah to the Triumphant Christ — *James Grier* 229

Contributors 239

Preface

At Puritan Reformed Theological Seminary, the beauty and glory of Christ evokes our strongest emotions and deepest convictions. By the Spirit's grace, we longed to have the mind and soul of each attendee of our 2010 conference—including ourselves—saturated with this glorious theme. For Christ is the hope of our glory and the glory of our hope.

I am convinced that to be truly evangelical, one must embrace doctrinally and experientially the Reformation's major tenets: *sola gratia, sola fide, solus Christus, sola scriptura,* and *soli Deo Gloria.* Is not our salvation based on Scripture alone, through Christ alone, received by faith alone, worked by grace alone, to the glory of God alone? At the heart of these stalwart truths is *solus Christus* (Christ alone). "Christ alone" is our life and salvation, our beauty and glory. Christ Jesus is the beautiful, glorious Savior and Lord, whose "legs are as pillars of marble" (Song 5:15), for He is strong and steadfast and is "altogether lovely" (v. 16). As Thomas Brooks said, "Christ is lovely, Christ is very lovely, Christ is most lovely, Christ is always lovely, Christ is altogether lovely."[1] Brooks also said, "Christ is the most sparkling diamond in the ring of glory."[2]

Many people from all over North America made the journey to Grand Rapids to be nourished by God's Word. The conference exceeded our expectations. The messages delivered by various men of God were a spiritual feast. As they led us into the green pastures of God's Word, they set before us the unsearchable riches of the Lord

---

1. "Heaven on Earth," in *The Complete Works of Thomas Brooks,* ed. Alexander B. Grosart (Edinburgh: James Nichol, 1866), 2:476.
2. Brooks, "The Unsearchable Riches of Christ," in *Works,* 3:57n3.

Jesus Christ. In expounding the written Word of God, they displayed the beauty and glory of the Living Word—the Son of the Father's good pleasure and His unspeakable gift to us.

On Thursday, August 26, David Murray preached on the prophecy of Isaiah, showing us the beauty and glory of the Father's Servant. The Scottish minister David Carmichael took us to the Gospels to show us Christ as the "Master of Storms," then later presented Jesus as the "Master of Stress" during His inexpressible suffering prior to and on the cross. Another minister from Scotland, Iain Campbell, spoke about the beauty and glory of Christ as displayed in the Song of Solomon. I offered some insights of the great Puritan theologian, Thomas Goodwin, regarding the beautiful heart of Christ, who ministers to His church as her exalted Mediator at the Father's right hand.

On Friday, Richard Phillips spoke about the preciousness of Christ as the incarnate Word of God. Jerry Bilkes then gave us helpful insights on Christ's parables. Al Martin proclaimed the beauty and glory of Christ in His death and resurrection. James Grier concluded the day by giving us a glimpse into the throne room of heaven, where we beheld the beautiful Lamb of God, to whom has been given all power in heaven and on earth.

On Saturday, Ray Pennings talked about our obligation to display the beauty and glory of Christ by living Christ-centered lives. James Grier ended the conference by drawing attention to the triumphant Christ and stirring us to say with the church of all ages, "Come, Lord Jesus, come quickly!"

Seminar addresses were also delivered by William VanDoodewaard on "Christology in Marrow Theology," Richard Phillips on "Glorying in the Imputed Righteousness of Christ," and Ray Pennings on "Christology: Calvin, Kuyper, and Politics."

The conference affirmed that our beautiful and glorious Christ is the Father's unspeakable gift to us. We are grateful to Chris Hanna and the staff of PRTS for organizing this conference, which proved to be one of the best I have ever attended. If you weren't able to join us, you can do so now belatedly through the pages of this book. In editing this volume, which is primarily designed for educated laypeople and ministers, I have let the speakers decide to what degree to retain the spoken style in their respective chapters, which explains why some chapters are a bit more formal than others. Generally speaking, the seminar papers are written in a slightly more academic style.

I heartily thank all the speakers for their diligent work on their excellent addresses. Taken together, these addresses provide an informative and heart-warming book about our precious Savior. It is our prayer that God will bless this volume to enhance your walk with Christ.

I thank Rebecca VanDoodewaard and Kate DeVries for their most helpful editorial assistance on the entire volume, Stan McKenzie for his meticulous proofreading, Gary and Linda den Hollander for their able typesetting and proofreading, Amy Zevenbergen for another great cover design, and Bartel Elshout for assisting with part of this preface. Thanks, too, to Lois Haley for transcribing two of the messages and to Phyllis TenElshof for assisting me in moving them from transcripts to manuscripts. I also thank my amazingly patient and dedicated wife, Mary, and my cherished children, Calvin, Esther, and Lydia, who without complaining allow me the extra time needed to work on producing sound literature like this book.

As I write, we are eagerly anticipating this year's conference—August 25–27, 2011, at the same site, the Prince Conference Center, Calvin College, in Grand Rapids, Michigan—on the beauty and glory of the Holy Spirit. The messages will address a variety of ways in which the Holy Spirit leads, guides, convicts, and comforts believers. Please join us. You'll be glad you did.

—Joel R. Beeke

CHRIST'S BEAUTY PROPHESIED AND TYPIFIED

PART 1

CHAPTER 1

The Beauty of God's Servant

David Murray

"In these passages we are not far from the highest New Testament Christology, such as that found in the fourth Gospel."[1] Henri Blocher refers to the so-called servant songs—although there is no evidence they were ever sung—in Isaiah 42:1–9; 49:1–6; 50:4–9; and 52:13–53:12. Some have also argued for a fifth servant song in Isaiah 61:1–4. That would be a fitting climax to the series, as the speaker there has many parallels with the servant and Christ confirms its fulfillment in Him (Luke 4:16–21). However, that passage is more usually understood as Isaiah speaking autobiographically, although he does so in such a way that he prophetically foreshadows the person and work of Christ.

We shall survey these four passages and ask two questions about the servant of these songs: first, who is he? And second, what is he like? We shall answer these two questions under two subject headings: the identity of the servant and the beauty of the servant.

The Identity of the Servant

The first question we must ask is, who is the servant? There are four main answers to our question:

- The servant is Israel.
- The servant is Isaiah.
- The servant is a second Moses.
- The servant is a prophecy of Jesus Christ.

Let us look at the strengths and weaknesses of each option.

---

1. Henri Blocher, *Songs of the Servant* (Downers Grove, Ill.: IVP, 1975), 55.

The Servant Is Israel

Some say that the servant was the nation of Israel, which suffered on behalf of the Gentile nations. A refinement of this view is that it was the faithful remnant in Israel. Arguments in favor of this identification are:

1. Isaiah addresses and describes Israel as the Lord's servant throughout (cf. 41:8–9; 42:19; 43:10; 44:1–2, 21; 45:4; 48:20).

2. The second servant song calls the servant "Israel" (49:3).

3. Israel and the servant are described similarly:

- "Whom I uphold" (41:10; 42:1)
- "My chosen" (42:1; 43:20; 45:4)
- "Formed you in the womb" (44:2, 24; 49:1)
- "Named" (43:1; 49:1)
- "A light to the nations" (49:6; 51:4).

4. Just as Ezekiel portrays Israel's history as a suffering, death, and resurrection (Ezek. 37), so Isaiah similarly portrays the servant in Isaiah 53:10ff. As the psalmist describes Israel as a sheep led to the slaughter (Ps. 44:22), so Isaiah describes the servant (Isa. 53:7).

5. Israel's "death" blessed the nations (Isa. 49:6) by the witness of faithful Israelites in exile (e.g., Daniel, Esther, Mordecai).

Objections to the view that Israel is the servant are the following:

1. The servant suffers and dies despite his sinlessness (50:5; 53:9), whereas Isaiah stresses that the people of Israel are sinners and suffer for their sin (40:2; 42:18–25; 43:22–28). Isaiah also describes the faithful remnant as sinners (43:22; 46:3; 48:1).

2. Although the servant figure is corporate Israel in other chapters of Isaiah, the chapters containing the servant songs all appear to be about an individual. That is how the Ethiopian eunuch understood the passage (Acts 8:34).

3. Isaiah 49:5–6 distinguishes Israel from the servant (see also 43:3; 53:8).

4. Whenever Isaiah speaks on behalf of the people of Israel, he uses "we," "our," "us," and usually introduces this very abruptly (1:9; 16:6; 42:24). In Isaiah 53:1ff, as Isaiah uses "we," "our," "us," without identifying the speakers, he speaks on behalf of Israel. Therefore, when Isaiah goes on to speak of the servant as a "he," it cannot be Israel.

5. Scripture portrays Israel as sheep going astray (Ps. 57:7–10; 119:176; Jer. 50:6), which is consistent with Isaiah 53:6.

6. Isaiah characterizes Israel as the blind and deaf servant (Isa. 42:19), but the servant of the servant songs is the perfect listener (Isa. 50:4).

The Servant Is Isaiah

If the servant is not Israel, then perhaps it is Isaiah himself. The Ethiopian eunuch also mentioned this as a possibility. Arguments in favor of this are:

1. Isaiah 20:3 explicitly identifies Isaiah as "my servant."

2. The servant of the servant songs speaks in the first person as "my...I...mine" (49:1).

3. The servant suffers physical affliction and rejection (42:4; 50:6–9; 53:3–12), just like Isaiah.

4. The servant has prophetic characteristics: he intercedes (53:12), teaches God's law (42:4; 49:2), and is endowed with the Holy Spirit (42:1).

Objections to the view that the servant is Isaiah are the following:

1. There are prophetic traits in the servant, but some things do not fit a prophetic identity. For example, the servant is commissioned to bring forth justice in the earth—a kingly function (42:1, 3). Also, a prophet can scarcely fit the victorious descriptions in Isaiah 52:13, 15; and 53:12.

2. There are first-person references (I, me, my) in songs two and three. However, in songs one and four, Isaiah speaks of the servant in the third person (him, he, his).

3. Isaiah keeps himself in the background throughout Isaiah, making his message prominent. He is the least biographical of the prophets.

Thus far, we have seen that the servant is not Israel (in whole or in part) or Isaiah. Other commentators have identified the servant as some historical or ideal priestly or royal figure like Ezra or Hezekiah. However, although the servant has some priestly and royal characteristics, he has other functions and characteristics that do not fit these roles. The servant's characteristics and functions are much wider than either of these two offices.

That leads some to see the servant as a "second Moses" (in fulfillment of Deut. 18:14ff), because although he was primarily a prophet, he also blends royal and priestly characteristics and functions. Let us next consider the evidence for that.

The Servant Is a "Second Moses"

Arguments in favor of this include the following:

1. Isaiah carries the "second-exodus" motif throughout the whole book, especially in chapters 40–55 with their repeated themes of redemption, recreation, theophany, pilgrimage, etc.

2. Some of the servant songs have very explicit "exodus" content.

3. Like Moses, the servant represents the people, mediates the covenant, delivers from bondage, intercedes for the people, is meek and gentle, and leads a model life.

4. Apart from David, Moses is the most frequently identified as the "servant." Scripture calls him a servant forty times, "servant of Yahweh" eighteen times, and "servant of God" four times—a title given to no one else.

5. Later in Isaiah, there is an explicit cry for a second Moses to arise (Isa. 63:11–19).

This is a helpful analogy, and insofar as Moses was a type of Christ, we would expect further prophecies to build on that, as Isaiah clearly does. However, the fact is that no one of Israel's offices of prophet, priest, or king can completely fulfill this servant motif. Neither can David, Ezra, Moses, nor Isaiah nor any of the greatest personalities in Israel fill the servant's shoes.

The Servant Is the Lord Jesus Christ

The servant is far greater than any of Israel's individual offices or of any of Israel's individual personalities. The servant is the fulfillment of Israel as a whole. He embodies and will fulfill everything that Israel was meant to be in the world. He is "ideal Israel" or "Israel fulfilled." Isaiah sums it up this way: "And said unto me, Thou art my servant, O Israel, in whom I will be glorified" (Isa. 49:3).

By giving him the same designation as Israel (servant) and even mentioning him in the same breath as Israel, Isaiah says that the servant is everything that Israel should have been by calling. That led Franz Delitzsch to portray Isaiah's servant theology as a pyramid.

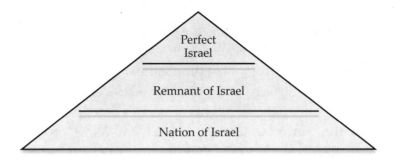

Sometimes Isaiah's servant was Israel as a whole, represented by the pyramid's base. Other times Isaiah uses "servant" to refer to the purified remnant of Israel, the middle section. But in the servant songs, Isaiah's servant is the coming Savior—the apex—who is the embodiment of Israel.[2] Significantly, Isaiah does not use the plural term for servant until after Isaiah 53. From chapter 54 onwards, the plural "servants" occurs eleven times, referring to God's people, including foreigners. His servant work produces servants, not just from Israel but from all over the world.[3]

Isaiah predicted that God would raise up Cyrus, a pagan king, to deliver His people from Babylon. But Cyrus was not the only deliverer to come. Isaiah predicted an exodus, a redemption, and a deliverer far greater than Cyrus. Cyrus's servant role was introductory; he was but a prelude to *the* servant and his better exodus.

Isaiah is pointing us towards Jesus Christ, who came not to be served but to serve and to give His life a ransom for many (Mark 10:32–45). Jesus was the first to see that He was the servant, and He saw it early on (Luke 2:49; 3:22). These servant songs gave Jesus the blueprint for His mission. Shortly after Pentecost, Jesus is called the servant four times (Acts 3:13, 26; 4:27, 30). In fact, Blocher remarks that the servant motif was so prominent in the New Testament church that Christology was primarily paidology (servantology).[4]

---

2. Franz Delitzsch, *Commentary on Isaiah* (Grand Rapids: Eerdmans, 1982), 2:174ff.

3. The New Testament repeatedly identifies this Servant-Savior as Jesus Christ (Matt. 8:17; 16:21; 27:26, 29, 31, 38, 57–60; John 10:11, 29; 3:17; 12:38; 19:1, 7, 18, 38–41; Acts 2:23; 3:13; 8:32–33; 10:43; Rom. 4:25; 8:34; 10:15–16; 15:21; Eph. 3:4–5; Phil. 2:9; Heb. 5:8; 9:28; Rev. 14:5).

4. From *pais*, the Greek word for "servant." Blocher, *Songs of the Servant*, 11.

The Beauty of the Servant

Having identified the servant as the coming Messiah, Jesus Christ, we shall now look at the beauty of the servant. What do we learn about Christ's beauty from these prophetic songs?

I will not take you on a verse-by-verse exegesis of these four songs. Rather, I will point to the highlights of Isaiah's descriptions and then show how the Lord Jesus Christ fulfilled them. As we proceed, you will notice that the songs follow the chronology of Christ's life.

The Servant Enjoys Beautiful Relationships
1. The Father/Son relationship: God the Father said of His Son, "Behold my servant" (Isa. 42:1). God called Adam to this role, but he disobeyed, rebelled, and failed. God called Israel to this role; Israel also disobeyed, rebelled, and failed. Nevertheless, here God predicts a servant who will succeed, a servant He will not be ashamed of, a servant He will call others to. When this servant appears, God will say to all, "Behold my servant," or "Would you look at that!"

God the Father will not only send His servant out on His own. He will also "uphold" Him, holding Him so firmly in His grip that nothing will defeat Him (42:1, 6). The Father's love for the servant is encapsulated in the Father's expression "my chosen." Hebrew culture viewed love as an act of the will, as a deliberate decision to bond with someone. It was not so much emotional but volitional. Love was not something you drifted into but a choice—"my chosen." This is underlined by the next phrase, "in whom my soul delighteth" (42:1). This is a highly unusual master/servant relationship.

The fulfillment of it was especially clear after Christ's baptism. As He came out of the water, God the Father effectively repeated Isaiah 42:1, filling Christ with His Spirit as Isaiah had promised in the same verse: "And Jesus, when he was baptized, went up straightway out of the water: and, lo, the heavens were opened unto him, and he saw the Spirit of God descending like a dove, and lighting upon him: and lo a voice from heaven, saying, This is my beloved Son, in whom I am well pleased" (Matt. 3:16–17). What a beautiful picture of intimate Trinitarian relationship—"Behold my servant!"

2. The Son/Father relationship: In the second song (49:1–6), the servant describes His experience of God, and especially His dependence upon Him. He speaks of His discouragement on a human level and of how He turned to His Father for support. "Then I said, I have laboured in vain, I have spent my strength for nought, and in vain: yet surely my judgment [personal vindication or work of restoring justice] is with the LORD, and my work with my God" (49:4). Many times throughout His life Christ expressed His dependence upon His Father in the midst of discouragement and setbacks (John 17). And, of course, at His greatest point of need, He committed His soul to His Father (Luke 23:46).

3. Covenant relationship: God established a covenant with Adam on behalf of the world, and then with Israel on behalf of the nations. Sadly, both of them broke relationship with God, proving unfaithful servants. But in the first servant song, God promises that He will give the servant "for a covenant of the people, for a light to the Gentiles" (42:6). Unlike Adam and Israel, this servant will become the covenant and keep the covenant, extending the covenant benefits beyond Israel to the whole world. Through the covenant of grace, sinners can enter into and enjoy a Father/son relationship with God.

The Servant Possesses a Beautiful Character
One of the servant's most prominent characteristics in the servant songs is His humble gentleness. This meekness is so appropriate for His servant role. Unlike the false prophets of Old Testament times, who were characterized by frenzied, hysterical, and self-promoting exhibitionism, "[the servant] shall not cry, nor lift up, nor cause his voice to be heard in the street" (Isa. 42:2). He will be quiet and modest; He will not be a publicity-seeker.

Neither would the servant follow the Cyrus pattern of deliverance through military might and power that crushed all before it. Rather, "a bruised reed shall he not break, and the smoking flax shall he not quench" (Isa. 42:3). How comforting this would be to broken, smoking Israel in Babylonian exile.

Isaiah also describes the servant as a tender shoot and a dry root (53:2). He is neither tall and handsome, nor strong and imposing. There is nothing attractive nor compelling about His appearance or physique. It is as if the prophet says, "We look at Him, but there is nothing to look at."

The whole picture is one of meekness. That does not, however, mean weakness. Though the servant will not break the bruised reed or extinguish the smoldering wick, He Himself will not be a smoldering wick or bruised reed (42:4). Weakness and fragility will not characterize Him. His light will not be extinguished. He beautifully merges gentleness and strength, meekness and courage.

As Matthew recognized, Jesus fit this description perfectly (Matt. 12:17–21). In fact, Jesus underlined how much He delighted in meekness (Matt. 11:29). He humbly refused publicity. He did not rant and rave. He sought out the weak and the discouraged and cherished the least signs of spiritual life. He tenderly healed the bruised reed and revived the smoldering wick.

The Servant Performs a Beautiful Work
1. Justice: A large part of the servant's work is to bring justice—just order—both to the Gentiles and to all the earth (Isa. 42:1, 3, 4). Justice was not so much about punishment but about re-ordering what had been disordered, bringing structure where there had been chaos.

2. Teaching: When Cyrus, another of God's servants, was on his way, the isles trembled in terror and dreaded his deeds (41:3–7). But with this servant, in contrast, the isles wait expectantly and hopefully. They look forward to this servant's clear, incisive, and penetrating teaching (42:4). Rather than plunge nations into darkness, He will be a light to the Gentiles (42:6). Scripture repeatedly underlines the servant's beautiful teaching and teachability (49:4–5).

3. Salvation: The servant will not only save from Babylon but also from sin. Isaiah describes something far greater than simply return from exile. It involves not just a return but a re-creation. It includes not merely Israel (49:3–4) but the Gentiles as well (49:6, 8). This servant will do much more than Moses ever did.

Paul saw the servant songs fulfilled in the life and death of Jesus Christ (Isa. 49:8; 2 Cor. 6:2). What a servant Jesus is! He effects justice, He teaches, and He saves!

The Servant Is Beautiful in Suffering

At this point, we expect onward, upward, and forward in the servant's career. However, the third song plunges us into what has been called the Gethsemane of the servant (Isa. 50:4–9), leading us into the Golgotha of the servant in the fourth song (Isa. 53). There was a hint of this painful possibility in the second (Isa. 49:4), but in the third and fourth songs, suffering becomes an increasingly intense and integral part of the servant's experience. Isaiah 53, the Golgotha of the servant, is the longest of the four servant songs and the most frequently quoted Old Testament passage in the New Testament. As it is also the song with which we are most familiar, I will not spend so much time on it apart from noting, first, that the servant would embody, fulfill, and finish all the Levitical sacrifices; second, that the suffering inflicted on the servant by Israel would become Israel's salvation; and third, that His sufferings were substitutionary—not for Himself but for us. "He was wounded for our transgressions, he was bruised for our iniquities: the chastisement of our peace was upon him; and with his stripes we are healed" (v. 5).

That such an excellent servant should have to suffer is shocking, but what Isaiah especially brings into focus is the servant's confident faith, patient endurance, and uncomplaining submission in the face of this suffering (Isa. 50:7, 9, 10; 53:7). Not once does He reject this part of His work or complain that it is unfair. In fact, He asks His adversaries to bring their charges and face Him at the judgment seat (50:8, 9). He is sure that He will be completely vindicated despite all appearances to the contrary. "For the Lord GOD will help me; therefore shall I not be confounded: therefore have I set my face like a flint, and I know that I shall not be ashamed. He is near that justifieth me; who will contend with me? let us stand together: who is mine adversary? let him come near to me. Behold, the Lord GOD will help me; who is he that shall condemn me? lo, they all shall wax old as a garment; the moth shall eat them up" (Isa. 50:7–9).

Not only does Christ, who "set his face like a flint" (Luke 9:51), fulfill these words, but Blocher also points out how Paul applies them to God's people in Romans 8: "Who shall lay any thing to the charge of God's elect? It is God that justifieth. Who is he that condemneth? It is Christ that died, yea rather, that is risen again, who is even at the right hand of God, who also maketh intercession for us"

(vv. 33–34).[5] Paul takes up the servant's confident words and gives them to God's people. Paul sees Christ's people standing in the same position as Christ, enjoying the same assured vindication as Christ. For the Christian, that turns the ugliest suffering in the world into the most beautiful suffering imaginable.

The Servant Accomplishes a Beautiful Victory
Despite the depth of the servant's suffering and humiliation, He will have the ultimate victory, as Isaiah emphasizes at the beginning and end of the fourth and final song (52:13–15; 53:10–12). The servant's mission is not completed with death but with His resurrection. He shares the spoils of what His death achieved with "the many" (Eph. 4:11–13). Kings will stand in dumbstruck amazement at His accomplishment (52:15), and their servants shall fall before Him.

The last servant song takes us behind the scenes to see that whatever sufferings the servant passed through, the Lord was behind it all. Everything is grounded in God's good pleasure. "Yet it pleased the LORD to bruise him; he hath put him to grief: when thou shalt make his soul an offering for sin, he shall see his seed, he shall prolong his days, and the pleasure of the LORD shall prosper in his hand" (53:12). It was the Lord's good pleasure to see the servant humiliated. But it is now the Lord's good pleasure to see Him exalted.

Conclusion
Let me leave you with five practical conclusions:

- *Believe in the Servant.* The third servant song ends with a call to faith (Isa. 50:10). Your eternal destiny depends on your response to the servant.
- *Preach the Servant.* Philip's preaching of Jesus from Isaiah 53 brought the first African disciple to Christ. The apostle Paul applies the fourth servant song as a warrant for evangelism of those who have "…not yet heard the gospel" (Rom. 10:16).
- *Imitate the Servant.* When faced with injustice and persecution, Peter sets forth Isaiah's servant as the example to follow (1 Pet. 2:20–25).

---

5. Blocher, *Songs of the Servant*, 52.

- *Be a Servant.* God calls us to serve this generation as Christ served His (Phil. 2:3–8). Paul's favorite self-description was "servant of Christ."

- *Praise the Servant.* The first two songs conclude with paeans of praise for the servant (42:10ff.; 49:13), as does the New Testament's "servant song" (Phil. 2:9–11). Let us pray for and strive to go forward praising this worthy Servant all our lifetime, and by grace, to all eternity.

CHAPTER 2

The Song of David's Son

Iain D. Campbell

The Song of Songs, which is Solomon's....
—Song of Solomon 1:1

An article published some time ago in the *Expository Times* said of the Song of Solomon that expositors "have not known quite what to do with this enigmatic book."[1] Any preacher on the Song of Solomon finds a variety of interpretive and exegetical difficulties when preparing to expound it. I do not pretend to be an expert. I read books and commentaries on the Song of Songs too, and, generally speaking, they espouse one of two views. Some take a purely horizontal view of the Song, believing that it tells us about human relationships and emotions; we can learn from it about relationships and marriage, but there is virtually nothing else here.

On the other hand, others say that everything in the Song is entirely vertical—that it is all about the relationship between God and His people, between Christ and His church. From this perspective, the guidance we have here about personal relationships is minimal, if it exists at all.

I suspect that preachers are nervous when they come to deal with the Song of Solomon; after all, God's name is notably absent from the text, and there seems at first glance to be no messianic import or allusion. How can one get from the Song of Solomon to the glory and beauty of Christ without committing the unpardonable exegetical sin of allegorizing and making the text say something that it does not mean?

---

1. C. Sedgwick, "Let There Be Love: A Sermon on Song 2:8–13," *The Expository Times* 108 (Oct. 1996–Sept. 1997), 310.

We approach the Song of Solomon as we approach any text of Scripture: with basic, fundamental presuppositions. First, *this is the inspired Word of God*. God gives us all Scripture, the Song included, by His inspiration. We come to this text as we come to any text of Scripture, believing it to be the product of God's outbreathing, sharing the characteristics of all Scripture. We do not shy away from it through embarrassment. We wrestle with it in order to take from it what God has revealed in it and what He therefore intends us to take from it because it is His Word.

For that reason, second, *this book is profitable* for us: all Scripture is given by inspiration and is profitable for our instruction in righteousness so that we will be equipped to live holy lives to the glory of God and be servants of the Servant. We fill our souls with this book, meditating on it so that we will better go and serve Christ in this world, not least in our own personal, familial relationships.

But, third, we come to this book remembering that Christ Himself said that *the Scriptures testify of Him*. Beginning at Moses and the prophets on the road to Emmaus, Jesus expounded from all the Scriptures the things concerning Himself (Luke 24:47). He is always the key to our interpretation. The text illuminates Christ from without because He illuminates the text from within. He is behind every word of the Song of Solomon. He is the Word, and the Word became flesh and dwelt among us, and we beheld His glory (John 1:14). Through the lens of the written Word in all its forms and parts, we too may behold the glory of the eternal Word, the glory of the only-begotten, the glory that is full of grace and truth.

With these presuppositions in mind, we come to the Song to see Jesus' glory. We want to revel in the beauty of Jesus in the Song. Dealing with this part of Scripture, as with the interpretation of any part of Scripture, requires that we pay attention to three particulars. First, we pay attention to the kind of writing we have before us, to the *literary genre*. The style of the writing is as much a product of inspiration as its content. Second, we pay attention to the *history*, because every book of Scripture is rooted and grounded in the history of redemption. Third, we pay attention to the wider *canonical placing and setting* of the Song, because no book of the Bible is an island. There are common threads and thematic trajectories that run right through the Scriptures—and through the Song, too.

The Song in Literary Context

Let us begin where the text itself begins. This is a *song*. It is poetry, and poetry in any language functions very differently than prose. This is not a historical record, notwithstanding the fact that this book reflects and is grounded in real history, where real personalities and issues exist. But this is not historical prose. It is a celebration, in poetry and in song, of something real and tangible in a historical context.

The Bible sets this poem alongside a sermon, both of which King Solomon authored. Both the sermon and the song are complementary. The sermon wants to highlight that without God, everything is empty and vain; it is a sermon that leaves its text to the end: "Let us hear the conclusion of the whole matter," says Solomon, "fear God and keep his commandments, for this is the whole duty of man. For God will bring everything into judgment" (Eccl. 12:14). The person who ignores this has the emptiest life. It may be full of possessions, pastimes, relationships, and wealth, but if God is not in it, then written over it all is "Vanity of Vanities."

For far too long, that is how many of us lived: without God, without hope (Eph. 2:12), without the thought of eternity and the perspective of the other world. We tried to fill our souls with everything the world could give us and discovered that the human heart is rapacious and capable of taking in everything the world can offer; the problem is that the world is not big enough to satisfy the heart of man.

The Song, however, that also leaves its principal theme to the end—"love is strong as death" (8:6)—alerts us to the fact that there is something that can fill the human heart. If we view life from the correct perspective, then written over it will not be "vanity of vanities" but "song of songs." We have the best song to sing if we catch this perspective: God can put a new song in our mouths, a song of praise to Himself (Ps. 40:3).

This, then, is a superlative song that points us to the superlative life. According to the opening verse, the song is Solomon's. The referent in the Hebrew, I think, means both that Solomon is the author of the song and that he is the principal subject of it. That ought not to surprise us. The Bible tells us that on account of the wisdom given to Solomon, he spoke "three thousand proverbs: and his songs were a thousand and five. And he spake of trees, from the cedar tree...unto the hyssop…: he spake also of beasts, and of fowl, and of creeping things, and of fishes" (1 Kings 4:32–33). The Song is part of the product of Solomon's wisdom. We come to it as the Queen of Sheba came to Solomon's court, marveling at the wisdom that God gave to him. As the Spirit of God sheds His own light on the text, we can say with her that "the half was not told" (1 Kings 10:7), because this song celebrates what it is to belong to God's covenant people, to sing the best song, the song of the best love. The songs of the world have "vanity of vanities" written over them, too; they are empty in comparison with this. In the covenant, we sing the song of songs.

In the Song itself, it is possible to trace a development of theme, from the initial desires and longings with which the first two chapters are full, to the call issued by the Beloved to his bride to come and follow him: "Let me hear thy voice, let me see thy countenance" (2:14). There is calling and enticement and allurement. Chapter 3 shows us how that love becomes formalized in Solomon's marriage union. The poem refers to a day—a coronation day, a day of the gladness of his heart, a day of his espousals. At the heart of the song is Solomon's marriage, after which the love matures and develops. The bride tells him what he is like to her, he tells his bride what she is like to him, and in that intensity the song moves forward into greater depths of experience and the great triumphant theme: "love is strong as death."

This poem is full of pathos, full of feeling, and full of affection. This is a beautiful song. As in other contexts, poetry paints a word picture with a wide range of imagery, color, and fragrance. These excite our senses as we read the material. To do justice to the text does not require us to find a spiritual significance in every fine detail of the picture. Nor does it require us to identify specific occasions; did the bride ever actually describe herself as "black but comely" (1:5)? How could the day of the coronation and the marriage be one and the same in 3:11? Poetry condenses time into its own forms of expression. It draws out feelings by heaping image upon image. This song is full of such movement, all centering on the marriage of the king. It is a celebration of real, personal, sovereign, monarchical love. But that begs the question: Whose love does it celebrate?

The Song in Historical Context

If this is a Solomonic celebration of the king's love, then we cannot do justice to it until we first examine the place and prominence of Solomon within the history of the people of God. We need to see Solomon's glory—less, according to Christ, than the glory of the lilies of the field, but great nonetheless. To do that, we need to look into the history of the king whom God Himself established upon the throne of His people.

First, we note *the glory of the prophecy* that was made about Solomon. When God established a covenant with David, David had desired to build a house for God. God did not permit him to do so. Instead, in a remarkable act of grace and condescension, God said to David, "Shalt thou build me an house for me to dwell in?…the LORD telleth thee that he will make thee an house" (2 Sam. 7:5, 11). God promised to raise up David's seed and establish his dynasty. God promised to be the builder and to make David the recipient of His blessing and grace. In addition, God promised that David's son would build the house that David could not build—a house for God and for God's worship.

This was the high watermark of the revelation of the covenant of grace in the Old Testament. It is a remarkable confluence of some of the themes of the Old Testament—God establishing the seed of His people and building a house for His name. The prophecy of the one to build a house for God focuses in the first instance on Solomon, whose calling and function it was to build the temple, where God's name and glory would dwell among His people.

This prediction, grounded in God's prophetic word in covenant with David, adds to Solomon's luster and glory. His place, prominence, and responsibility were the outworking of the covenant of grace, symbolic to the people of God of what He as their covenant Lord was doing for them.

Second, we need to remember *the glory of Solomon in his birth*. This may not strike us because of all the things that were going on in David's life that resulted in the birth of Solomon: the adultery with Bathsheba, the murder of her husband, the death of David and Bathsheba's baby son. This was all very tragic; how wonderful to read of the birth of Solomon. To him, Nathan gave another name, Jedidiah, meaning "beloved of the Lord" (2 Sam. 12:25). This was a remarkable intrusion of grace into the darkness of the preceding events. This son, born through a liaison that ought never to have been, and the seed of David upon whom God's promise has its immediate focus and application, is pronounced by heaven to be the Lord's beloved. Solomon is no ordinary child; he is God's beloved son before he is David's beloved son.

Third, there is *the glory of Solomon's accession to the throne*. What a marvelous moment that was: when the crown was placed on Solomon's head before a magnificent assembled congregation! Zadok the priest took a horn of oil out of the tabernacle and anointed Solomon. They blew the trumpet and all the people shouted, "God save king Solomon!" (1 Kings 1:39).

Interestingly, the Song asks us to pause at that. "Go forth, daughters of Zion," it says, "and behold King Solomon with the crown wherewith his mother crowned him in the day of his espousals" (3:11). People read this and say, Who is Solomon's mother? What are we to make of this? The text has just told us who his mother is: the address is to the daughters of Zion. Zion is Solomon's mother; he is a son of the covenant people and the daughters of Jerusalem are to behold their king! The call in the Song is for the daughters of Zion to go and see the crowning of the son of Zion.

There is an interesting parallel here in the gospel narrative of Christ, who was told on one occasion that His family wanted to see Him. Pointing to the disciples, He described them as His mother, sisters, and brothers (Matt. 12:49). The family of Jesus is the people of God, the children of the covenant. This is the very point the Song makes. The son of David is the son of God and he is the son of Zion. The covenant family is to behold him established in office, anointed to rule and govern them.

This is why it is important to remember the literary genre of the Song. At one level, the daughters of Zion as well as Zion itself, the mother of the king, represent the covenant nation. Poetry accommodates this apparent contradiction. The people set apart Solomon to the office of king according to God's command and therefore crown him.

So God has raised him up, but Zion has crowned him and poured the anointing oil on his head. The people came after him and piped with pipes and rejoiced with great joy so that the earth was torn in two because of the celebration of the accession to the throne of Solomon (1 Kings 1:40).

And so 1 Kings tells us that Solomon sat on the throne of David his father (1 Kings 2:12). But is that all that is going on? There is a reason why things are repeated in Scripture; there is a reason why we need Chronicles as well as Kings. The record of Chronicles—which does not focus on the latter sins of Solomon at all—theologizes on Solomon's life and reign and significance. As it does so, it does not say that Solomon sat on the throne of David, but that he sat *on the throne of the Lord* as king instead of David his father, and prospered, and all Israel obeyed him, submitting themselves to Solomon. The Lord magnified Solomon exceedingly and bestowed upon him such royal majesty as had not been on any king before him in Israel (1 Chron. 29:23–25). Second Chronicles 1:1 takes up the narrative: "Solomon, the son of David, was strengthened in his kingdom and the Lord his God was with him and magnified him exceedingly."

This is not simply a narrative of history about the succession of a king; this is a very deliberate historical theology, a very deliberate and precise theologizing of history. Yes, Solomon sits on the throne of his father; but the throne of his father is the throne of God. This is the beloved of the Lord sitting on the throne of the Lord, and he is king over the people of the Lord. The Song calls to the daughters of Zion to go and behold this king.

Fourth, there is *the glory of the work that Solomon does on the throne*. He builds a house for himself, but more importantly he builds a house for the Lord, just as the Lord had predicted. God has raised him up for this purpose—he is to build the temple, and Solomon's glory as the temple builder is written all over the history (1 Kings 5–9).

And so too, fifth, is *the glory of Solomon's marriage*. It is true that at a personal, moral level, the affections of Solomon's heart were his ultimate undoing. The text of the Old Testament does not offer any mitigation in Solomon's defense: God was angry with him because he married many foreign women (1 Kings 11:1–8).

But let us not forget what the text says about one striking relationship that Solomon forged early in his life. First Kings 3:1 tells us that Solomon made a treaty with Pharaoh the king of Egypt; he "took Pharaoh's daughter, and took her into the city of David, until he had made an end of building his own house and the house of the

Lord and the wall of Jerusalem round about.... There was no house built unto the name of the Lord until those days." The text introduces us to a particular marriage: the union between Solomon and Pharaoh's daughter.

Commentators generally dismiss this as a political expedient. The argument is that Solomon married the princess of Egypt because of all the benefits such a connection with Egypt would bring him. But what if the argument is flawed? What if we are meant to pause here and read what is a very positive statement about Solomon: he did marry this woman, who is mentioned five times in the narrative of Kings, and for her he built a house in Jerusalem. Solomon built a house for the Lord, for himself, and for the princess of Egypt.

When I read the Song in the light of this history, suddenly the power of the allusions comes alive. Why should the Beloved compare his bride to the best horse in Pharaoh's collection (1:9)? Solomon has this great illustration in the Song—the best of Pharaoh's horses is as nothing compared to his bride. And into her mouth he puts these words, "I am black but comely, O daughters of Jerusalem" (1:5). Is this an allusion to her African complexion and the pigmentation of her skin? Could it be that the Shulammite of the Song—the "Solomonness"—is actually the princess of Egypt, an allusion to Solomon's one positive marriage that the Old Testament text records and highlights?

After all, Kings tells us that Solomon spoke of virtually everything; he was so wise that "his wisdom excelled all the wisdom of the east country and all the wisdom of Egypt" (1 Kings 4:30). He was interested in Egypt. At the dedication of the temple, Solomon held a feast, "and all Israel with him—a great congregation from the entering in of Hamath to the river of Egypt" (1 Kings 8:65). The fourteen-day feast included Egyptians! They were among those whom he sent away on the eighth day and who "blessed the king and went to their tents joyful and glad of heart for all the goodness that the Lord had done for David his servant, and for Israel his people" (1 Kings 8:66).

The historical context of the Song is the history of Solomon, the king promised by God, beloved of God, established on the throne of God, anointed with the holy oil of God and set apart over the people of God. Through him, Israel is blessed and benefits from his wisdom, which excels that of the ancient world. And he enters into a marriage with the princess of Egypt! The contact with Egypt becomes itself a means of blessing—the princess of Egypt is brought to Jerusalem. She is not by nature a daughter of Jerusalem, but she has come to Jerusalem. In the Song, Solomon has her dialogue with the daughters of Jerusalem, and she feels very different from them—she is well aware that they already have Solomon as their king. They benefit from his position and elevation, but she does not. However, Solomon loves her and marries her, and this great poetic composition celebrates her union with him.

This is a royal romance; so we agree that there is something going on here at the horizontal, personal level of human relationships. That is what distinguishes allegory from type as we handle the text of the Old Testament: typology is always bedded in history. There is symbolism here, rich and deep, which in the light of the whole Bible story yields a gloriously fertile typology. The superlative Song that Solomon composes—in which we are invited to see his glory and rejoice with the congregation in his marriage, to celebrate a love that is sovereign and strong as death, a love that is on the throne, that is monarchical, unique, unprecedented, and blessed by heaven—is a wonderful thing. The symbolism of this is what opens the door to the typology. In the Song there is a greater-than-Solomon; the son of David is a type of David's greater Son, Jesus Christ.

Some may object to this, arguing from Solomon's later failures that he could not possibly be a type of Christ. But read the Old Testament; *all* the types of Christ failed miserably. Jonah is a type of Christ while failing miserably, as a result of which he found himself in the belly of the fish. Christ says that this was a sign, a type of the duration of time which He, the obedient prophet, would spend in the heart of the earth. Moses is a type of Christ, yet he has blood on his hands. David is a type of Christ, yet he, too, has blood on his hands. Go right back to the very beginning: Paul says explicitly that Adam is a type of Christ (Rom. 5:14), and he failed spectacularly. The types of the perfect One are not perfect types.

Solomon stands before us in history as a type of Jesus. He is not merely a king, but the promised seed of David. It is in that light that we must come to this Song. After all, what is the first historical fact that the New Testament teaches us about Jesus? It is that He is "the son of David" (Matt. 1:1). And what is virtually the last fact that the

New Testament teaches about Christ? From His own lips we hear, "I am the root and the offspring of David" (Rev. 22:17). How can He be both? If He is the root of David, David comes from Christ. If He is the offspring, Christ comes from David.

Yet in the economy of redemption, both things are true; everything in David's life, with regard to his position over the people of God, derives from the ultimate fulfillment of God's purpose in Christ. Yet, according to the flesh, Christ is also the "son of David" (Rom. 1:3), who derives His human nature, and therefore the legitimacy of His succession to the throne of the Lord, from His physical descent from David. Like others, we must come before this Christ and say, "Thou son of David, have mercy upon me!" (Matt. 9:27; Mark 10:48).

The Song in Canonical Context

This fact leads us to our third consideration: the place of the Song of Solomon on the trajectory of biblical revelation. The New Testament itself opens our eyes to the fact that these great covenant predictions that God made to David, focused in the first instance on Solomon, actually had a much greater horizon in view. They derive their efficacy, authenticity, depth, and meaning from the One who was the ultimate fulfillment of all the covenantal revelation and dealings of God from the very beginning; Christ was always the promised seed of the woman who would crush the head of the serpent (Gen. 3:15). He was always the seed of Abraham, in whom God would establish the salvation of His covenant people (Gen. 12:3; Gal. 3:16). He was always the Son of Judah, to whom the scepter of God's kingdom rightly belongs (Gen. 49:10). And He is the Son of David, anointed and exalted to take His rightful place at the right hand of the majesty on high. Solomon is anointed and the earth is torn by the people shouting, "God save King Solomon!"

After all, there was a day in the New Testament, too, when the earth tore again at the accession and exaltation and coronation of David's Son. There were no people around, no human voices were heard, but when Jesus was "justified in the Spirit and seen of angels" (1 Tim. 3:16), an angel came down and caused an earthquake as a greater-than-Solomon succeeded to the throne of the Lord over the people of God (Matt. 28:2). In that exaltation, the Lord of David says to the Lord of David—the Father, to the Son, in covenant with one another for the redemption of His people—"Sit thou at my right hand, until I make thine enemies thy footstool" (Ps. 110:1). The Father highly exalts David's Son to a position of eminence and glory that He occupies even now, until at last every eye will see Him and every tongue will confess that He is Lord to the glory of God the Father.

God's covenant promises have their ultimate focus on Him, on Jesus, the great King and deliverer of God's people, our great Solomon, the Son of David before whom we fall and say, "My Lord and my God!" (John 20:28). We may sing the great psalms that had their immediate interest in Solomon and say, "His name shall endure for ever; his name shall be continued as long as the sun" (Ps. 72:17); as we do, we know that they speak of a greater One than Solomon. These great messianic psalms that speak of the promised seed focus our attention on the Lord Jesus Christ. This is why the church ought to retain psalms in our Christian worship. This is the age in which the Psalms have come into their own and are filled with the dignity and glory of the son of David.

Related to this is an interesting fact that all the successive revelations of God's covenant in the Old Testament seem to be illustrated by marriage. Right at the beginning, God made a covenant with Adam in which He gave him promises of life on condition of obedience. *Then* He created Eve, who became one flesh with Adam and shared the same covenant standing before God as a consequence.

After the flood, God made a covenant with Noah; by saving Noah's family, he made them heirs of the same covenant promises. He promised to be the God of Shem and to bring the Japhethites into Shem's tent (Gen. 9:27), making a union through which the families of the earth will be blessed. Only as the Gentile seed of Japheth "marries" the seed of Shem can it enter the covenant blessing. It is through union with the Semitic seed that the Gentile seed will be saved.

Then God enlarged the promise to Abraham in a great act of grace by which God called another idol worshiper, establishing a covenant with him and promising that his seed would be blessed. What is the longest narrative of Genesis? It is the pursuit of a bride for Abraham's son (Gen. 24). This is what preachers of the gospel are doing every Lord's Day: they are looking for a bride for Abraham's Son because it belongs to the very essence of God's covenant grace to bring others into the orbit of the covenant blessing through union with the covenant heir.

Then the covenant of grace is administered through Moses, with the promises of the covenant focusing on the line of Judah. Do you know why the book of Ruth is in the Bible? It is to illustrate the same principle: here is a woman from Moab, by nature a stranger to the covenants of promise, without God and without hope in the world (Eph. 2:12). But what the law could not do, because it was made weak through her flesh, God did (Rom. 8:3)! He provided a redeemer for her, and she married her redeemer! Through her union with the son of Judah, Ruth the Moabitess becomes an heiress of God and a joint heir with Boaz of the blessings of God's covenant.

And now the Song, celebrating the marriage of David's son to someone who was as far from these covenants and promises as it was possible to be: the daughter of Pharaoh. It was out of Egypt that God brought His son (Hos. 11:1); but out of Egypt God will bring a daughter, too. His chosen king, His beloved Solomon, loves her, and unites her to himself. Consequently, in some remarkable way, she herself becomes an heiress of the covenant promise. Jesus' words to His disciples could almost be a message from Solomon to his Egyptian princess as he plans his building program in Jerusalem: "I go to prepare a place for you, so that where I am there you will be also" (John 14:2).

This "enigmatic little book" is the Holy of Holies of Old Testament literature, as it celebrates the possibility of a stranger becoming a child of the covenant through union with the son of David. If you are a believer, you are the Shulammite, you are the Moabitess, you are the Japhethite; you who were "not my people" are now the people of the living God (Hos. 2:23; Rom. 9:25–26). For no merit of your own but by virtue of your marriage to David's Son, you have come into the bond of the covenant.

That is the spiritual dimension to the Song; let us free this book from the Babylonian captivity of modern critical scholarship and of evangelical exemplarist moralism and set it as the jewel that it is against the backdrop of the canonical revelation in which God says to me, "Behold I show you the bride" (Rev. 21:9). At last, I see the church coming down out of heaven from God. She is the heavenly Jerusalem, adorned with the glory of God. She fulfills all the biblical trajectories anticipated in the garden of Eden and found in the Paradise of God at last, when the Lamb in the midst of the throne enjoys the company of His Shulammite, His Solomonness.

The glory of it is that the marriage begins here in this vale of tears, this world of sadness, where the Son of David comes to His people and says, "I have loved thee with an everlasting love: therefore with lovingkindness have I drawn thee" (Jer. 31:3). He has made us His own. It is in union with Him—in an unbreakable marriage bond that is a covenant—that He, the royal King, gives all that He has and all He is capable of to you. In your struggles and situations, in your sins, in your disappointments and frustrations, He says there is nothing in death or life or in all creation that can break the bond: "Love is strong as death!"

Go and behold your King! Sing the Song of Songs! He is yours! You are His! Nothing can separate what God has joined together.

> He and I in that bright glory
> One deep joy shall share
> Mine to be forever with Him
> His that I am there.[2]

What a day that will be, when the Song finally comes into its own, and we see the King in His beauty in the land that is very far off (Isa. 33:17). We will then sit, in union with David's Son, at the marriage supper of the Lamb. The song of heaven will be the song of Moses and of the Lamb, the Song of Songs, the song of David's Son!

---

2. Francis Ridley Havergal, "The Welcome to the King," Christian Articles and Sermons, http://articles.ochristian.com/article5691.shtml (accessed May 23, 2011).

CHAPTER 3

He Is Altogether Lovely

Iain D. Campbell

I am my beloved's....
—Song of Solomon 7:10

In our previous study, I tried to set the Song of Solomon in the context of biblical theology to see it as a composition by Solomon about himself. In it, Solomon celebrates his marriage, which occasions this great song. It is not designed to illustrate the beauty of marriage, but the beauty of the marriage of David's son as a type of the marriage of Christ to His people.

I also tried to set this great book of Scripture on the line of canonical revelation to show that the theme before us in the Song of Solomon is a developing theme throughout Scripture: God, through the union of His covenant heir and another party who is a stranger to the covenant, brings that stranger into His covenant family. In the Davidic covenant, Solomon is the promised seed; eventually, he will sit on God's throne in place of his father David. In the light of everything we are told about Christ in the New Testament we are warranted to read the Song and say, "A greater than Solomon is here" (Matt. 12:42).

Part of the Song's effect is to reveal the king's beauty to us. So the book sets before us the king in all his beauty. Indeed, the theme of this study comes directly from Song 5:16: "He is altogether lovely."

One of the things that Solomon does in this composition is show us how the loveliness of the king unfolds in the experience of his bride. In all that she experiences, in the situations that are registered in the Song's development, the bride comes to discover the beauty and see the loveliness of her royal lover in different ways.

There is a refrain that runs through the Song that is, I think, crucial to this theme. In 2:16, the bride says, "My beloved is mine, and I am his." That is echoed in 6:3: "I am my beloved's and my beloved is mine." Then, as the Song moves towards maturity, the refrain appears in a slightly different way in 7:10: "I am my beloved's, and his desire is toward me." This refrain is an important element in the Song because it registers the bride's subjective experience. This is her response to the revelation of the king's glory. In the early chapters, the emphasis is on *her possession of him*: "My beloved is *mine*" is followed by "and I am his." The emphasis is on what she has and what she owns. He is hers before she is his. But the emphasis changes as the Song progresses and develops. In chapter 6, the accent falls not on what *she* has, but on what *he* has: "I am *my beloved's*" comes before "and he is mine." The alteration of the refrain is significant; she has moved in her understanding of what is important. At the beginning, *her* experience and possession were important; now what *he* has become is primary. That is what comes to the fore in the end, too, as her possession hardly matters at all. What matters is that she is her beloved's, and "*his desire* is toward" her. At the beginning, her desires mattered; at the end, *his* desires matter.

My Beloved Is Mine

There is something deeply spiritual being registered in this movement. The emphasis at the outset is on her possessing her beloved. He has called her and spoken to her; he has allured her and shown himself to her. She looks at him and glories in the fact that all that is true of him belongs exclusively to *her*. His loveliness, his glory—they are *hers*! He has covenanted himself to his bride. Everything he possesses is now hers.

In a sense, this is what grace enables us to do. It enables us to take Jesus as He is freely offered in the gospel. God breaks down all resistance by His irresistible grace. Some people have a problem with the concept of irresistible grace because, they say, sinners always resist the offer of the gospel. But it is not grace that is offered in the gospel so much as it is *Christ* who is offered. People do resist Christ, and they do so willingly and freely because of the power that sin has to bind them and to keep them in bondage. But when grace frees the will from that bondage, it comes with irresistible force and makes

Christ irresistible, too. By nature, a sinner sees no beauty in Christ; he will not and cannot come to Him unless enabled and persuaded to do so.[1] The natural mind is enmity to God. It is utterly impossible, left to itself, for the human heart to choose Christ. The servant song of Isaiah expresses it magnificently: there is no beauty in Him that we should desire Him (Isa. 53:2).

The problem is not that Christ is devoid of beauty; the problem is with us, with our inability to see and respond. But grace makes the world of difference: it breaks down every barrier and removes all the resistance. It opens the eyes of the understanding, illuminating the heart and moving the will. It persuades us that we must have Christ, and it enables us to have Him. When the gospel makes its impact on our soul, we see Christ in the gospel and say, "Yes! He is mine! I have Him—everything He is, I have; everything He has done, I embrace."

By faith, we see *the loveliness of Christ's person*. We take all that He is in His unique, glorious, incomparable self. John Owen reminds us that only by faith can we see this:

> The Beauty of the Person of Christ as represented in the Scripture consists in things invisible to the eyes of flesh. They are such as no hands of man can represent or shadow; it is the eye of faith alone that can see this king in his beauty. What else can contemplate on the untreated glories of his divine nature? What eye can discern the communications of the different properties of his natures in the same Person?... It is in these things that the loveliness of Christ consists.[2]

What a vision for the eye of faith! Faith sees this glorious, unique Jesus, this one who was always God, who was with God, who is the delight of God. Everything that was true of God is true of Him; there is no God but Jesus. All the luster of divine perfection and beauty resides in Him: in Him all the fullness of the Godhead dwells (Col. 2:9). His person, revealed in His human nature, shows His altogether

---

1. To the question "What is effectual calling?," the Westminster Shorter Catechism (Q. 31) answers, "Effectual calling is the work of God's Spirit, whereby, convincing us of our sin and misery, enlightening our minds in the knowledge of Christ, and renewing our wills, he doth persuade and enable us to embrace Jesus Christ, freely offered to us in the gospel." Cf. John 6:44–45.

2. John Owen, *Christologia*, "The Nature, Operations and Causes of Divine Love, as It Respects the Person of Christ," chapter 13. Available at http://www.ccel.org/ccel/owen/christologia.xvii.html.

loveliness as the God-man. This one came to be what He was not without ceasing to be what He was. He always was God, His Godhead uncompromised by the addition of a human nature by which, in humiliation, He was impoverished when He took the form of a servant. In all of this, Jesus is altogether lovely to the eye of faith. This is "my beloved"—beautiful in what He is.

But faith also enables us to see *the loveliness of Christ's work*. He is altogether lovely in what He has done. In the gospel, the Son of David has mercy on sinners, so much so that every path He treads has the cross in view. "This is my Father's will which sent me," He says, "that of all that he has given me I should lose none" (John 6:38). To gain all of them, He has to go to Calvary where He will stand alone and be made a curse so that the blessing of Abraham will rest on the Gentiles through Christ (Gal. 3:13–14).

In this work, Christ, contracted to a span in the womb of the virgin but now grown to perfect manhood, gives that manhood over to God in an act of divine worship and sacrifice on Calvary's cross. He came for sinners; He lived among men to give His life as a ransom (Mark 10:45). The gospel sets Jesus before me as the Savior whose life is given for me, and He is all the more attractive to me for that reason.

A colleague of mine recently published a poem in memory of his father, one of whose occupations was to weave tweed cloth on his loom. In my youth, on the Isle of Lewis in Scotland, there were many people who made their living that way. The poet describes how his father used to sing Gaelic psalms as he wove the cloth:

> Dad used to fill the room with praise
> These hours spent bowed above his loom,
> Precenting[3] over patterns, weaving belief
> Deep into both weft and warp
> Till wool was flecked with psalm
> As each song shuttled, threading verse
> Through two-by-two or plain
> Until his finished tweed retained

---

3. In the tradition of unaccompanied psalm singing, the precentor is the one who strikes up the tune and leads the praise.

Rhythyms of Kilmarnock, Stornoway[4]
Deep within the tightness of the cloth
For a stranger to put on, unaware how faith
Was sewn within the garment; bright stitch
Among both checks and herringbone;
An active work of worship, prayer
With which my father laboured to prepare
Fabric fit for other souls to wear.[5]

As I read it, I thought instinctively of Jesus on the cross in His "active work of worship," laboring to prepare fabric fit for other souls to wear. His work on the cross is done with an eye to His Father's glory—His death is His supreme act of worship. All the sacrifices were ordained and appointed within the context of worship in the Old Testament; Calvary is Christ's greatest offering, His greatest act of piety, prayer, and praise.

All the time, as Christ is engaged in the worship of His Father, He is weaving a robe of righteousness which we could never have woven for ourselves. As we lean on Him and embrace Him in the gospel, we say, "My beloved is mine, and this robe of righteousness He wove for me at Calvary!"

He is altogether lovely *in all the offices He undertakes as my Savior*. He is my Prophet, the last great messenger of the covenant. He is the final word from God who would seal up the vision and the prophecy (Dan. 9:24), the great eschatological prophet of whom God said, "This is my beloved Son: hear him" (Mark 9:7). The greatest prophet of the Old Testament is eclipsed by God's final prophet; there was no prophet like Moses to whom God spoke face to face, and the world waited for the prophet whom Moses himself foretold (Deut. 18:15). This prophet did not appear in all eras of the Old Testament. However, on the Mount of Transfiguration, where the only two prophets of the Old Testament who spoke to God on Mount Sinai appear in Jesus' presence, God says that the last prophet has come. "Hear him!" God says, He is heaven's final word to earth; God has no more to say, until at last the veil lifts and every eye sees Him, every tongue con-

---

4. These are the names of psalm tunes.

5. Donald S. Murray, "Weaving Song: In Remembrance of Angus Murray, (1922–81)," in *Stone Going Home Again: New Writing Scotland 28*, ed. Alan Bisset and Carl MacDougall (Glasgow: Association for Scottish Literary Studies, August 2010), 65.

fesses Him, and every knee bows. In these last days, the last word has been spoken (Heb. 1:1–3).

He is also the great Priest, and altogether lovely in His priestly office. He finished a great work on earth, but the finishing of His earthly work was not the end of His work; it was only the end of what could only be done on earth. In the Old Testament tabernacle, there were two altars: one of brass in the outer courtyard and one of gold inside the veil. Only when he was finished at the first could the priest officiate at the second. That is what Christ has done for us. He first, in view of all the world, offers Himself. Once that was finished, He stepped within the veil (not without blood) and went to the golden altar of incense to offer up His intercession before the Father. That is where He is, still my Priest, still exercising that office in intercession for me (Rom. 8:32).

And He is the King, my Solomon, the son of David, crowned and exalted. God has set Him apart, notwithstanding the opposition to Him (Ps. 2:6–8; Phil. 2:5–9). The Lamb of God is now in the midst of the throne. He is Prophet, Priest, and King, complete and eminent in them all. He is altogether lovely in all of this, and I embrace Him and say, "He is mine!"

He is also lovely in *the way He applies that redemption through His Holy Spirit*. He actually saves us! He does so by applying to us, personally, existentially, individually, in our space/time history the benefits of the redemption that He secured for us at Calvary. The robe that He wove is a perfect fit; He puts it on me and prepares me for glory! I could not otherwise be fit for glory apart from the fact that He works on me and in me what He worked for me at Calvary. He will not stop until that work is done; where He began it, He will continue it (Phil. 1:6).

He was a carpenter once; He is a carpenter still. He is taking the raw material of my sinful heart and shaping it into something glorious. He will not lose any of those for whom He died. This is His covenanted obligation to the Father: to lose none of His people, and to raise them all up at the last day. He will redeem them, protect them, preserve them, and at last present them without spot or wrinkle or any such thing (Jude 24–25). He will account for every last one of them.

This Christ is mine! "My beloved is mine." Can we say this? Can we say that this greater than Solomon is ours? This Son of David who calls and saves sinners in the gospel—is He ours? There is no more important issue in the whole of the world than that we should be able to echo the claim of the bride and say that we have this King as our own. Is He to us like the apple tree among the trees of the wood, under whose shadow we have sat with great delight and found His fruit sweet to our taste (Song 2:2)? Have we a testimony to tell of how this Christ became ours?

I Am My Beloved's

To be able to say "My beloved is mine!" is a glorious response. Yet, in a sense, for the maiden of the Song, it is a very inadequate response. Not only has the king been giving himself to his bride, he has also been calling her to follow him. "Rise up, my love, my fair one, and come away. The winter is past, the rain is over and gone; the time of the singing of birds is come, and the voice of the turtledove is heard in our land…rise up my love, my fair one, and come away!" (Song 2:14). That is his call to his bride. She ought to have risen up and followed him, but all she has done is declare, "He is mine!"

It is never enough to stop with the mere possession of Christ. Do not misunderstand me: once you can say that Christ is yours, you are safe for time and for eternity. But the Christian life is not only about initial conversion; it is about discipleship. It is about rising up and following Him. It is not enough to stay where you are and say, "He is mine." We are called to serve this King, to rise up from where we are, to take up our cross, and to follow Him. Here, in this Song, Solomon pictures the bride simply responding by exulting in her possession and then discovering that he has to deal with her gently, uniquely, and personally so that she will discover his beauty and loveliness all the more.

In chapter 3, the bride says, "By night, on my bed, I sought him whom my soul loveth; I sought him, but I found him not." What was the reason for this? He had previously called her to rise and follow but she had simply stayed and said, "He's mine." So then he withdrew in order to teach her—and us—that the thrill of the experience of possessing Christ is not an adequate substitute for the depth of the blessing of obeying Christ.

He leaves her yearning for him, pining for him. She has nowhere to go but about the city streets, seeking the one whom her soul loves. She seeks him, but she does not find him. She finds the daughters of

Zion who are rejoicing in the king's crowning, but the bride in this Song does not belong to the number of the daughters of Zion. The more she goes on, the more she feels alienated and like a stranger in Jerusalem. She longs to know that this king loves her. He speaks about her in chapter 4, still calling her to follow. By the time we reach chapter 5, she is conscious not only of his voice calling, but also of the loss of his nearness and presence; she says, "I opened to my beloved, but my beloved had withdrawn himself and was gone" (Song 5:6).

Sometimes, in order to make us obedient disciples, our Beloved withdraws Himself. We lose our conscious sense of His nearness and presence; He leaves us seeking Him in order to draw us into living and vital obedience. I know that it is true that those who seek Him find Him, but it is also true in the life of grace that those who find Him seek Him. There are times when those who have found Him are seeking Him not because they do not have Him, but because they do. His withdrawal and seeming absence is training them to seek Him and follow Him all the more earnestly. So here is the bride, in the middle of the Song, when she ought to be enjoying His conscious presence and fellowship, going about the city streets, longing like Mary in the garden to recover her absent King (John 20:13).

Let us bear in mind the principle of the previous study; this is poetry. We do not have to interpret this literally, as if there was a point when Solomon's bride actually went about the streets of Jerusalem saying the things she says in the Song. This is a magnificent portrayal of being in love with David's Son, and there are rich depths of spirituality here. The bride is portrayed as being lost and alone; she does not know where her Beloved is. She calls and there is no response; the watchmen on the city walls wound her and take away her veil. She simply says, "If you find my beloved, tell him that I am sick of love" (Song 5:8).

It is interesting that she had used this language of lovesickness in 2:5. But in chapter 2 she was sick with love because of how *much* she had of these first waves of excitement and of discovery and the freshness of her possession of him. Now she is sick with love not because of his nearness, but because of his absence.

The contrast could not be more stark. In chapter 2, she tells the daughters of Jerusalem where he is; in chapter 5, she asks the daughters of Jerusalem where she might find him. In chapter 2, she is sick with love because she has so much; in chapter 5, she is sick with love because she has so little. In chapter 2, she is sick with love as he calls her, but she does not respond. In chapter 5, she is sick with love as she calls him, and now *he* does not respond. In chapter 2, she is sick with love because of how much she had around the banqueting table in the banqueting house of her beloved, but in chapter 5 she is sick with love out on the streets, and there he is—on the other side of the door. In chapter 2, she is sick with love because he is so close to her; in chapter 5, she is sick with love because he seems so far away.

In his hymn "O for a Closer Walk with God," William Cowper asks these questions:

> Where is the blessedness I knew
> When first I saw the Lord?
> Where is the soul-refreshing view
> Of Jesus and His word?

It was all so bright at the beginning, that first moment when my dungeon filled with light and my chains fell off; when I was freed to follow Jesus, the sense of Him was so overwhelming. But maybe it is not like that now—then we were overcome with love because of how much we realized we had in Christ; now we have been on the pilgrimage some time, and we do not seem to have so much. Time seems to have robbed us of many of these blessings and feelings and experiences and senses of His nearness. We are now sick with love and cannot even put our feelings and experiences into words. All we can say is, "Just tell my beloved that this is how I am."

I do not know of anyone who has expressed this more beautifully than Ralph Erskine in his "Paraphrase on the Song of Solomon":

> The love, the love that I bespeak,
> Does wonders in my soul;
> For, when I'm whole, it makes me sick,
> When sick, it makes me whole.
>
> More of the joy that makes me faint
> Would give me present ease;
> If more should kill me, I'm content
> To die of that disease.[6]

---

6. Ralph Erskine, *The Poetical Works of the Reverend and Learned Ralph Erskine* (Aberdeen, Scotland: G. & R. King, 1858), 333.

This is a most remarkable insight into our spiritual experience. This is where we are so often: more of the joy that we cannot bear would actually help us in our present condition! The love that so overwhelmed us when we first saw Christ and embraced Him in the first moments of faith seems to have disappeared. These heightened feelings and exaggerated experiences seem a thing of yesterday.

The nineteenth-century Scottish preacher, John MacDonald of Ferintosh, wrote a Gaelic elegy in memory of his father, a deeply spiritual man. He says that his father never wanted to be alive merely *on* his feelings, but he did want to be alive *in* them. There are such things as religious affections—"whom having not seen you *love*" (1 Peter 1:8). You fell in love with Christ once, when the brightness of His person and glory and work became so radiant in the gospel and it was blessed to your soul. You danced when your burden rolled away and said with Bunyan's Pilgrim:

> What a place is this!
> Must here be the beginning of my bliss?
> Must here the burden roll from off my back?
> Must here the strings that bound it to me crack?
> Blest cross! Blest sepulchre! Blest rather be
> The man that there was put to shame for me![7]

You do not want to live on your feelings, but you would love to dance with spiritual joy again.

Sometimes, however, you simply cannot put your experiences into words. A remarkable thing happens at this point in the Song. When the bride in the Song tells the daughters of Jerusalem that they should tell her beloved that she is sick of love, they ask her, "What is your beloved more than any other beloved?" (Song 5:9). In response, this bride, who previously found it so difficult to put her experience into words, cannot stop the torrent of words that comes out in answer to the question, "What does he mean to you?"

When she cannot speak about herself, she will speak of her king: "My beloved? You want me to speak of him and tell you what he means to me more than any other beloved? He is white and ruddy, the chiefest among ten thousand.... Supposing you were to fill the arena with ten thousand of the choicest men of Jerusalem, my

7. John Bunyan, *The Pilgrim's Progress* (Edinburgh: Banner of Truth Trust, 1997), 36.

beloved would stand head and shoulders above them all. He has a head like most fine gold in its preciousness and value; his hair is raven black; there is no hint of age or grayness in his hair because he retains the beauty and glory and dew of his youth. His eyes are so gentle, like doves' eyes—they have a way of piercing my soul right through to the very depths." Have you ever experienced that? Do you remember how Peter experienced it? "The Lord turned and looked upon Peter" (Luke 22:61). Christ who was dumb like a lamb before the shearers spoke more in His silent look at Peter than He could say with words!

And still the bride speaks. She describes the cheeks of her beloved as a bed of spices; his lips are like lilies; his hands that bless and caress and do not break bruised reeds, perhaps because they are bruised hands, are like gold rings set with beryl. His legs are like pillars of marble; his face is like Lebanon, and his mouth—ah! It is the sweetest mouth! Grace is poured into his lips (Ps. 45:2)! All he has to do is open his mouth and grace comes out—that is the experience of the bride.

That is your experience of Jesus, too, is it not? No man spoke like this man (John 7:46). "Whom have I in heaven," said the psalmist, "but thee?" (Ps. 73:25). Of all the choice saints in glory, some we know and many we do not, Christ stands out in the company. Maybe some of you have been on the pilgrim way a long time, and now you count more of your Christian friends among the dead than among the living—you have more in glory than on the earth—but still, none compare with Him.

"This is my beloved...this is my friend" (Song 5:16). Do you see? The bride cannot find words to convey her own experiences, but when she is asked what her beloved means to her, she cannot stop talking! There are not enough words! She cannot explain her own heart, but when she is asked to explain her king, she paints a word portrait that conveys the excellence of his attractiveness and the brilliance of his person. She finds him altogether alluring and desirable and attractive.

I have to confess that I am on something of a campaign to stop testimonies—at least, the kinds of testimonies that people often tell. I hear people standing up to give their testimony, and they tell us about things that happened ten, twenty, or thirty years ago when they could say, "My beloved is mine!" That is good, of course; I am not decrying it. But I want to know how much more beautiful Jesus has become with the passing of the years. I want to hear how He sometimes dimmed the lights with dark providences and robbed you of much so that you were left with nothing but Him. I want to know how much more beautiful He has become to you, when God in His providence removed so much else on which you leaned once, and left you leaning only on Him. I want to hear of how altogether lovely He has become as He has brought you along roads that made you say, "O that I knew where I might find him! I look up and He is not here. I call to heaven and heaven is silent. On my left hand and on my right hand, and He is not there. O that I knew!" Those moments when He left you saying, "But he knoweth the way that I take" (Job 23:1–10).

In all these afflictions and trials, in the things that came into your life since you came to Christ, in the things that shaped you, not by the choices you made for yourself, but by the providences you would never in a million years have chosen for yourself—I want to know how much more lovely He has become in these things. That is the testimony I want to hear. What have you learned in your pilgrimage that makes Him attractive still? You have left behind so many of your dreams and prospects in what has gone by of your wilderness journey. He has stripped you just as the bride in the Song seems to have lost everything in her search for her beloved in the way he has dealt with her. Yet all the time for her, and for you, the experience is designed to elicit an even more sweet appreciation of His beauty and loveliness and magnitude.

So if, with all these valleys behind you, you can still say that "he is the chiefest of ten thousand to my soul," then I will listen to your testimony gladly. In *Pilgrim's Progress*, Bunyan has his pilgrims pass over Enchanted Ground and come into Beulah land, out of the reach of Giant Despair; they could not even see Doubting Castle. But they did hear the voices from the Celestial City saying, "Say to the daughter of Zion, Thy salvation cometh." And with a more perfect view of the city and the streets of gold, Christian with desire, began to grow sick, and Hopeful also had a fit or two of the same disease and said, "If you see my beloved, tell him that I am sick with love."[8]

Having been in Doubting Castle, having come through the Slough of Despond, having your heart weaned away from the world and all

---

8. Bunyan, *Pilgrim's Progress*, 179.

its prospects, do you have a clearer view of the City now? And does that leave you with a soul sickness of love for Christ? Is your testimony now not so much "He is mine," but "I am His"? Have you come to realize that you would gladly continue the pilgrimage knowing that you are in His hands? Your maturity and growth of grace are seen precisely in this: whatever the cost of following Him has been in real terms, with the loss of your initial experiences and of much else, too, you can still rejoice to know that you still belong to Him.

His Desire Is for Me

But the refrain will change again. In 7:10, she is going to say, "I am my beloved's and his desire is towards me." How does she know that? She knows it because virtually everything that is said in chapters 6 and 7 of the Song are his words, describing her beauty to him. She knows now that his desire is for her.

I think there is a sense in which this is the end of all our Christian experience: that we will know that the King's desire is for us. We discover Christ in the gospel to be altogether lovely, and we discover Him in our experiences to be altogether lovely. But the Song points us to this: His loveliness has the end in view that we will be His entirely, for His desire is for us. He has a testimony, too, of what He did to save souls, of the work that He performed in human lives. He says, "See that man kneeling down to pray? I did that! See that woman over there weeping over her sins? I did that! She never wept before, but she cannot stop now! I did that! See this person who has sacrificed it all to take up the cross and yield his life to me? I did that"—that is His testimony. If a conference on the beauty and glory of Christ does not leave us marveling at what He did and the claim He has upon us now, then we have not begun to see Him clearly. His desire is that we will give everything about us and everything in our lives—all our dreams and hopes and aspirations—to Him who gave His all for us.

What a blessing it would be for us if our meditation on the beauty of Christ would leave us longing that His desire would be accomplished, and leave us saying as He said Himself, "Not my will but thine be done!" (Matt. 26:39). He wants you, my Christian friend, because He loves you. His desire is for you every day. He wants to give Himself to you, and He wants you to give yourself to Him.

Supremely, He wants you to be with Him where He is, to see His glory (John 17:24). Here, we see through a glass, darkly, but then we will see face to face (1 Cor. 13:8). We have begun to glimpse Jesus' loveliness amid earth's shadows, but one day we will see it in its fullness in the glories of heaven. May we through the gospel anticipate the day when all desires will meet and be fully satisfied around the marriage supper of the great King!

CHRIST'S GLORY FROM BETHLEHEM TO GOLGOTHA

PART 2

CHAPTER 4

The Glory of Christ's Victorious Incarnation

Richard D. Phillips

And the Word was made flesh, and dwelt among us, (and we beheld his glory, the glory as of the only begotten of the Father,) full of grace and truth.

—John 1:14

The exodus of Israel was one of history's great mass migrations, with over two million people leaving their bondage in Egypt.[1] At first, this great caravan would have had a certain splendor, laden down as it was with the treasures of the Nile. But before long, in the desert, the Israelites would have looked more and more like refugees: they were dirty, disheveled, and increasingly disorganized. Even then, however, the Israelites possessed a glory that made them the marvel of the world. At the center of their camp was the tabernacle of the Lord, over which rested the cloud of fire that God sent to guide His people. Inside was the ark of the covenant, with the glory of the presence of the Lord filling the tabernacle.

Christians are likewise unimpressive during our pilgrim journey through this desert world. But like the Israelites, the Christian church has the glory of God in her midst. John writes, "The Word was made flesh, and dwelt among us, (and we beheld his glory, the glory as of the only begotten of the Father), full of grace and truth" (John 1:14). In light of this and other statements about the glory of Christ's victorious incarnation in the Gospel of John, I intend to unfold this theme in four points: the glory of Christ *as the Word*; the glory of Christ as

---

1. Numbers 1:46 lists 603,550 fighting men over twenty years old. This likely indicates a whole population between 2 and 2.5 million people. See Timothy R. Ashley, *The Book of Numbers* (Grand Rapids: Eerdmans, 1993), 65.

the revelation of true man; the glory of Christ as *the fullest revelation of God*; and the glorious privilege of knowing the incarnate Christ as He *dwells among His people*.

The Glory of the Incarnate Word

John 1:14 states the doctrine of the incarnation. Jesus Christ was born of the Virgin Mary in the stable at Bethlehem. But the second person of the Trinity did not come into being through this birth. John says, "In the beginning was the Word," and then at a certain time, "the Word became flesh." God the Son—the Word—did not come to existence in His incarnation, but He then took on our human nature in addition to a divine being. The Westminster Confession explains, "The Son of God…being very and eternal God…did, when the fullness of time was come, take upon him man's nature, with all the essential properties, and common infirmities thereof, yet without sin" (VIII.1). Christ's incarnation means that the Son of God became a human in the fullest sense, but without losing any of His deity. Paul says, "In him dwelleth all the fulness of the Godhead bodily" (Col. 2:9). Likewise, Jesus is sinless without losing His full humanity. His is uncorrupted, true humanity.

The apostle John often selects words that have layers of meaning. There is no better example than his use of "the Word" to describe Jesus. The Greek is *Logos*, which refers to Jesus in terms of the mighty creative Word of the Father which was in the beginning. John's gospel glorifies Christ as the Word by whose power the new creation comes through the cross and empty tomb. But this same word, *Logos*, was also one of the most significant terms in Greek philosophy. By using this word, John built a bridge from the Greek philosophical world to the Jewish thought-world of the Old Testament.

One of the earliest Greek philosophers was Heraclitus (sixth century). He thought about the fact that things constantly change. His famous illustration was that you can never step twice into the same river; it is never the same because the water has flowed on. Everything is like that, he said. But if that is true, how can there be order in the world? His answer was the *Logos*, the *word* or *reason* of God. This was the principle that held everything together in a world of change. There is a purpose and design to the world and events, and this is the *Logos*.

The *Logos* fascinated Greeks from Heraclitus onward. What keeps the stars in their courses? What controls the seasons? The world is full of order and purpose. Why? The answer is the *Logos*, the divine logic, the Word. Plato said, "It may be that some day there will come forth from God a Word, a *Logos*, who will reveal all mysteries and make everything plain." In a stroke of divine genius, John seizes on this background and says, "Listen, you Greeks, the very thing that has most occupied your philosophical thought and about which you have been writing for centuries—the *Logos* of God...has come to earth as a man and we have seen him."[2]

Jesus, the incarnate Word, is every bit the answer that men and women need today, just as the philosophers of old did. Psychologist Erich Fromm argues that three unsolvable dilemmas, existential problems, plague modern man. First is the dilemma of life versus death. We want to live, but we all die. Jesus answers that problem, giving eternal life to all who believe on Him. He said, "I am the resurrection, and the life...whosoever liveth and believeth in me shall never die" (John 11:25–26). "The second of Fromm's dilemmas is the dilemma of the individual and the group. Jesus is the answer to that problem too, for He has come to break down all walls and to make of His followers one new man which is His mystical body (Eph. 2:14–16). The last of Fromm's dilemmas is that arising from the conflict between our aspirations and our actual achievements. We all fall short of what we would like to be and believe ourselves intended to be. Is there an answer? Yes, Jesus is the answer to that problem also, for He promises to make us all that God created us to be in the first place. We are to be conformed to Christ's image."[3]

The industrialist Henry Ford once had a breakdown on his assembly line that no one could fix. In desperation, he called Charlie Steinmetz, the mechanical genius who had designed and built Ford's plant. Steinmetz showed up, tinkered for just a few minutes, threw the switch, and everything started running again. Days later Ford received a bill for $10,000, an exorbitant sum in those days. He wrote back, "Charlie, don't you think your bill is a little high for just a little

2. James Montgomery Boice, *John* (Grand Rapids: Baker, 1999), 1:35.
3. Boice, *John*, 1:239.

tinkering!" So Steinmetz sent back a revised bill: "Tinkering—$10. Knowing where to tinker—$9,990."[4]

Our world today is terribly broken down, and there is no one able to fix it other than the One who made it. Our nation cannot be fixed by anyone but Christ. Our churches and our marriages cannot be fixed by anyone other than the divine Creator Word. The same is true of our corrupted hearts, which apart from Christ have no peace or satisfaction. The glory of the incarnation is that our world has received the long-awaited Word, the answer who has come to reveal salvation in the glory of His person and work. Our lives are restored to working order only when saving faith receives Christ the Word.

Christ's Incarnation Revealing True Humanity

When Jesus took on our flesh, He gained a human body, which enabled Him to suffer death for us. Jesus also possessed a human mind and heart: He felt all that we feel, including sorrow and joy, weariness and temptation. Because of this, He is able to sympathize with us in our trials (cf. Heb. 4:15). Moreover, Jesus lived a human life in the same world in which we live. He was born and grew up as a boy. He learned a trade in His father's carpenter shop. He had friends and neighbors; He paid taxes and was subject to the governing authorities. "Lo, within a manger lies/He who built the starry skies.... Thus to come from highest bliss/Down to such a world as this!"[5] Because He truly lived as we live, Jesus sets an example of true humanity for us to follow.

John describes Christ's incarnation by saying that Jesus "dwelt among us" so that we "beheld his glory" (John 1:14). The Greek word for *dwelt* is better translated as *tabernacled*: it is a verb form of the noun for the tabernacle that served as the tent of meeting during Israel's exodus sojourn. This description relates not only to Jesus' divine glory but also to His glory as true man in the incarnation. God gave the tabernacle as a way in which God's glory could dwell among His people and travel with them, and this is the very reason Jesus became man and came to earth. Moreover, the tabernacle was humble in appearance: a canvas structure about forty-five feet

---

4. R. Kent Hughes, *John: That You May Believe* (Wheaton, Ill.: Crossway, 1999), 18.
5. Edward Caswall, "See, amid the Winter's Snow," in *Christian Hymns* (Brynitirion, Wales: Evangelical Movement of Wales, 1977), no. 178.

long and fifteen feet wide, it had none of the outward visual appeal of the pyramids of Egypt or the ziggurats of Babylon. So it was for Jesus. The Christmas hymn says, "Veiled in flesh the Godhead see."[6] A. W. Pink remarks: "He came, unattended by any imposing retinue of angels. To the unbelieving gaze of Israel He had no form nor comeliness; and when they beheld Him, their unanointed eyes saw in Him no beauty that they should desire Him."[7]

So what glory does John have in mind when he says of the incarnate Christ, "we beheld his glory" (John 1:14)? Theologians give different answers. Some think this refers to the transfiguration, where Jesus was revealed in full splendor on the mount before three of His disciples. This certainly was a display of glory, but the fact that John omits it from his gospel suggests that he has other things in mind. Others point to Jesus' miracles: His healings, His ability to feed thousands with a few fish and loaves, and His power even to raise the dead. John tells us that the miracles "manifested forth his glory" (John 2:11), showing His divine power and sublime compassion. John devotes the first half of his gospel to presenting what has been called the Book of Signs, that is, a record of the miracles that pointed to Christ's glory.

But there is another answer to this question about Jesus' glory. Jesus showed His glory as true man through His humble, obedient, servant life. To us, a glorious person is one who rises above the crowds, ascending to a place of wealth and prominence. But Jesus showed us a higher human glory. Though He had the power that created galaxies, He was born in humble circumstances. He allowed His heart to break as He wept over Jerusalem. He allowed His body to be broken and His hands and feet to be nailed to a cross by creatures He had made; He also gave up His life so that we might live.

The truth is that, humanly speaking, Jesus was not very glorious. He had His moments, but what did He accomplish? Leon Morris assesses Jesus' earthly achievement: "He preached to a few people in an outlying province of an ancient, long since vanished empire. Even there he was not often in the capital, the center of affairs, but in

---

6. Charles Wesley, *Hark! the Herald Angels Sing,* in *Psalter Hymnal* (Grand Rapids: Board of Publications of the Christian Reformed Church, 1976), no. 339.

7. Arthur W. Pink, *Exposition of the Gospel of John* (Grand Rapids: Zondervan, 1975), 35.

a remote country area. He taught a few people, gathered a few disciples, did an uncertain number of miracles, aroused a great number of enemies, was betrayed by one close follower and disowned by another, and died on a cross. Where is the glory?"[8]

We tend to think that glory requires the pomp and glitter of this world—gold medals, trophies, great stock portfolios, and showy houses. But God shows us through Jesus that real glory is not like that; it does not depend on pageantry and show. Real glory lies in humble service out of devotion to God. This points to a way of glory that Christians are to recognize and pursue. What will give significance to your life? Is it fame and fortune, fleeting and unsatisfying as they are?

Jesus' incarnation says that we, too, can lead glorious lives. We do not possess His divine power to perform miracles, although we do have great power through prayers offered in Jesus' name. And through the Holy Spirit, as Christ lives in us, we have power to deny ourselves, serving sacrificially out of God-given love. We, too, can help. We can heal. We can teach. We can give. We can take in the lost. We can bind up broken hearts. Through faith, we can be Christlike, bearing His glory before the world.

The night that I came to faith in Christ, I met Lawrence Dow, a deacon at Tenth Presbyterian Church in Philadelphia, who was greeting at the door before the evening service. I remember how his joyful demeanor made me feel accepted and welcome. Lawrence was an aging African-American man who never had a good formal education and worked as a doorman in a downtown hotel. Over the years that followed, I got to know Lawrence well, and he showed how God's glory and grace are revealed through humble obedience and gospel servanthood.

To tell about Lawrence I only have to describe his funeral, when he died after a long struggle with cancer. Our church sanctuary was jam-packed and the service was long. Person after person came to bear testimony to how God had used Lawrence in their lives. Some had come to faith in Christ through his personal witness and received his mentoring in their early Christian growth. Some had been discouraged or faltering, and Lawrence had noticed them and given the encouragement they needed. Three different ministers spoke about how Lawrence had led them to Christ and equipped them in their service to their Lord. Lawrence's children and grandchildren spoke of his legacy of faith and love in their lives. The whole service, recounting the glory of this humble servant life, was simply overwhelming.

Afterwards, I was sitting in the office of my fellow minister at the church. We were both dazed by what we had just seen; the funeral had been a glorious experience, and we were awestruck. After several minutes of silence, my friend said, "It just goes to show what God can do in the life of anyone who yields himself unreservedly in humble service to Jesus." That is exactly the glory that Jesus showed through His own obedient, humble, and servant life. This is why Jesus saw the event of His greatest earthly humiliation—the apex of His servant obedience—as His true glorification on earth: "The hour has come," Jesus said of the cross, "that the Son of Man should be glorified" (John 12:23).

The Incarnation as Revealing God's Glory

Christ's victorious incarnation glorifies our Lord as the long-awaited answer who alone can give hope and meaning to the world and by setting before us an example of the glory of true humanity. A third glory, the glory most on the apostle John's mind, is Jesus' revelation of the glory of God in His incarnate life. John writes, "The Word was made flesh, and dwelt among us, (and we beheld his glory, the glory as of the only begotten of the Father)" (John 1:14). The tabernacle, which John compares to Christ's incarnate person, was called the tent of meeting because there the people met with God and saw His *shekinah* glory, the radiant light of God's majesty. We likewise see the radiance of the glory of God in Christ's incarnation.

Prior to the incarnation of His Son, God had of course revealed Himself to mankind. Hebrews 1:1 states that God "at sundry times and in divers manners spake in time past unto the fathers by the prophets." There are all kinds of different ways that God revealed Himself to Israel prior to Jesus' coming. But with the coming of His Son, God gave us the truest and most effectual revelation of Himself. Hebrews continues, saying that God "hath in these last days spoken unto us by his Son" (Heb. 1:2). The incarnate Christ is "the brightness of his glory, and the express image of his person" (Heb. 1:3). John Calvin compared the revelation of God prior to Christ to a pencil sketch. Such a drawing will enable us to recognize a person. Now that His Son has come in the flesh, however, God has given us a revelation in living color. In Christ, we may really know God personally.

John makes the comparison between the prior revelation and the living revelation of God in Christ at the end of his prologue: "No man hath seen God at any time; the only begotten Son, which is in the bosom of the Father, he hath declared him" (John 1:18). All through the Old Testament, godly men and women longed for an intimate knowledge of God. But God could not be seen, for He dwelt, Solomon said, "in thick darkness" (1 Kings 8:12). Elijah heard only a still, small voice. Abraham dealt with angels and saw God as a smoking fire pot. Moses had the most intimate dealings with God, standing before the burning bush and having the divine light shine on his face. Yet his greatest longing was to see God Himself. "I beseech thee, shew me thy glory," Moses pleaded. But God said, "Thou canst not see my face: for there shall no man see me, and live" (Ex. 33:18–20).

Jesus came to provide the perfect revelation of God that men *could* receive. John describes Him as "the only begotten Son, which is in the bosom of the Father" (John 1:18). This is why Jesus is greater than John the Baptist or Moses, not to mention Mohammed or the pope. Jesus is Himself very God of very God, one in the divine Trinity. He is in intimate fellowship of love with God the Father. Christ, then, is the One who can truly show us God.

This means that Jesus is the unique and only Savior for all who long to know God. The Greek word translated "made known" (*exegesato*) gives us our English word *exegete*, a word that scholars use for Bible interpretation. We exegete Scripture to give a full account of its meaning. This is what Jesus does: He interprets and explains and exposits God to us. Jesus gave a full revelation of God in what He taught and what He did. To know what God is like and what God intends for the world, we need only study Jesus. This is what we most greatly need and what we should most fervently seek: to know God through Jesus Christ.

John characterizes Christ's revelation of God in two specific terms: "(and we beheld his glory, the glory as of the only begotten of the Father), full of grace and truth" (John 1:14). Considering the second of these first, Jesus reveals God to us in *truth*. This means not only that Jesus is Godlike in His revelation, it also means that the God we long to know is Christlike in all things. If you want to know what God is like—what is His manner, His character, His attitude, and His heart—you should look at the portrait of God's incarnate Son in the Bible. Because of our alienation from God in sin and because of our own idolatrous tendency to erect false images of God, our race had lost contact with our Maker. But Jesus came into the world and His posture, His tone of voice, His attitude, and His reaction to events were those of God. To see Jesus and comprehend His mind and heart, His character and His habits, is to comprehend God. God is always and only Christlike, so that the more we know of Christ the more we know of God. Jesus Himself stated, "He that hath seen me hath seen the Father" (John 14:9). This revelation of God is the impetus to our faith, for to comprehend God in Christ is to trust and adore Him.

A passage that wonderfully shows the importance of seeing the truth about God in Christ is found in Luke 7. Jesus was having a meal in a Pharisee's house when a sinful woman came in and began perfuming His feet, washing them with her tears, and wiping them with her hair. We were reading this passage in our family devotions recently, and I asked my children if they were uncomfortable with this behavior; they admitted that they thought it socially bizarre. I pointed out that the woman had seen that the incarnate Jesus is God in the flesh and the revelation of God. It was the woman who was acting appropriately by abandoning herself in adoration, not the Pharisee who tried to treat Jesus as an equal. Seeing the truth about God in Jesus, this woman who had spent her life being mistreated and used by men, was perfectly comfortable opening her heart in the presence of Christ. Because of the truth she saw revealed in Jesus, she was able to trust God, despite the hard experiences of her life. We likewise will learn to trust God, draw near to Him, and open our heart fully in adoration if we see God as He is revealed in His incarnate Son, Jesus. God is Christlike and therefore we can trust Him.

Moreover, John says, Jesus also revealed the *grace* of God: "full of grace and truth." I have described a number of ways in which we should understand the tabernacle, John seeing it as the Old Testament model for Christ's glorious incarnation. The tabernacle represented

God's presence among His people, compared favorably to Christ's earthly humility, and was the place where Israel met with God and saw His glory. But there is one more vital thing to know about Israel's tabernacle: it was the place where the sacrifices were made to atone for sin. The tabernacle revealed God's holy hatred of all sin, for there sin could be atoned for only through sacrificial blood. The tabernacle also revealed God's marvelous grace in providing a sacrifice to die in our place. The animal sacrifices of Israel's tabernacle pointed forward to Jesus Christ, whose cross is the true tabernacle, revealing the grace of God to sinners by His death for our sins.

The sinful woman of Luke 7 who wet Jesus' feet with her tears and wiped His feet with her hair, seeing the truth of God in Christ, trusted Jesus enough to open her heart and draw near in the most vulnerable way. But Jesus says that she also was drawn to the grace of God she saw revealed in Him. He explained to the Pharisee and the other guests, "Seest thou this woman? I entered into thine house, thou gavest me no water for my feet: but she hath washed my feet with tears, and wiped them with the hairs of her head. Thou gavest me no kiss: but this woman since the time I came in hath not ceased to kiss my feet. My head with oil thou didst not anoint: but this woman hath anointed my feet with ointment. Wherefore I say unto thee, Her sins, which are many, are forgiven; for she loved much: but to whom little is forgiven, the same loveth little" (Luke 7:44–47).

If seeing divine truth revealed in Jesus is the key to trusting in God, seeing the divine grace of Jesus' cross is the key to loving God. John said in his first epistle, "We love him, because he first loved us" (1 John 4:19). How did God love us? "In this was manifested the love of God toward us, because that God sent his only begotten Son into the world, that we might live through him. Herein is love, not that we loved God, but that he loved us, and sent his Son to be the propitiation for our sins" (1 John 4:9–10).

Jesus most fully revealed God's grace at His cross, a fact which reminds us that Jesus became incarnate so as to die for our sins. The incarnation finds its glory in the atonement. Jesus was born *as* man in order to die *for* man. This is why any idea of "incarnational ministry," in which good deeds take the place of the preaching of Christ's cross, is a complete misnomer. It is wrong to say that we must preach Christ constantly, and only when necessary to use words. We must always preach Christ through words that point to His cross, where the grace and truth of God are displayed to win the faith and love of sinners. The only way for us to see God's glory is ceaselessly to proclaim the person and work of Christ for the salvation of sinners.

This is one reason why we must preach the atoning work of Christ in all of its fullness. It does not glorify God's grace to teach that Christ died so that all might have the possibility of salvation. But it does glorify God's grace to teach the gospel truth that Christ died to atone effectually for His people's guilt, to deliver them from their sins, and to redeem them for eternal life. Christ's glory is greater than that of a Socrates, who suffered death for a principle. Christ's glory is greater than that of Nathan Hale, the colonial American patriot who lost his life for the great cause of freedom, regetting only that he "had but one life to give for his country." Christ's glory is higher than either of these. He died not for a principle or a cause, but, revealing God's grace, Christ suffered death for us. He died, every Christian can say, "for me." Seeing this kind of glory revealed in the incarnate Christ's victory on the cross changes our approach to Him from one of admiration to adoration.

The movie *Saving Private Ryan* tells of a rescue operation immediately after the Allied invasion of Normandy, in June 1944. The War Department learned that three out of four boys in a family named Ryan had died in battle on the same day. The Army's top general ordered that the fourth son be rescued from behind German lines, where he parachuted on D-Day. An elite squad of Army Rangers was assigned to find Private Ryan. Their search led to a bridge where German tanks were trying to break through Allied lines, and there the squad was destroyed just as their quest finally succeeded. As the captain who saved Private Ryan lay dying on the bridge, surrounded by the bodies of the men from his squad, he drew Ryan close and gasped, "Earn this. Earn it." The movie concluded with Ryan, now an old man, returning to the cemetery where the men who died for him were buried. Falling to his knees at Captain Miller's grave, he said to the white plaster cross, "Every day I think about what you said to me that day on the bridge. I've tried to live my life the best I could. I hope that was enough. I hope that at least in your eyes, I earned what all of you have done for me." Turning to his wife, who came up beside him, he stammered, "Tell me I have led a good life. Tell me I'm a good man."

We praise God that we are not required to earn what Christ has done for us, nor could we ever. We receive His death not as those who have led a good life but as sinners who trust in His blood for our salvation. But, like Private Ryan, looking at the white plaster cross of his earthly savior's grave, we look at the wooden cross of our divine, incarnate Savior, and we adore Him not as one who merely died for a principle or for a cause, but as one who died for us. We say in faith, "He died for me." Seeing this, we glorify Him in return in how we live. We live not to prove ourselves or merely for a principle or even for a great cause. We live for a person in whom we glory and in whom we see the grace and truth of God for our own salvation, the Lord Jesus Christ. Christians can say of the God revealed in His Son Jesus: "I live for Him, because He died for me."

The Glory Dwelling among Us

Through His victorious incarnation, Christ revealed Himself as the Word from God to man, as the revelation of true humanity, and as the ultimate revelation of God in all His grace and truth. Lastly, we must note that Christ became incarnate so that this glory might dwell among us.

This raises three essential questions. The first is this: Do you see the glory revealed in Jesus Christ? This serves as a workable definition of a Christian. A Christian is someone who sees in Jesus the glory of God. Others may see Him as a valued teacher, a social reformer, or even a pitiful victim. But a Christian reads the Gospels and sees glory in Jesus Christ so that he worships Him and yields his life as Jesus' disciple. We speak as did Peter; when the crowds were leaving Jesus because He didn't teach what they wanted to hear, Peter said, "Lord, to whom shall we go? thou hast the words of eternal life... thou art...the Son of the living God" (John 6:68–69). Embracing this by saving, Spirit-worked faith makes you a Christian and gains eternal life.

A second question is for Christians: Do we in fact make the glory of Christ dwelling among us the chief glory in which we delight? What, for instance, are we seeking in our churches? What makes us excited about coming to church? Is it the music, the fellowship with Christian friends, or even the excellence of the preaching? John points to the true definition of Christian success: to see the glory of Christ tabernacling among us in the grace and truth of God. If we seek this glory, we have Christ's promise to grant it. "I, saith the LORD..., will be the glory in the midst of her" (Zech. 2:5), Jesus said of old. Let His be the glory that we seek in our churches; as the Scripture says, "He that glorieth, let him glory in the Lord" (1 Cor. 1:31).

The same must be asked of us as individual Christians: What is the glory we are seeking? How are we defining success in our lives and in the lives of our children? Is it through advanced education, career advancement, or material possessions? Jesus says, "This is life eternal, that they might know thee the only true God, and Jesus Christ, whom thou hast sent" (John 17:3). Do we believe that? John reminds us that "the Word was made flesh, and dwelt among us, (and we beheld his glory, the glory as of the only begotten of the Father,) full of grace and truth" (John 1:14). Let that glory be our passion and desire, that we might live beholding that glory, growing always in the grace and knowledge of God.

Lastly, how does the incarnate Christ dwell among us in His glory? Is there some emotional or spiritual state we must attain by means of a certain kind of music? Is there a ritual that will place us in a glory-attuned state? Will the setting—the elegance of vaulted ceilings and stained glass or the repetitive strains of liturgy—cause the glory of the incarnate Christ to shine among us? No, says Paul. "Say not in thine heart," Paul warns, "Who shall ascend into heaven? (that is, to bring Christ down from above): or, Who shall descend into the deep? (that is, to bring up Christ again from the dead.) But what saith it? The word is nigh thee, even in thy mouth, and in thy heart: that is, the word of faith, which we preach" (Rom. 10:6–8). Christ in His glory is present among us as His means of grace are received by humble hearts that seek to know and serve Him as Lord. As the Emmaus Road disciples said of the victorious Christ, who had shown them His glory, may we learn to say with rejoicing, "Did not our heart burn within us, while he talked with us by the way, and while he opened to us the scriptures?" (Luke 24:32). The glory of Christ will be among us as through God's Word when we fulfill the command of the psalmist: "Glory ye in his holy name: let the heart of them rejoice that seek the LORD. Seek the LORD, and his strength; seek his face forevermore" (Ps. 105:3–4).

CHAPTER 5

The Glory of Christ's Parables[1]

Gerald M. Bilkes

Christ's parables are among the best-known and much-loved parts of the Gospels. Who can forget such parables as the prodigal son, the ten virgins, the good Samaritan, or the lost sheep? People like these brief, simple, well-crafted stories. They are colorful, human, and engaging. And they often include elements of surprise that foster an impact, especially in attitude and behavior.[2]

However, when we speak of the *glory* of the parables, we mean more than just the attractive style and memorable character of these parables. Many human orators and authors have displayed an ability to impress and attract people with their stories and poetry. With the parables, however, we have something far greater going on—something that is far more glorious.

---

1. Recent years have seen considerable fresh work on the parables, including Klyne Snodgrass, *Stories with Intent: A Comprehensive Guide to the Parables of Jesus* (Grand Rapids: Eerdmans, 2008); Richard N. Longenecker, *The Challenge of Jesus' Parables* (Grand Rapids: Eerdmans, 2000); Craig L. Blomberg, *Interpreting the Parables* (Downers Grove, Ill.: IVP Academic, 2000); Terry Johnson, *The Parables of Jesus* (Fearn: Christian Focus, 2007); Richard D. Phillips, *Turning Your World Upside Down: Kingdom Priorities in the Parables of Jesus* (Philadelphia: P&R, 2003). Some older works that are still relevant today include James Montgomery Boice, *The Parables of Jesus* (Chicago: Moody Press, 1983); Simon Kistemaker, *The Parables of Jesus* (Grand Rapids: Baker, 1980); Herman C. Hanko, *The Mysteries of the Kingdom: An Exposition of the Parables* (Grand Rapids: Reformed Free Publishing Assoc., 1975); John Laidlaw, *Studies in the Parables of Our Lord* (Minneapolis: Klock & Klock Christian Publishers, 1984); Richard Chenevix Trench, *Notes on the Parables of Our Lord* (London: John W. Parker and Son, 1857).

2. Adapted from Snodgrass, *Stories with Intent*, 17–21. Cf. Johnson, *The Parables of Jesus*, 17–27. See also John W. Sider, *Interpreting the Parables: A Hermeneutical Guide to Their Meaning* (Grand Rapids: Zondervan, 1995), 93–170, for different literary components in Jesus' parables.

After all, when the Bible speaks of glory, it means the weightiness of royal splendor; the Hebrew word for *glory* literally means "weight" or "heaviness." It is what you feel when a king or other dignitary is in your presence.[3] Today, we might use the word *gravitas*, or the importance or dignity that someone has or with which someone speaks. It is something that you cannot see per se, but you sense it. It makes you feel small in comparison.

Of course, there is a glorious weight or importance to everything Christ said—whether it was His preaching in the synagogue or the sermon He gave on the mount or His discourses to His disciples. Not a word He spoke on this earth was without purpose, authority, and effect. But there is something distinctively glorious about the parables, and that is what we want to trace in our time together. I believe there are essentially three reasons why the parables are glorious, and thus also show the glory of Christ: their splendid scenery, their kingdom focus, and their transforming effect.

Their Splendid Scenery

A parable has a unique form. It is not meant to give you a historical or factual account of some event or process; at base, it is a comparison, short or long, with scenarios and stories drawn from everyday life.[4] It tells a story or describes a process in order to suggest something spiritual.[5] Actually, the word *parable* comes from a word that means "to carry alongside of." And the point is that the person telling the parable aims not to speak simply of earthly things, but

---

3. See also Leland Ryken, James C. Wilhoit, and Tremper Longman III, eds. *Dictionary of Biblical Imagery* (Downers Grove, Ill.: InterVarsity Press, 1998), s.v. "glory."

4. For a history of interpretation and brief explanation of parables, see Joel B. Green, Scot McKnight, and I. Howard Marshall, eds., *Dictionary of Jesus and the Gospels* (Downers Grove, Ill.: InterVarsity Press, 1992), s.v. "parable." For an extended treatment of the genre of parables and the modern discussion, see Stein's chapter in Longenecker, *The Challenge of Jesus' Parable*, 30–49.

5. This way of reading the parables stands in opposition to the allegorical method. See Longenecker, ed., *The Challenge of Jesus' Parables*, 3–29 for a historical overview of the allegorical method. For a contemporary appraisal of the use of allegory in interpreting parables, see Blomberg, *Interpreting the Parables*, 29–49. His conclusion is that the "anachronistic" use of allegorizing is a thing of the past. But depending on one's definition of "allegory," it is permissible to see elements in the parables as allegorical. See also Herman Ridderbos, *The Coming of the Kingdom* (Philadelphia: P&R, 1962), 121–23.

through them to speak of *other* things. In the parable, the earthly things are "carrying along" a spiritual message, which you may or may not understand.

Though we might overlook this fact as elementary, this is already part of the glory of the parables. Christ saw creation and life as a ready vehicle to convey theological truths and spiritual lessons. Think of the rich and varied scenery He used in parables. There are agricultural scenes—a sower going out to sow or a fig tree being examined by the husbandman to see whether it is bearing fruit. There is a threshing floor. There are vines and vineyards. There is a shepherd with his sheep. There is a woman in her house. There is a wedding scene, where bridesmaids are waiting to attend a bridegroom. There is a marriage banquet, where guests come dressed in wedding clothes. There is an estate, on which a father lives with his two sons and hired servants. There are two men building houses in different locations—one on rock, one on the sand. There is a traveling scene where a man is attacked by robbers as he makes his way from one place to another. All everyday scenes! Think of His use of the common stuff of life: pearls, leaven, oil, coins, sheep. Jesus did so much with the ordinary things of life!

In this way, Christ reminds us of Solomon, the wisest man of the Old Testament. Scripture records of him that "he spake of trees, from the cedar tree that is in Lebanon even unto the hyssop that springeth out of the wall: he spake also of beasts and of fowl, and of creeping things, and of fishes" (1 Kings 4:33). Solomon was a student of creation, and his teachings in the book of Proverbs refer often to the created world. He taught spiritual lessons from common created beings, inspired by the Holy Spirit. Think of some of the things on which his proverbial teaching is based: "Go to the ant, thou sluggard—consider her ways, and be wise" (Prov. 6:6). He speaks of going after a strange woman "as an ox goeth to the slaughter" or "as a bird hasteth to the snare" (Prov. 7:22–23). Or "the spider taketh hold with her hands, and is in kings' palaces" (Prov. 31:28). Note the things Solomon used to give a comparison of a lazy person: "As the whirlwind passeth, so is the wicked no more.... As vinegar to the teeth, and as smoke to the eyes, so is the sluggard to them that send him" (Prov. 10:26).

Some might imagine that it would be fitting for the Savior, while He was on earth, to have buried Himself in scrolls, synagogues, or ancient libraries. But more than anyone, Christ understood the great value of the first book of revelation, namely, creation.[6] Scripture makes it abundantly clear that the heavens and all of creation declare the glory of God (Ps. 19:1). By nature, our minds are so darkened by sin that we cannot read this "most elegant book, wherein all creatures, great and small, as so many characters leading us to contemplate the invisible things of God, namely, His eternal power and divinity, as the apostle Paul saith (Rom. 1:20)" (Belgic Confession, art. 2). With Christ, however, the exact opposite was the case.

As the Son of God, Christ Himself *had created* all these things, seen and unseen. But in His human nature, He studied this glory that His own eternal hands had made. Luke notes that Christ "grew, and waxed strong in spirit, filled with wisdom" (Luke 2:40). Surely that means that He must have observed and learned from the world around Him. He recognized the world and the creation for what they are, and He did so infallibly, perfectly. In this light, is it any wonder that He reached for this created world when He spoke the parables? In His doing so, these common things take on brilliant meaning, which no human author could extract from the things of nature. Edward N. Kirk writes:

> When the Most High comes among us himself as a teacher, calling on nature and life to reflect the light of his glory, then they obey. This call they answer truly. And gloriously can the lily then teach. The stars, the stones are full of truth.... The instant he bids them speak, they utter words of heavenly wisdom, or eternal truth, or infinite grace.... The tares have a lesson to teach; not something forced upon them; not some artificial mnemonics, by which the memory should retain the divine truth. But the divine teacher opens to view the intrinsic and real analogy between them and man's spiritual relations.... He who created the grain of mustard-seed, is the Author and King of the heavenly world.[7]

---

6. See the differences between Jesus' parables and those of His day in Arland J. Hultgren, *The Parables of Jesus: A Commentary* (Grand Rapids: Eerdmans, 2000), 5–11.
7. Edward N. Kirk, *Lectures on the Parables of Our Savior* (New York: J. F. Trow, 1856), 9.

So the parables are glorious because Christ used the subjects of His own creation and handled them most splendidly and infallibly —which cannot be said of any other noninspired writer.

Christ not only knew and observed and used the natural realm around us, but He also referred to people, men as well as women, God's image-bearers, in most of the parables. Christ understood man perfectly, both as the crown of God's creation as well as deeply sinful. He knew how these facets of humanity show themselves in human actions. He had watched men and women in the country-side of Galilee, and in the shops and houses of Nazareth. More than anything, the parables occupy themselves with human beings, their abilities, their industry, and their relationships.

Christ spoke of people working: building houses, building a tower, and managing a fig tree (Matt. 7:24, 26; Luke 14:28; 13:6). He spoke of people engaged in commerce: finding a very costly pearl, losing a silver coin, being given talents, and a master's steward (Matt. 13:46; Luke 15:8; Matt. 25:16; Luke 16:1).

He spoke of people in relationships: fathers and sons, servants and masters, subjects and kings (e.g., Matt. 21:28; Matt. 25:14; Luke 19:14). Think of how His teaching gleaned meaning from the rela-tionship between the rich man and a poor man at his gate, dogs licking his sores (Luke 16:21), or of the wounded traveler and a per-son of another ethnicity passing by (Luke 10:33). He had observed the dynamics between the Pharisees and the publicans (Luke 18:10).

As He described the people in His parables, notice how per-fectly He understands man's fallen condition. He spoke of the blind leading the blind or the fickle children in the marketplace always changing their tunes in their games (Matt. 15:10; Luke 7:32). He had seen scenes of conflict. He spoke of agreeing quickly with one's adversary, of a widow who needed protection from her persecutor, and of going to war (Matt. 5:25; Luke 14:31; 18:6).

In fact, Christ showed in the parables that He knows man's thoughts within himself. His knowledge of the human heart strikes that deep. Think only of the parable of the rich fool, in which Christ gave an infallible testimony of the man's inner thoughts: "And he thought within himself, saying, What shall I do, because I have no room where to bestow my fruits? And he said, This will I do: I will pull down my barns and build greater; and there will I bestow all my fruits and my goods. And I will say to my soul, Soul, thou hast much goods laid up for many years; take thine ease, eat, drink, and be merry" (Luke 12:17–19). It is no wonder that we read elsewhere that Christ "needed not that any should testify of man; for he knew what was in man" (John 2:25). After all, He could say, "I the Lord search the heart and try the reins" (Jer. 10:7).

Many anthropologists and sociologists have written large volumes on the development and character of human beings and on how they relate to people around them in their social relations. But nowhere do we find such a glorious insight into the nature of human beings as in Scripture; Christ's parables are certainly no exception. Whenever Christ spoke of people in His parables, He did so in a way that not only respected the glory of men and women as God's creation, but also recognized the depth of our fall from glory.

Christ, however, did not just speak of us in our relationship to other people. Think of how Christ also showed His infallible awareness of our relationship with God, and of God's verdict upon us. Think, for example, again of the parable of the rich fool where Christ gave us insight into what God says about him: "Thou fool, this night thy soul shall be required of thee" (Luke 12:20). Or in the parable of the publican and the Pharisee, Christ told that the one man is rejected by God, while the other goes to his home justified (Luke 18:14). The rich man, who received his good things in this life, is sent to hell, but the beggar Lazarus is welcomed into heaven. How profoundly honest Christ is in dealing with souls when it concerns their relationship to God!

And so Christ, despite what we might have expected, did not focus on life in the halls of important personages of the day like Caiaphas, or on the material of the ancient myths and fables, or temple rites and ceremonies.[8] Christ gave no place to the disjunction between the sacred and the secular. As far as His parables were concerned, His eye was actually more on the farmer sowing his seed and the woman making bread than on the priest doing his work in the temple. After

---

8. Jesus was not the only one to use parables as a mode of teaching. Though scholars do highlight many similarities between Jesus' parables and those of other traditions, there were also many differences. For a scholarly critique of these similarities and differences between Jesus' parables and those of rabbinic literature, see Blomberg, *Interpreting the Parables*, 58–69. See also Evans's treatment of parables outside the New Testament: Longenecker, *The Challenge of Jesus' Parables*, 51–75; and Snodgrass, *Stories with Intent*, 37–60.

all, did He not take upon Himself flesh and blood to be born among common men and women and live in the backcountry of Galilee (Matt. 4:13, 15)? It was precisely thus that Christ determined to dwell among us and thus for people "to behold his glory" (John 1:14), also in how He told the parables.

Their Kingdom Focus

Christ's teaching in parables did not just concern general lessons and morals without any coherence. Instead, when Jesus began teaching in parables, He did so in order to reveal *the kingdom* of God.[9] So many of the parables begin exactly that way. "Again, the kingdom of heaven is like..." (e.g., Matt. 13:24, 31, 33, 44, 45, 47).

Moreover, when the disciples asked Christ, "Why speakest thou unto them in parables?" He answered, "Because it is given unto you to know the mysteries of the kingdom of heaven, but to them it is not given" (Matt. 13:12–13). What is meant by the term "the kingdom of heaven"? Simply put, it refers to the domain in which God rules by His grace through His Holy Spirit.[10] The kingdom of heaven is where God manifests His gracious reign in bringing sinners into fellowship with Himself through Christ.

In the opening pages of the New Testament, John the Baptist announced this kingdom. As He started His earthly ministry, Christ began developing the idea of what the kingdom of heaven is. His Sermon on the Mount is a kind of constitution or kingdom charter; it describes the character of the citizens of the kingdom, the standard of righteousness for the kingdom, and how members of the kingdom should live. Then, too, as Christ performed miracles, He

---

9. Cf. David Wenham, *The Parables of Jesus* (Downers Grove, Ill.: InterVarsity Press, 1989), 232.

10. I like to define it as follows: The domain of God's salvific dominion at the climax of redemptive history, effected by the death, resurrection, and ascension of Christ, wherein He overthrew all principalities and powers, triumphing over them. He manifested this kingdom in His preaching and parables, calling for willing subjects of this reign, and He will consummate this reign when He returns on the clouds. Herman Ridderbos writes, "The coming of the kingdom is first of all the display of the divine glory, the re-assertion and maintenance of God's rights on earth in their full sense" (*The Coming of the Kingdom*, 20–21). John Laidlaw says it like this: "That kingdom is just the Gospel of Jesus, or Christianity considered as a power—a cause, an influence, a moment, the power of God unto salvation. And that King is none other than Jesus the Lord" (*Studies in the Parables of Our Lord*, 52).

pictured the kingdom.[11] People's circumstances changed; life came from death. Something new and radically restorative was here. It was the kingdom.

However, it was especially in the parables that Christ showed the mysterious and hidden inner working of this reign of grace—the kingdom of heaven. Particularly in the parables the Lord unveiled how different the kingdom of heaven is from all the other kingdoms of this world. It does not come by might or force, but by the Word and Spirit. It comes like seed sown in the ground. It works like leaven. It is discovered like a merchant finding a most extraordinary pearl.

Notice, moreover, that the parables are more than just nice doctrinal descriptions of the kingdom. They are reports from the King Himself.[12] They do not comment on the kingdom from the outside, but they aim to invite into the kingdom and promote the kingdom. After all, the prophets had brought this news of the kingdom. John the Baptist had preached the kingdom. But now the great King Himself had come to unfold the kingdom.

Imagine this scenario that has occurred many times throughout history. A conquering king subdued a neighboring country, banishing the original king. That original king, however, sends emissaries who speak to the rank and file about his plans to retake the country. Often these reports had to be in code so that if the occupying king got wind of it, he would not necessarily understand all the dynamics that were in the works. But imagine that the king himself would come, veiled, and move among the people and announce the imminent return of his kingdom and how he would accomplish it. Likewise, Jesus came veiled in flesh and spoke about the kingdom in parables—in code. He announced it, explained it, and gained subjects of His kingdom. Would that not have been glorious to those who, like Joseph of Arimathaea, "waited for the kingdom of God" (Mark 15:43)?

This is especially glorious when we think about the fact that this is no earthly kingdom, but, as Christ makes clear, the kingdom *of God* or *of heaven*.[13] The reign that had its origin in heaven with God

---

11. Miracles were a demonstration of God's glorious power over creation. They served as a display of God's authority. See Phillips, *Mighty to Save*, 1–20 (esp. 3–4), and Ridderbos, *The Coming of the Kingdom*, 65–70.

12. Cf. Eugene S. Wehrli, *Exploring the Parables* (Philadelphia: United Church Press, 1963), 111–19.

13. For a biblical theological understanding of the kingdom of God/heaven,

had now come close—yes, in disguise—and yet, through the para-bles and other means, Christ unfolded its splendor and glory.

Notice how Christ did not do it all at once. He unfolded it gradually. Many parables build upon each other, and the whole body of the parables follows a discernible pattern.[14] Take even the first day of parables, recorded for us in Matthew 13. There we find seven parables with an order in them. First, there is the great intro-ductory parable of the sower, dealing with the first contact that the heart has with the Word of God. Then Christ continued with the tares, where we hear of the work of the kingdom of darkness as it sought to counter the kingdom of heaven. Next there are the parables of the leaven and the mustard seed, identifying the might of the kingdom, both internal and external. Then come the parables of the hidden treasure and the pearl merchant, both of which deal with the all-consuming love and esteem the citizen of the kingdom has towards the gospel of the kingdom. And then, finally, there is the parable of the net and fisher, indicating the final completion of the kingdom.[15]

If you consider this order, you realize how the focus remains on the kingdom through these seven parables, but within this sequence is the gradual shift from the origin of the kingdom to the final con-summation of the kingdom, and along the way Christ explains the opposition as well as esteem for the kingdom. John Laidlaw remarks: "These parables begin with a man's acceptance or rejection of the Word of God and ends with God's acceptance or rejection of men."[16]

---

see Geerhardus Vos, *Biblical Theology of the Old and New Testament* (Edinburgh: Banner of Truth, 1975), 372–87. See also Geerhardus Vos, *Redemptive History and Biblical Interpretation: The Shorter Writings of Geerhardus Vos,* ed. Richard B. Gaffin, Jr. (Philadelphia: P&R, 1980), 304–16.

14. To see an example of a similar methodology used here in dividing the parables, see Robert F. Capon, *The Parables of Grace* (Grand Rapids: Eerdmans, 1988), 7–18. Other methodologies are prevalent in New Testament studies and range from simplistic to very complicated. Snodgrass does not follow a chronological development, but rather what appears to be a topical methodology. He has divisions such as "Grace and Responsibility," "Parables of the Present Kingdom," "Parables Concerning God and Prayer" (Snodgrass, *Stories with Intent,* viii–ix, 576–77). For an overview of historical methods and approaches, see Blomberg, *Interpreting the Parables,* 29–169. For literary divisions see Sider, *Interpreting the Parables.*

15. Laidlaw, *Studies in the Parables of our Lord,* 52–53.

16. Laidlaw, *Studies in the Parables of our Lord,* 53.

It is as if Christ revealed the whole panorama of the kingdom over the course of the day's teaching.

The same gradual unfolding of the kingdom takes place over the span of the whole body of the parables. It was near the end of His time in Galilee that Christ began teaching in parables. At first, He dealt largely with the idea of the kingdom of heaven coming into this world, such as the sower sowing, the strong man bound, the seed growing secretly in the earth. Then Christ traveled through Palestine from Galilee to Jerusalem, a journey of about six months. During this time, His parables spoke often of the grace of the kingdom. Think of the parables of the good Samaritan, the great supper, and the prodigal son. It is by grace that God draws people into the kingdom. He invites them graciously, without respect to their condition, and in the kingdom they continue to live dependent on grace, in turn showing grace to others. Quite a few of the parables from this time, interestingly, also deal with money, showing how the love of money is a force that is opposed to the kingdom. The Pharisees, whose religion was based on principles of works and rewards, showed themselves to be covetous even in everyday life (Luke 16:14). Their religion and their lifestyle meshed perfectly. Christ showed the error of both, coordinating the generosity of God's grace with a life of faithful stewardship under God. Both were concepts that would have been alien to the Pharisees to whom Christ spoke. The operating principle of the kingdom is not money or man's works, but God's gifts through Christ.

As Christ neared Jerusalem, the focus of the parables seems to shift again—this time toward the judgment, which will cause division in the kingdom.[17] There is the man without the wedding garment (Matt. 22:1–14); there are five wise and five foolish virgins (Matt. 25:1–13); there are sheep and goats (Matt. 25:14–30). The need to be watchful is clear. God's kingdom will be victorious, and all who falsely claim to be part of the kingdom will be destroyed.

---

17. Morgan states this idea well. "There were the final days in the life of our Lord on earth, and these parables all move in that realm. On this third day, he was there in the Temple as the great Prophet of God, the King, and the Prophet, dealing with the nation in august majesty and dignity. The two parables we have considered had dealt with privilege." G. Campbell Morgan, *The Parables and Metaphors of Our Lord* (New York: Fleming H. Revel, 1943), 128.

We would be remiss, however, if we did not show that Christ also revealed Himself as the King of the kingdom. After all, when Christ began to teach in parables, He was beginning in earnest to prepare to suffer and perform His final work, and so He cannot but reveal Himself to a lesser or greater extent in the parables. Ultimately, He is the One who came to sow the Word of God (Matt. 13:37). He is the One digging around the fig tree (Luke 13:8). He is the treasure in the field and the pearl of great price (Matt. 13:44, 46). He is the One who through His messengers is graciously inviting to a great supper of God (Luke 14:23). He is the Bridegroom who will soon come for His church (Matt. 25:13). He is the Shepherd who goes out to find the lost sheep (Luke 15:5). Who is the father in the parable of the prodigal son other than God through Christ, looking while prodigals are still a long way off (Luke 15:20)? And all those parables that speak of grace—that grace would be dispensed at His expense. Listen to these prophetic words from the parable of the wicked husbandmen: "Last of all he sent unto them his son, saying, They will reverence my son. But when the husbandmen saw the son, they said among themselves, This is the heir; come, let us kill him, and let us seize on his inheritance. And they caught him, and cast him out of the vineyard, and slew him" (Matt. 21:37–39). When you look in the rearview mirror over all the parables, you realize that it is the King of the kingdom whose portrait is like a watermark throughout. What rich insights there were in the parables into the person and work of the Redeemer for those who believe!

Yet there is another side. In these very parables in which He revealed himself as King, Jesus also concealed Himself. He says it Himself in Matthew 13: "Therefore speak I to them in parables: because they seeing see not; and hearing they hear not, neither do they understand" (Matt. 13:13). It may be puzzling to imagine how Christ could conceal Himself in the very parables He spoke in order to reveal the kingdom and Himself as king. The explanation for this quandary lies in faith. For those who believe, the parables reveal Christ and His kingdom. For those who do not believe, all that is there are stories that are partly interesting, partly mysterious, and partly offensive. The overall effect on those who do not believe is that the truths remain hidden in terms of real knowledge and persuasion. Unbelievers never look at the parable from the "inside." At best they stand outside of its significance and import. It is like a veil of common stories has been drawn over the full reality of the kingdom, and without faith, the glory of the kingdom and the glory of Christ are hidden.

After all, when Christ began to teach in parables, He was beginning in earnest to prepare to suffer and perform the final work that was given to Him. It was time for those who expected only an earthly kingdom and salvation to go. As He physically began to withdraw and conceal Himself, His parables drew a veil of words—a veil of parables—over Himself.[18] In the parables, He hid Himself and His cross and the kingdom that would come through His death. In a way, the parables are like the ancient tabernacle. The tabernacle was a symbol of God's reign of grace among His people; there He showed forth His glory as He sat enthroned between the cherubim. The tabernacle used many coverings and veils which hid the mystery from those who were blind to it. To them it was but a little tent with a whole lot of curtains around it. Even if they could take a look within and see the various symbols—the altar, the shewbread, the laver, the candlestick, and so on—they would never understand what they truly meant and would thus derive no spiritual benefit from them. The mystery of God's gracious kingship was hidden from their eyes.

Proverbs 25:2 explains what Christ was doing when it says, "It is the glory of God to conceal a thing: but the honour of kings is to search out a matter." As the divine Son of God, Christ has the prerogative to conceal. He is the inscrutable One who is all the more glorious because He hides Himself. Let me give a simple example. Think of how much more intriguing it is to receive a gift that is wrapped, even if the wrapping is plain, than it is to receive a gift without wrapping. The wrapping begs to be taken away so the gift can be seen. Similarly, the parables have no glory to those who are blind to the Savior. They just see the plain "wrapping"; because there is no humble, teachable faith, they never receive what is in the wrapping of the parable. Those people might find a certain measure of attraction in these simple stories, but the mystery of the kingdom is hidden from them, and the King of the kingdom is hidden from them. But just as the veiled tabernacle contained glorious revelation, so the parables reveal God's grace and glory as they transform those who do believe.

---

18. Compare Johnson, *The Parables of Jesus*, 14–26.

Their Transforming Effect

When God revealed His glory on Mount Horeb to instruct the people of Israel and establish His kingdom among them, the people were unable to bear the sights and sounds of His glory. They pleaded with Moses that he would speak with God and then speak to them in turn. The royal splendor of the sovereign Lord was too great for them. Even the great Moses had to hide in the cleft of the rock, and only then, sheltered by the hand of the Lord Himself (Ex. 33:22), could he glimpse the glory of God from behind. But these glimpses were so powerful that Moses' face shone to such an extent that he had to cover his face when he came down from the mountain.

Like the Israelites who preferred to stand at a distance from God, many seem to prefer to stand afar off from the parables. They may see them as interesting stories, but they are not transformed by them. They cannot understand the things of the Spirit. But to those who believe, these very same parables are power and glory and riches, and have a transforming effect on the heart. How do the parables do that?

They Read Our Hearts

Have you ever thought when you read the parables that, from a certain perspective, they are reading you? As I indicated earlier, the parables were spoken by the omniscient Savior, the infallible interpreter of every man and woman's life and heart. He knew not only creation, but the crown of creation—man—and everything that lives in his heart. And so the parables unmask and expose the evil in our own hearts. In the parable of the sower, for instance, the stony ground exposes the hardheartedness that is so common in hearers of the Word, and the thorny ground exposes how the cares of this world choke out the seed of the Word. Think of how the parable of the rich fool exposes our greediness and selfish spirit, thinking we have it all in order with goods stored up for many years. Think of how the parable of the good Samaritan indicts us for our coldness in the name of religion and our lack of mercy to those in need. Think of how the parable of the Pharisee and the publican uncovers our pride before God, like the pride that is in the Pharisee's heart. Think of how the parable of the great Supper exposes our natural tendency "with one accord to make excuses." Think of how the parable of the prodigal son exposes our native desire to wish that we could leave the Father's house and pursue our own desires. Think of how the same parable exposes our censoriousness and critical spirit toward those who do receive the grace of God. Think of how the parable of the man who buried his talent unveils for us the tendency in us to say to God, "I feared thee, because thou art an austere man: thou takest up that thou layedst not down, and reapest that thou didst not sow" (Luke 19:22). Think of how the parable of the ten virgins exposes our tendency to fall asleep and to be unprepared for the coming of the Lord. Think of how the parable of the wicked husbandman reads our hearts; by nature, we want to remain in charge of our own lives and get rid of the heir to whom it is due.

Do you see how the parables are like a laser beam into our hearts, reading us exactly? That is the first part of this transforming work that the parables aim at—to uncover us to what we are.

They Write upon Our Hearts

These glorious parables do more than read our hearts. They begin to write God's glorious truth upon our hearts, as Paul says in 2 Corinthians 3:3: "Ye are...written not with ink, but with the Spirit of the living God; not in tables of stone, but in fleshy tables of the heart."

Through the work of God's Spirit, the parables bring us to agree with God about who and what we are. They draw confession from us. Think of how many of the parables end with a question or a challenge. For example, the parable of the good Samaritan ends this way: "Which now, of the three, thinkest thou, was neighbor unto him that fell among the thieves?" (Luke 10:36). Or the parable of the wicked husbandman, which ends, "When the lord therefore of the vineyard cometh, what will he do unto those husbandmen?" (Matt. 21:40). Or the parable of the workers in the vineyard, where the Lord asks, "Is it not lawful for me to do what I will with mine own? Is thine eye evil, because I am good?" (Matt. 20:15). Christ is requiring a response, and the parables already suggest what this response should be. In this way, they could be said to do more than "read" us; they aim to write upon our hearts the proper response to God's truth.

Even where the parables do not end with rhetorical questions, their sudden or open endings encourage a certain response. Think of how the parable of the prodigal son demands a response with its final statement: "It was meet that we should make merry and be glad: for this thy brother was dead, and is alive again; and was lost, and is found" (Luke 15:33).

The parables can also guide us in our response by detailed confessions. Rather than simply stating that the prodigal repented, the parable gives us direct speech, thereby putting on our lips the words, "I have sinned against heaven and before thee" (Luke 15:18). Likewise, the parable of the Pharisee and the tax collector leaves us with the prayer of the tax collector: "God be merciful to me a sinner" (Luke 18:13).

Finally, the parables can guide our response by specific encouragements, warnings, or exhortations. The parable of the friend at midnight includes this encouragement: "Ask, and it shall be given you, seek and ye shall find, knock, and it shall be opened unto you" (Luke 11:9). The parable of the ten virgins ends with the solemn exhortation: "Watch, therefore, for ye know neither the day nor the hour wherein the Son of man cometh" (Matt. 25:10).

This is also how Christ's parables are gloriously effective in the lives of believers. They read us, and they write upon us until our own hearts become living epistles of "the Spirit of the living God" (2 Cor. 3:3). That is how the glory of Christ in the parables transforms believers. The glory of the Lord cannot but change us: "But we all, with open face beholding as in a glass the glory of the Lord, are changed into the same image from glory to glory, even as by the Spirit of the Lord" (2 Cor. 3:18). Our hearts need to become places where Christ's glory and cross reside like glory in earthen vessels — veiled in a certain sense, yes, yet also reflecting the beauty and kingly glory of Christ.

True disciples of the Lord are not content to stay on the outside of the parables. They are drawn by the loveliness of Christ, who hides Himself in His parables. He stands ready to open them and explain them and show Himself to inquiring disciples, who humbly come and say like the disciples in Matthew 13:36: "Declare unto us the parables." Through His Spirit, He takes them by the hand and brings them all the way to Calvary to see by faith what it all means. He opens up their eyes to behold the glory of the crucified Redeemer; through the cross to the portals of the open grave and the glory that was concealed, then to the open tomb, bringing them on their faces to say like Job, "I have heard of thee by the hearing of the ear, but now my eye seeth thee" (Job 42:5). His glory lays them down at His feet, there to admire and reflect the glory of the crucified Redeemer in the parables.

CHAPTER 6

Jesus: Master of Storms

David Carmichael

It seems clear to me, beyond any shadow of a doubt, that Scripture gives to believers due warning of stormy days to be endured while en route to glory. Passage into the heavenly presence of God will not be easy or danger free. The Lord Himself makes this very point: "If they have persecuted me, they will also persecute you" (John 15:20). Nothing in these words, or others relating to cross-bearing (Matt. 16:24) or life-cost counting (Luke 14:28), gives to any thinking, sensible believers even the slightest cause to imagine that they have been called to a life of ease or that it is their guaranteed right to know protected health or abundant prosperity this side of glory. Reality takes a different form altogether.

God's people must expect to know trials, tribulations, tragedy, or tears in many forms—not to mention the hatred, opposition, and antagonism of a fallen and unbelieving world, one clearly intent on self-destruction. And what of the age we live in? It is challenging, to say the least, marked by:

- *Terrorism*, with evil, cowardly attacks made on innocent and unsuspecting people in the name of nationalism or false religion.

- *Tension* caused by financial meltdown, job loss, broken relationships, and a disintegrating society, all rooted in the sinful soil of greed or selfishness.

- *Tragedy*, in which voices describe as good what God has designated as bad; people favor or fear Islam while they sneer at or suppress Christianity. Personal honesty and dignity are shrugged off while we become foolishly enamored with the lifestyles of so-called celebrities, who are often nothing more than shallow, self-loving, superficial people. Nor must we forget the arrogance and smirking of the "new atheists" who believe that they stand on higher ground, as this world encourages them to attack and mock the Christian faith. The devil is at large!

- *Tears* as we see people falling deeper into the ruining captivity of darkness and sin and as the world rages against the rule of God. We cry with the psalmist, "How long, Lord? Wilt thou hide thyself for ever?" (Ps. 89:46).

Clearly, we live in difficult and stormy days with no immediate relief on the horizon. In such days, preachers need to speak a word in season (2 Tim. 4:2)—not a cold, dry, scholarly word, no matter how well-rooted it might be in Scripture, but a word that will engage our minds, excite our hearts, and command our wills as it inspires our spiritual imaginations. Our need today is for a word that will uplift and thrill our souls, making our spiritual heartbeat strong and steady, simultaneously bringing holy dynamism to our lives.

Yes, preachers will properly give focus to the great doctrines of Scripture, but that will never be enough to satisfy the spiritual needs of God's people. Our chief need is to see Christ, to see Him in His beauty and glory, to be enamored by Him, to have passion for Him, and to know that He is truly the fairest among ten thousand (Song 5:10). The Lord should take our breath away as Scripture presents Him to us in all of His supernatural beauty and awesome glory. The grandeur and grace of His being should captivate us. So let those who preach do so as men whose humble and chief desire it is to focus on Christ, to exalt Him and exult in Him so that believers have cause to glory in Him. Let preachers avoid the trap of feeling the need to consciously or otherwise parade their learning in a manner that often numbs the minds or deflates the souls of their listeners.

We live in stormy days, and we need in our pulpits neither comedians nor heart-tugging storytellers nor smooth and slick entertainers. What we need are preachers who agree with Archibald Alexander that "the Word of God should be delivered with the utmost solemnity under a deep impression that what we speak is indeed a revelation from God."[1] These preachers will draw us to an

---

1. James M. Garretson, *Princeton and Preaching* (Edinburgh: Banner of Truth, 2005), 186.

exalted Christ. They will fill our minds, bless our hearts, and thrill our souls with Christ. They are preachers who will focus on the One we need to see in the dark days in which we live, the One who is the *Master of storms.*

How, then, are we to survive in stormy days? Let me draw your attention to Mark 4:35–41, which contains an inspirational and uplifting message of splendid, spiritual truth. This passage reveals Jesus in all of His breathtaking glory as not only a wonderful Savior but also as a magnificent champion of His people. He is one whose life promises to us that we will know, possibly when we least expect it, victory in the midst of spiritual trials, troubles, or warfare. I am persuaded that our Lord would have us know something of a sane and sensible victory dynamic at work within us that will consistently warm and inspire our hearts, shape and power our thinking, and energize our living.

Thus we come to a portion of Scripture designed in precise, spiritual ways to deeply thrill, encourage, and stir those who are the true people of God: men and women undeservedly saved by Almighty God's compassionate love and outpoured, amazing grace, who are numbered among the redeemed, owning the guarantee of being glory bound. Simultaneously, though, as ever with this gospel, we find a strong challenge pressed upon the hearts and minds of those who, captives of the present darkness, are dead in their sin. They belong by choice not to the kingdom of God but to our depraved, diseased, and dying world.

Our chief interest, then, is the study of the very short passage found at the end of Mark 4 from verse 35 to the conclusion of the chapter. But before we go any further, it will help us to know that a special section in Mark's gospel begins at verse 35, one that runs right through to the very end of chapter 5. This extended portion of Scripture, fifty verses long, is given over to declaring and proving that to all who believe in Him, Jesus Christ is the fairest among ten thousand, the great King, the gracious Master, and the glorious Lord who reigns supreme. This is for the strengthening and encouraging of our faith, the uplifting of our souls, and the increasing of our resolve to press on in the Christian way, come what may.

Let these two words echo in your hearts and reverberate in your minds: He *reigns supreme.* These are spiritually delicious words and we should delight to savor them. You see, it is Mark's determination to give us good cause to exult in Christ because Mark would persuade us of the fact that our King and Lord reigns supreme and is indeed the Master of every situation, the conqueror, in His own time frame, of every enemy. To be a friend of the Son of God is to have cause to blaze with spiritual confidence, knowing that in Him we need never be afraid of life, this world, or the powers of darkness, because in Him victory is ours. And it is not a partial victory, but full and complete—consummated victory! Guaranteed victory! It is wonderful victory that brings to fulfillment the promise in the first Old Testament preaching of God's gospel, namely, that God's champion, our Savior, would come and crush the devil (Gen. 3:15).

What does Mark do in these verses and those that follow as he continues developing his thinking through to the conclusion of chapter 5? Well, he gives himself to the task of illustrating the fact that Christ is the great and all-conquering defender, protector, and champion of His people. He does this by a fourfold emphasis. The illustrative flow of Mark 4:35 through to the end of chapter 5 can be detailed as follows:

1. In the presence of danger, Christ is our Champion: the story of the calming of the storm (Mark 4:35–41).

2. In the presence of darkness, Christ is our Champion: the healing of Legion, the demon-possessed man ("Come out of the man, thou unclean spirit") (Mark 5:1–20).

3. In the presence of disease, Christ is our Champion: His meeting with and healing of a sick woman ("Thy faith has made thee whole") (Mark 5: 25–34).

4. In the presence of death, Christ is our Champion: the raising of the daughter of Jairus ("Talitha cumi...Damsel, I say unto thee arise") (Mark 5:21–24).

"Christ our Champion" is the great unifying theme of Mark 4:35 right through to 5:43. By means of perfect and precise illustration, Mark makes his point that Christ is the Master who reigns supreme in every situation. It is my intention to focus our minds on the details of the first of Mark's four historically rooted illustrations. So we look at Mark 4:35–41, keen to be reminded that because our Lord is the Master who reigns supreme, it is ours to glory in the reality that in

Him there is victory over danger. Now, looking at the disciples in the verses before us, notice first their predicament.

They Faced a Storm (Mark 4:35–37)

Such is life even for loyal followers of Jesus living in faithful obedience to His will. Life can be calm one moment and beset with troubles the next. Many are the storms of life that suddenly blow up and violently rage against us, usually when we least expect them. I have in mind wild and stormy circumstances that seem determined to bring wreckage to our trust in Christ or a gaping hole to our faith in Him; we might begin to sink deeply into and under the tumultuous waters of spiritual fear, doubt, distress, disillusionment, or unbelief. Think of how such an experience might potentially arise as the result of a fierce storm of grief, blowing and raging within us, after a heart-rending, unexpected bereavement. Or consider the storms of illness that can damage us spiritually by threatening our physical well being. What of the focused storms of temptation that seem intent on blowing personal ruin our way?

Many and varied are the sudden and sometimes savage storms of life; they often seem powerful enough to blow our lives off their glory-bound course. Drowning our faith and leaking out our hope in the Lord Jesus Christ of whom we begin to think badly, the storms close in on us. We can wonder if the lack of action on His part has to do with His either being ignorant of or indifferent to our predicament of life. At times He seems to be fast asleep as the storms of life rage against us, taking their heavy spiritual toll. But we need to learn the primary lesson that the verses before us teach, namely, that Jesus can be trusted whatever storms of life we find ourselves in because He is the Master who reigns supreme.

This is a glorious fact, but when you come to think about it we can only discover its reality for ourselves in the midst of a storm. For this very reason, Christians are nowhere taught in Scripture that we will have an easy and smooth passage from earth to glory—that ours will be a journey exempt from life's storms. Indeed, the opposite is the case. Think of our Lord's words of warning to His disciples: "In the world ye shall have tribulation" (John 16:33). Yes, we are glory-bound, but our passage home will not be smooth sailing. Like all men, we will know the storms of sickness, stress, loss, bereavement, worry, or disappointment. We need to be realistic. As Christians, our journey to the promised land of glory and gain, even as we walk in the path of duty doing the will of God, will not be one empty of stormy moments.

But someone might ask the question: "Why does God allow the storms of life to blow so furiously against His own people—His beloved?" Well, you see, storms test our faith for good reason. It is one thing to say that we love Jesus on a calm, pleasant, peaceful day, but another thing altogether to actually trust Him when the day is dark, difficult, or stormy, full of life's troubles. Storms of affliction have a way of touching us, ultimately for our own spiritual good. They remind us of our own human frailty and weakness and give us cause to properly and trustingly lean on our Savior, drawing from the resources of His love and grace, so as to be strengthened, sustained, and satisfied. And when we receive such help, does it not ensure that we grow in love for our Master? Our trust moves from the realm of mere theoretical expression—"I trust Jesus"—to the realm of marked practical experience—"I am trusting in Jesus." Storms that God allows in His providence to blow our way activate and energize our trust, mature our faith, and wean us from the world as there develops within us an ever-increasing longing for heaven.

Now, in terms of the storm the disciples found themselves in, it was a savage one. It was so fierce that it had the power to cause experienced fishermen, who had battled through many a storm, to fear for their lives. But you know that there were good reasons why, in the midst of such a dreadful and dangerous storm, they should have been without fear. We need to give measured thought to these reasons, for they can make all the difference in the storms of life.

They Had a Promise for Their Lives
Jesus had said to them, "Let us pass over to the other side" (Mark 4:35). We find in these words, if we weigh them carefully enough, the tones of implicit guarantee and strong promise in relation to the reality of *safe arrival*. Note that Jesus does not make promise of an easy or calm journey. But what He does promise is guaranteed, safe arrival. Our Lord's words were not "Let us attempt to pass over to the other side" but rather, "Let us pass over to the other side." This is the Lord of Glory speaking. What power known or unknown to man could have prevented Him from making safe passage to the

other side? When Jesus invited His disciples to go, they should have realized that safe arrival was a given. Traveling in Jesus' company always means assured arrival at His stated destination.

We need to register this truth, for it is a glorious gospel reality. As believers, ours is the privilege of being Jesus' traveling companions. In essence, it is the invitation of the gospel that by grace and faith we walk with Jesus, that we journey with Him, knowing that ours is the privilege of traveling to the other side. This world is not our home; we are foreigners in a strange land. We sense that we belong to another kingdom, high, glorious, and majestic, against which this world pales in comparison.

Having responded by grace to the wooing call of the gospel, we find ourselves departing from the shores of a dying world. And this we do in the company of Jesus, traveling with the guarantee that we will pass over to the other side. Ours will be safe arrival on the distant shores of glory. Our journey will not be easy, but as we travel home we are much encouraged, even in the storms of life, because we have the promise of the Lord girding our hearts. Ours is the promise of safe arrival on the shores of the heavenly kingdom (John 14:1–3).

Do you hear the gospel promise again (Matt. 11:28)? Christ is emphatic in His teaching and promise: we *will* reach the other side. When we travel in the gospel boat, we travel with our Savior. We are the crew and He is the Captain. He will take us home, and we will dwell with Him in the kingdom of heavenly grandeur, the place of everlasting glory and majesty. Bliss and blessing will be ours to enjoy, time without end. It is guaranteed (Rev. 21:1–5). Yes, the world is dark and the storms are many and wild, blowing furiously against us. Nevertheless, we are glory bound because we believe the gospel promise that all who travel with Jesus will, in guaranteed, assured, and victorious fashion, pass over to the other side.

The world will haunt, hunt, and harass the people of God (2 Tim. 3:12). It will oppose, mock, scorn, and persecute, subtly and flagrantly. Believers will find themselves living through terrible times in the last days (2 Tim. 3:1). Men, given to the ways of evil and darkness, will be lovers of themselves, lovers of money, lovers of pleasure, but resolutely *not* lovers of God (2 Tim. 3:2–4). God's people must expect to be on the receiving end of the storms of this world's hatred of and opposition to God's glorious gospel. But know this: the people of

God, though they bear the wounds, bruises, and scars inflicted by the storms of spiritual warfare, will at the end safely pass over to the other side. There is no power that can keep us from the love of God, snatch our salvation away, or prevent us from entering the eternal kingdom (Rom. 8:35–39; John 10:27–30; 1 Peter 1:3–9). The other side is our destination, and upon its shores we will safely arrive.

And what is the gospel of God if it is not an invitation to the lost men and women of this world who, being unregenerate, are steeped in sin, without good purpose or any real, saving hope in life? The gospel is without doubt a wooing invitation to sinners that they, with God's help, might with great haste make their way into the company of Jesus. They may board the gospel boat of salvation to safely travel with Him to the other side, to the place of everlasting glory and gain. When Jesus reaches out His hand to sinners, He says to them in the invitation of His gospel, "Sinner, take My hand, and together let us journey to the other side." If your hand is in the Lord's hand, then know that whatever the storms of trials or troubles, or the wearying spiritual aches and pains that assail you at this time, that you will reach the other side. What a glorious promise belongs to believing people: we will reach the other side.

They Had a Presence in Their Lives

Think about it: the Lord was with the disciples, so what had they to fear? They were in the company of awesome power. Had He not driven out demons, setting people free to live new lives? Had He not miraculously healed many people? Was He not the very Son of God who had won their hearts? Yes, yes, and yes again! Rather than knowing fear of the storm, they should have had deep and firm confidence in Him. In their defense, though, we might say that despite all of the spiritual advantages they had known, they were still young and growing in their faith, yet to learn that Jesus reigns supreme as the Master of every situation. In the outworking of God's providence, the experience of the storm would teach them much.

We need to remind ourselves that we, too, enjoy the supernatural presence of the Lord in our lives. The Lord is with His people; He will never leave or forsake us (Heb. 13:5). Such is His awesome might that He is able to confidently declare that no power, known or unknown to man, has the ability to snatch from His hand the people who are His beloved (Rom. 8:38–39). Do you not see that as Christians, ours is the privilege and pleasure of knowing the Lord and enjoying the reality of His power in and around our lives? What joy is ours to know, even in the midst of the storm!

They Had a Pattern for Their Lives
The disciples could see that Jesus was perfectly at peace, even in the midst of the storm. The reason for His behavior was that He knew He was at the center of God's will for His life. God the Father, in whom His trust was anchored, was the one He knew would care for Him. So it was easy for Jesus to sleep, even in the midst of a savage storm.

He is a pattern for our lives. We too can know peace in the midst of the storm when we ensure, following our Lord's example, that we are living and trusting in the will of God for our lives. Then we can say with the psalmist, "I will both lay me down in peace, and sleep: for thou, Lord, only makest me dwell in safety" (Ps. 4:8).

We have noted that the disciples faced a storm. Secondly, we observe that:

They Focused on the Savior (Mark 4:38)
We need to be reminded that this is the appropriate action for people caught up in trouble. Full of anxiety and fear, they turned to Jesus. Short on trust, reverence, and patience, they roused Him from His sleep in order to make complaint: "Master, carest thou not that we perish?" (Mark 4:38). Notice that their chief concern was their own safety and not their Master's. However, we do hear the note of faith in their cry. It was clearly their belief and hope that, with Christ awake, their physical lives might yet be saved.

The storm had done its work by giving the disciples fresh cause to look to Jesus, draw close to Him, lean on Him, and learn and know again their great need of Him. However, we should take a moment to remind ourselves how unacceptable our own behavior is if it has become our practice to turn to Jesus only when we find ourselves in trouble. He should be the focus of our spiritual gaze and the foundation upon which we build our lives every day.

So the disciples cried unto Jesus. It was a cry of faith, albeit little faith. In essence, the cry was a frightened plea for help. By implication, their plea was "Save us!" Angry, menacing clouds were heavy and dark overhead; the storm was wild, powerful, and threatening as it gave tumult to the waves that lashed the boat and held it captive. The disciples' fear was high, water was pouring over the side, and the boat was filling up. They sensed that they were in a storm that had the beating of them.

It was a terrifying experience. Nevertheless, God in His providence allowed it for their spiritual good so that their faith would grow, develop, mature, and be educated. The storm would help them discover wonderful truths about Jesus in a moment when He would exercise His awesome power. Such truth would be pressed upon their hearts and communicate to them the great truth that Jesus is the Master of every situation and circumstance. He is and always will be the source of victory for His people.

Blessed, then, was the storm that taught the disciples this important lesson as it moved them away from a self-sufficiency to the better place of reliance and dependence on the Lord's grace and power. Is it not heartwarming to note that while the storm did not have the power to wake Jesus, the touch of their trembling hands and faith did? This proved beyond question that He was sensitive to their needs! In the boat, even as the storm raged and roared, Jesus was at rest with His head upon a pillow. The storm did not and could not trouble Him or rouse Him from His peaceful sleep. But the need of His disciples could and would rouse Him.

You must never imagine that the Lord is disinterested in your situation, be it big or small. Nothing could be further from the truth. I tell you that, in your moments of need, when life's storms rage against you and seem to have the power to overwhelm or submerge you in the spiritually drowning waters of dilemma, dismay, doubt, or defeat, a faith-filled touch will bring Him to you. Yes, a touch, a cry, a plea, a groan will bring Him to you. To focus on the Savior when we find ourselves in the midst of a storm is to discover that He is with us and for us in loving, gracious, and powerful fashion (Deut. 31:6).

How foolish we are, then, when we ask in the storms of life if God cares for us. Of course He does! Remember that it was for our sake that He came into our world, knowing all that would happen. His would be a lowly birth followed by a life that would become the focus of the world's hatred, opposition, and rejection. He would know what it was to be hunted, persecuted, forsaken, beaten, scourged, and crucified. And still He came! Do not doubt His care for your life or your soul.

So we have noted that the disciples faced a storm. We have also noted that they focused on the Savior. Now, in response, as we have cause to look at our Lord, we need to notice that:

He Created a Stillness (Mark 4:39–41)

It was for Him the easiest of things to accomplish. Think of Paul's knowledgeable and encouraging words: "For by him were all things created, that are in heaven, and that are in earth, visible and invisible, whether they be thrones, or dominions, or principalities, or powers: all things were created by him, and for him" (Col. 1:16). He is the Lord of glory, the Master over all and of everything.

So we see Him standing in the boat, the mighty Creator and Ruler of all that He surveyed. With great authority, He rebuked the wind and commanded the waves, "Peace be still" (Mark 4:39). Immediately, all was calm because the Master had spoken. On that day of storm, Jesus made all the difference, securing His disciples' safety. What a glorious and awe-inspiring picture Mark presents to our spiritual imagination. Can you see it?

I see Jesus rising to His feet, unfazed by the pitching or rolling of the boat. His hair and robes are billowing in the wind. The huge, heavy waves are drenching Him with their spray, determined to knock Him to His knees. I see the disciples with fear and anxiety written large on their faces as the savage storm, ugly and dangerous, left them persuaded of nature's destructive power. But in all of what I see, my eyes find their best focus on Jesus the Lord, who in the midst of storm made all the difference. What glorious and thrilling reality! He spoke and all was calm.

Life will not be without its storms, but for our encouragement let us learn well the truth that Jesus is in the boat of life with us. He is the One to whom we can always turn for wisdom, guidance, courage, power, and rescue. Do you remember what our Lord said to the Sadducees in relation to their rejecting the reality of resurrection? "Do ye not therefore err, because ye know not the scriptures, neither the power of God?" (Mark 12:24). To know the Word in its richness and detail is to know the Lord in all of His beauty, glory, and awesome power. He has sovereign and perfect control over all that He has created. Fill your eyes with the Lord who is the Master over storms.

When the psalmist looked at the ways of evil men he was distressed and felt overwhelmed, but how different things became when he looked to the Lord. A cry formed on his lips: "The Lord is King for ever and ever: the heathen are perished out of his land" (Ps. 10:16). Jesus has not promised us that we will go through life without difficulties, but He has promised us His hand, His strength, His love, and ultimate rescue. We must never despair of reaching the end of our journey—heaven's shores. The Lord will ensure our arrival. He will carry us through every danger till at the end we are delivered to glory.

With Christ, we can conquer every foe. Our relations or friends might oppose us, our neighbors may laugh or scorn, our temptations are many and great, and governments the world over legislate against God's people. But He that is for us is greater than the one who is against us (1 John 4:4).

There is no storm in your life—be it of despair, tears, or guilt— that Jesus Christ cannot deal with. He is the Master. He reigns supreme. He can turn storm into calm! So be done with little faith and instead be people of much faith, indeed, of great faith. Fill your eyes with the beauty and glory of Jesus Christ, the Son of God. He reigns supreme. In Him there is victory—glorious, wonderful, and everlasting victory.

CHAPTER 7

Jesus: Master of Stress

David Carmichael

I am persuaded that focused study of the fifteenth chapter of the Gospel of Mark should leave us thoroughly convinced that we dilute our understanding of the details it contains, particularly in relation to our Lord's experience on Calvary's cross, if we fail to mark God's use of divine and dramatic punctuation.

God's Use of Divine Punctuation (Mark 15:33–41)

The event of the cross is full of deep meaning and rich doctrinal message. It channels to our minds a vital, vivid, and spiritual communication from heaven—a message so powerfully and precisely punctuated by God as to ensure that it has the greatest impact upon our souls. Just as good punctuation gives structure, logic, and rhythm to the written word, highlighting its intrinsic use of emotion, nuance, or contours of emphasis to facilitate readers' engagement, education, or excitement, so God brings the message of the cross wonderfully, strikingly, and pertinently alive. He does this by means of His skillful and careful divine punctuation: the use of doctrinal detail and demonstrable drama to engage minds and touch souls with the message of the cross—all to reveal the breathtaking beauty and glory of Christ.

If we are to see Jesus at His best, as the one who is the *Master of stress*, then we need to see Him upon the cross of Calvary, where He experienced stress to the utmost degree! That is stress of such spiritual and emotional magnitude as to be beyond our fullest comprehension. It was deep and dangerous stress, so extreme in its manifestation that it had the power to break a man; undoubtedly, it would have broken a lesser man than Jesus Christ. It was stress that would find its awful climax in the momentous event of Calvary's cross. He would know the hatred of a world that lusted after His death. Oh, the unimaginable stress and the ever-intensifying strain that our Lord endured during His last moments on earth.

Think of Gethsemane where He began to be "sore amazed, and to be very heavy" (Mark 14:33). His was the experience of being deeply distressed and much troubled as He contemplated the dark hours that lay ahead of Him. The very weight of the prospect was almost more than He could humanly bear. Hence the scorching honesty of His emotional outburst: "My soul is exceeding sorrowful unto death" (Mark 14:34). There was a cup to be drunk: the one containing the wrath of God against sin!

In terms of His experience of the ever-increasing stress that engulfed His being, think of the trials He endured before judges who were anything but honest, objective, and impartial (Mark 14:53–65; 15:1–15; Luke 23:6–12), and how they made disgraceful use of those who "bore false witness against him" (Mark 14:56).

Think of the aftermath of His wrongly being found guilty of blasphemy by the Sanhedrin: He was spat upon, blindfolded, struck, and mocked (Mark 14:64–65). Without an iota of doubt, our Lord experienced such intense and magnified personal stress as potentially had the power, knowing as He did the hatred of the world and the focused attention of the Evil One, to break His spirit, diminish and corrupt His faith, and destroy His trust in His heavenly Father. This stress, though, would not even begin to reach its climax until some Roman soldiers had enjoyed their evil way with Him. It would be theirs to scourge Him and to mock Him, dressing Him up as their "comic" king, using a faded purple robe and a crown of cruel thorns (Mark 15:16–19). It was the behavior of these same soldiers that gave Pilate cause to utter the words, "Behold the man!" (John 19:5). These were necessary words of identification because Jesus' face had been beaten beyond all recognition (Matt. 27:29–31).

Surely, now, enough had been done by a fallen, wicked world to give expression to its malignant hatred of Jesus! Evil, though, is never satisfied. Enough is never enough! Listen, at the cross, to the passersby as they berated Jesus with their scornful mocking. In essence, they said: "You are no prophet" (Mark 15:29–30). Listen to the chief priests who mauled Jesus with the accusations: "You are not a priest, and You are no king" (Mark 15:31–32). What a storm of stress our

Lord endured. Gethsemane (Matt. 26:36–46)! Gabbatha (John 19:13–16)! Golgotha (Mark 15:22–39)! As the Son of God, He was mauled, mocked, and rejected in all of His saving offices. The world would not have Him as its prophet, priest, or king. What wicked, complete, and determined rejection!

The point must be made again: if we are to see Jesus at His best, as the one who truly is the *Master of stress*, then we need to see Him in His dying moments upon the cross of Calvary. And seeing Him there, it is absolutely essential that we pay the closest attention to God's use of divine punctuation recorded in Mark 15:33–41, determined as He is in His communication with us to drive home the real meaning and rich message of the cross of Calvary.

Consider, then, His use of the punctuation of drama, dignity, and demonstration and declaration.

The Punctuation of Drama (Mark 15:34)
There was clearly dramatic effect when suddenly, in the oft-quoted words of Spurgeon, there was "midnight at mid-day"—the moment when the cross and surrounding area suddenly and unexpectedly found itself bathed in the deepest, almost suffocating, eerie darkness. It was a punctuating moment of supernatural wonder. Thirty-three years earlier, the midnight of the birth of Jesus had known angels (Luke 2:8–9), brightness (Luke 2:9), and music (Luke 2:13); now, at the midday of His death, a starker moment—one with an absence of angels and portentously marked by prevailing darkness and loud silence. What a striking, solemn contrast! His birth marked by heaven's celebrating, His death marked by heaven's mourning! Dramatic punctuation, indeed, revealing the deepest mourning for the sin and wickedness of the world and, therefore, the need for the death of the beloved Son of God (Amos 8:9–10).

By use of the evocative punctuation of dramatic darkness, God was issuing a symbolic warning to those who, on behalf of a fallen world, had hunted Jesus to the cross. It was a warning with its roots in the events of the first Passover (Ex. 12:1–7). He would have the minds of Jesus' tormentors recall another moment of darkness—a time when their ancestors had survived the plague of death as it swept inexorably over Egypt by smearing the blood of the Passover lamb on the sides and tops of the door frames of their homes. When the judgment of God came upon the land, killing the firstborn, the angel of death would "pass over" the homes of the people of God. By an act of grace, God saved His own people, those under the protection of the blood of the Passover lamb. And the warning in the cross of Jesus, made explicit by God's punctuation of darkness, lets a sinner know that, come the day when he will know the judgment of God upon his sins, that his salvation and the safety of his soul will be utterly dependent upon his enjoying the covering of the blood of Jesus, the ultimate Passover lamb (1 Cor. 5:7). For this to happen, there needs to be faith in Jesus Christ and His redeeming work upon the cross. Without such, a sinner's lot will be the darkness of eternal doom (Jude 13). God's punctuation highlights the strikingly pertinent and pressing message of the cross: judgment is coming and men have a need to be prepared.

But we also find great punctuating drama in the emotional and spiritual moment when Jesus' voice unexpectedly and abruptly broke and pierced His self-imposed three hours of solemn silence upon the cross. It had been, in no uncertain terms, a dramatic silence, indicative of the mysterious and deep emotions He was experiencing in the stress-filled, tormenting moment of being made sin and knowing its terrible punishment (2 Cor. 5:21). Dramatic silence, shattered, by a dramatic shout! It was loud; it was the loudest of cries, strong and full of vibrant, overflowing passion. It was a soul cry! And it erupted from the depths of His being, knowing the focus of His mind and the fire of His heart. It was a striking cry with the searing, scorching power to rend the heavens and be heard in the very throne room of God. It was a cry that would suffer no muffling, a shout determined not to be ignored. It was an emotional eruption, one demanding to be heard, as dramatic a cry as the world has ever known. Listen to it again, "Eloi, Eloi, lama sabachthani?... My God, my God, why hast thou forsaken me?" (Mark 15:34). What a dramatic moment in the history of the world—indeed, in the history of heaven, in terms of God outworking His mysterious providence. What could be more dramatic than *God the Son*, at the zenith of His suffering and anguish, crying unto *God the Father*, "My God, why?" Dramatic indeed!

In due course, Jesus would get His answer, and it would be, unsurprisingly, an outstandingly dramatic one. It would know the dynamic of the punctuation of dramatic demonstration when the temple curtain was torn in two and an earthquake shook the countryside. In essence, God said to His Son:

> Thou askest Me why Thou hast been forsaken. Here is Thy answer. I have accepted the sacrifice of Thy life for the sins of the world. With My own hands, I have torn the curtain that has kept sinful man at a distance from Me. Now the way into My presence is open and I bid sinners come. They must approach in Thy name, having been washed and cleansed in Thy blood, for Thou art their Passover Lamb (1 Cor. 5:7). Thou didst take their place under My holy judgment. Thou hast borne their sins, every last one of them. Thou hast suffered sin's punishment and died in the place of those who were undeserving of a Savior. I tell Thee, My Son, the way to salvation has been opened.

What a dramatic exchange between the Father and the Son, as suggested by the punctuation of demonstration. Let us solemnly note, though, that our Lord's experience of desertion on the cross is a stark reminder and warning to sinners that sin brings terrible consequence: terrifying distance from God.

However, it is important that we note in direct relation to the punctuating, dramatic cry which erupted out of our Lord's soul, that it was powered by loving, focused, and unwavering trust in God. The cry affirms that our Lord's sense of desertion was real. He was forsaken of God when for a season He became sin for us; He was the one destined to be the bearer of our punishment. It is a stark and unassailable fact that God the Father stood back from God the Son, His eyes being too pure to look on evil (Hab. 1:13).

It is a fact, though, that, in the bleak darkness and sore desertion of the moment, at no point did Jesus rail against God with anger or petulance. Nor did He ever lose His trust in God. The truth is that His dramatic cry gave expression and amplification to the trust He felt in His heart. Do you hear what God is saying in the punctuated language and message of the cross? It is that we should learn well from His beloved Son to hold on to our trust in the stressful trials of life. Unwaveringly, Jesus trusted His Father in heaven. Even in His moment of being forsaken, He knew unerringly that He was still the beloved of God, the one who, as He did the work He had been given to do, left His Father well pleased. His words reverberate with unequivocal trust: "My God, my God." Do you register the glorious emphasis? "*My* God, *my* God." Hearing these words, we may be sure that the Father loved His Son as much as ever.

Yes, there was distance and a tangible sense of frightening desertion, but the Son never stopped *trusting* the Father. And the Father never stopped *loving* the Son. What a dramatic, punctuating cry, "My God, my God!" In essence, Jesus was saying: "My God, I cry to Thee because I continue to love and trust Thee even in this My moment of greatest stress and need. Yes, I feel the distance between Us, such as emotionally bruises My heart, psychologically disturbs My inner peace, intellectually troubles My mind, bringing trauma to My soul. But know this: in My pain and anguish there is no other to whom I would turn. Even if, once again, the evil one was to come offering rescue from the cross and the prize of all of the kingdoms of the world becoming Mine to rule over, I would still refuse him My loyalty. I remain committed to Thee with every aspect and fiber of My being. I cling to Thee in the stress and strain of the moment. Thou art *My* God; yes, *My* God! To Thee I turn and cling and to no other."

In the midst of great trial, His was great trust, and so He mastered His moment of greatest stress. We must learn from His example. Are there not times when, to a much lesser or modified degree, we find ourselves feeling forsaken? In foolish moments, we feel as though God has turned away from us. Such moments are brought on possibly by the sore experience of unexpected illness, unrelenting affliction, the wearying and constant struggles of life, knowing and suffering the consequences of our own foolish actions, or by God being mysteriously at work—all to the eventual teaching of important life lessons, designed, in time, to draw us closer to Him.

It is possible that many a believer will be heard to utter a cry tantamount to "My God, my God, why hast Thou forsaken me?" That is, in effect, "I am struggling in the present moment. I miss the sense of Thy presence. I feel the lack of Thy comfort and consolation. I feel so alone!" But while we might know the drama of such a cry in our lives, we must not give way to despair! We must not foolishly imagine that we are without hope, or that God has forever turned away from us; that we will never again know the help or blessings of His outpoured grace. Such thinking would further weaken us spiritually, as well as leave us emotionally embittered.

Rather, we serve ourselves in better fashion when we reach out to God in trust, casting ourselves upon His care, showing that we are accepting of the outworking of His providence despite mysterious, wounding, stressful, and challenging times. In the moments when our groans and cries effectively amount to "My God, my God, why hast Thou forsaken me?" we must find ourselves showing forth our trust by our emphatic use of possessive pronouns in relation to God—"*my* God, *my* God."

In the darkness of life, or in the midst of any sense of feeling lost or deserted, it should be our way to cry unto heaven with lively hope and trusting faith: "My God, my God, I look to Thee and no other." Let it also be the case that Job's wise words will be found upon our lips, when, if like him, we find ourselves in the midst of distressingly stressful and trying circumstances: "Though he slay me, yet will I trust in him" (Job 13:15). In moments of darkness and desertion we would also do well to remember the words and example of the psalmist David: "Why art thou cast down, O my soul? and why art thou disquieted within me? hope thou in God: for I shall yet praise him, who is the health of my countenance, and my God" (Ps. 42:11).

Moving now from the punctuation of drama, we need next to consider the punctuation of dignity.

The Punctuation of Dignity (Mark 15:35–37)

I want you to notice Jesus' dignified behavior in the midst of the drama of deliberate misdirection. Some of those who heard His plaintive cry of abandonment—uttered, I believe, in the very moment of His emptying the last dregs of the cup of suffering, the very thought of which had so disturbed Him in the garden of Gethsemane (Mark 14:32–42)—claimed that He was calling out to the prophet Elijah for help. I am sure that they knew full well that He was doing no such thing. They were, however, trying to capitalize on a belief current in their day that Elijah played a role as the patron saint of sufferers or those in need of being rescued. It strikes me as a crass attempt to cheapen Jesus' cry.

They were making a joke at His expense as they deliberately mistook His use of the Aramaic "Eloi, Eloi" (in Hebrew, *Eli*) as a cry not to God but to the prophet Elijah—a cry not for the help of the greater but for the lesser! They mocked Him. But it was a punctuating moment that would lead to even greater drama. John tells us in his gospel that it was following this moment of mockery that Jesus spoke His fifth word from the cross, namely, "I thirst" (John 19:28).

Here were words that gave prophetic fulfillment to the fifteenth verse of the psalm, which we have good cause to believe was in Jesus' mind as He hung on the cross: "My tongue cleaveth to my jaws" (Ps. 22:15). Our Lord's punctuating cry, then, fulfilled prophecy. It was a cry that did not go unnoticed in heaven, for God heard the anguished cry of the Son He loved and determined that He would be ministered to in His need. In the final moments of the accomplishing of His greatest work—dying for the sins of the world, while retaining His trust in God—He would know the soothing ministry of relief for His parched lips and throat with greater joy, blessing, and victory to follow. Mark tells us that a man, touched and moved by the cries of Jesus (some believe him to have been the centurion mentioned in verse 39), took a sponge and, having soaked it in wine vinegar, a popular and cheap thirst-quenching drink in those days, offered it to Jesus on a stick, or, more precisely as John tells us in his gospel, the stalk of a hyssop plant (John 19:29).

Jesus was glad of the drink, and as He sucked on the sponge, He enjoyed the refreshment that it brought to Him (John 19:30). Now He was ready for His last moments on earth. Raising Himself up, He gave breath to another piercing cry. Yet again it was one given to the dramatic punctuating of the message of the cross. It was His sixth cry: "It is finished" (John 19:30). In the Greek text, there is but one word—*tetelestai*. What wonderfully ringing and thrilling tones this word has! It seems to reverberate with the spiritual music of triumph and the lyrical cry of assured victory. "*Tetelestai*: finished!"

It was not a word spoken in defeat or weakness, as though He were bearing testimony to the fact that He had been beaten by the forces that had assailed Him and nailed Him to a cross, mocked Him, and watched Him die. No, His point was not that He had been finished by His enemies—not remotely! The truth is that His cry knew much spiritual vigor and vitality as He gave loud and clear testimony to the fact that His mission was finished. Even more than that, it was successfully finished. And despite all the signs to the contrary, He was far from being in the depths of the experience of defeat. Rather, His was the cry of an exultant man standing on the elevated heights of the dramatic reality of victory won over the powers of darkness, whose determination it had been to break Him and turn Him against God.

"Tetelestai!" was His cry. He did not say, "I am finished." He said, "It is finished." He was testifying that His work was finished. He was declaring that He had accomplished, without failure, all that the Father had given Him to do and all He had come to do. *Tetelestai!* Nothing left undone, nothing at all. Finished! He had come from glory, commissioned by God to do a great work—the work of salvation. It was a work that only He could accomplish, and it knew His complete commitment, even from the earliest of years. Do you remember the words He spoke as a twelve-year-old when He said, in determined and disciplined tones, to those who thought He was lost? "How is it that ye sought me? wist ye not that I must be about my Father's business?" (Luke 2:49). He spent His whole life serving and pleasing His Father and ultimately, in the perfect timing of heaven, to the blessing and saving of men. We find the proof of this in our Lord's own words of testimony: "My meat is to do the will of him that sent me, and to finish his work" (John 4:34). And again: "For I came down from heaven, not to do mine own will, but the will of him that sent me.... And this is the will of him that sent me, that every one which seeth the Son, and believeth on him, may have everlasting life: and I will raise him up at the last day" (John 6:38–40).

Clearly, Jesus was a man on a saving mission. It could not, however, be rushed. Everything was designed and destined to happen in accordance with the perfect plan and time schedule of God. John tells us of a moment when God's providence knew challenge: "Then they sought to take him: but no man laid hands on him, because his hour was not yet come" (John 7:30). But when it did come, He knew exactly what the Father expected of Him in the way of obedience. "And it came to pass, when the time was come that he should be received up, he steadfastly set his face towards Jerusalem" (Luke 9:51). Does that register with you? He set His face towards Jerusalem, knowing exactly the experience He was walking into.

Had He not prophetically told His own disciples that "the Son of man must suffer many things, and be rejected of the elders, and of the chief priests, and scribes, and be killed" (Mark 8:31)? However, He not only told them what would happen, He also told them why it would happen. "For…the Son of man came not to be ministered unto, but to minister, and to give his life a ransom for many" (Mark 10:45). Jesus knew that in paying the ransom by sacrificing His life for the sins of men, all of the Old Testament prophecies relating to the Messiah's saving work would find complete and precise fulfillment in Him.

- He was the Savior promised in Genesis 3:15 who defeated the devil.

- He was the One spoken of by Micah whose origins were old and of ancient times (Micah 5:2).

- He was the One who owned the titles Wonderful, Counselor, Mighty God, Everlasting Father, and Prince of Peace (Isa. 9:6).

- He was also, in fulfillment of the prophecies of Isaiah, the One who was wounded and bruised as He bore the sin of many and made intercession for transgressors; by His stripes they were healed (Isa. 53:5, 12). His would be supernatural suffering, beyond our comprehension.

All that Jesus came to do, by way of holy service to God unto the saving of the lost, had been wonderfully accomplished. He had obeyed God's will, He had preached God's Word, and, on the cross, in line with God's will and Word, He had done God's work. No wonder He cried out in relation to the work He had come to do—the work of salvation—"*Tetelestai!*" His was without doubt a finished work. *Tetelestai*, in its fullest sense, means "it is finished, it stands finished, and it always will be finished." He had done the greatest work ever: He had paid the full cost of our salvation.

In the deep darkness over the cross, the sins of the world had been placed on and pressed down upon Him. It was a heavy, crushing weight no man but He could bear. And as He was made sin on our behalf (2 Cor. 5:21), so to bear our punishment, He experienced a sense of soul-destroying desertion as no person had ever known before. But it was an emotion and a moment He would conquer. Therefore, He was able to shout in victory, "*Tetelestai!*" Price paid in full, saving work done, God honored, redemption unto salvation accomplished. *Tetelestai!*

You cannot add to the finished work of Jesus. So let the truth be heard, near and far, that any who think that they can add to Christ's work to the meriting of the saving of their souls are trapped in a delusion, one that will be their eternal death. Salvation comes by trusting in the finished work of Jesus, and nothing and no one else. There is no other way into heaven (John 14:6). The work of salvation belonged to Jesus and He finished it. Hence His cry of victory: *"Tetelestai!"*

To know Him in His finished victory is to have cause to exult in Him and to lift up our voices with Philip Bliss, singing to the glory of our Lord, with all the passion of our being:

> Lifted up was he to die,
> It is finished was his cry
> Now in heav'n exalted high
> Hallelujah, what a Savior.

Yes, indeed, what a Savior, what a wonderful Savior! And as He hung on the cross there was one final word that He would utter. Luke records it for us in his gospel. "Father, into thy hands I commend my spirit" (Luke 23:46). Do you understand the implications of this seventh word from the cross? It is this: there was no longer any distance between the Father and the Son. The cry of desertion was behind Him and He no longer thirsted; He had finished the work God had given Him to do. Now His was a cry of confident and assured delight, for He had regained the consciousness of the Father's loving, caring, and protecting presence. Hence the rich and trusting tone of His heartfelt words: "Father, into thy hands I commend my Spirit." Thus it was that He returned to the glory that He had with the Father from eternity (John 17:5, 24). Mark puts it like this: "And Jesus cried with a loud voice, and gave up the ghost" (Mark 15:37). What punctuation of dignity!

Our Lord's death was a dignified one, not at all what His enemies had planned for Him. They had wanted Him to die as others normally died on the cross. They lusted for Him to know progressive loss of strength, to fall into unconsciousness, to die in embarrassing, unheroic, undignified, weak, and feeble fashion. But they would have no such satisfaction. For in dignified manner at the end, His was a loud cry: the cry of a man dying in strength, not weakness; the cry of a man mastering stress by trusting in God and bowing to His will; the cry of a man dying in His own time, and not the world's; the cry of a man tasting victory!

He was not a martyr. Rather, He was the beloved Son of God making the willing sacrifice of His life for the sins of the world. Of His own free will, He gave up His life. Paul tells us of Jesus that "He humbled himself, and became obedient unto death, even the death of the cross" (Phil. 2:8). Jesus gave His life; nobody took it.

No man ever lived as He lived, and no man ever died as He died. With a loud cry, nothing less than a dignified cry of victory, Jesus, in strength, in His own time, full of trust in God, breathed His last. The apostle Paul has this to say: "Wherefore God also hath highly exalted him, and given him a name which is above every name: that at the name of Jesus every knee should bow, of things in heaven, and things in earth, and things under the earth; and that every tongue should confess that Jesus Christ is Lord, to the glory of God the Father" (Phil. 2:9–11). Oh, the thrilling wonder and glory of it all!

Having noted in the language of the cross God's use of the punctuation of drama and dignity, we need to end by also noting His use of the punctuation of demonstration and declaration.

The Punctuation of Demonstration and Declaration (Mark 15:38–39)

Use your imagination for a moment. Take yourself back to that first Good Friday. You are standing in the temple. You are aware that, outside on Calvary's hill, a man called Jesus of Nazareth is hanging, dying on a cross. Absentmindedly, you are staring at the temple curtain. The artistically designed cherubim embroidered into it remind you that the way into the Holy of Holies, into the symbolic presence of God, is well and truly barred. For you, a sinner, there is no access. Dare to go behind that curtain and you know that you would meet with death under the holy judgment of God. To stand uninvited on holy ground would be an act of arrogance and rebellion, deserving of the severest of punishment—death itself!

The curtain's message, then, is loud and clear, "No Access: sinner, stay on your side; you are not welcome on God's side!" But then you hear a distant cry, the likes of which you have never heard before, carried to you on zephyrs of wind. At the very same moment, the ground shakes in terrifying fashion beneath your feet. You hear the awesome noise of breaking rocks and heaving, rupturing earth (Matt. 27:51). And then, before your eyes, you see the temple curtain beginning to tear in the most amazing, unexpected, and unexplainable fashion—from top to bottom.

You begin to sense that God is speaking in the dramatic, punctuated language of heaven. But what is He saying? And then suddenly, you know. For you see the curtain hanging open before you—a curtain supernaturally torn by the unseen hand of God! And now there is, clearly and wonderfully in response to the atoning death of Jesus Christ, a new message, a wonderfully glorious message, being declared: *Access!* By an amazing and undeserved act of grace, God has opened the way for men and women to come into His presence. The separating curtain is no more. In response to the atoning, sacrificial death of His Son, God rent it apart. Now the way is open for people believing in Jesus and trusting in His atoning work upon the cross, whereby He has borne the punishment of their sin, dying in their place, to enter into the kingdom of heaven. Glory, hallelujah!

As Jesus offered Himself upon the cross as the ultimate sacrifice for sin, it followed that in the very moment of His body being torn apart by death, God tore the temple curtain in two. He was making use of the punctuation of demonstration to leave sinners in no doubt that the body of Christ is, in effect, the parted curtain. If a sinner would enter into the saving presence of God, then he must come by way of Christ. There is no other way under the sun into the presence of Almighty God (John 14:6).

In Christ, God has made a Savior available to sinful men and women. Standing by the cross, the centurion, who had seen much and heard much, found his heart and mind compelled to make declaration. In the providence of God, the moment would know divine punctuation: "Truly this man was the Son of God" (Mark 15:39).

Conclusion

Jesus mastered the stress of His life as He faced it in the form of the opposition of the powers of darkness, His enemies' hatred, the world's rejection, His disciples' failure, the cross, darkness, desertion, and His impending death. And He did so because He used every breath that He took to live at the very center of the will of God for His life in trust and faith, unto the glory of God. Thus it was that our Lord, as the Master of Stress, triumphed in everything.

The centurion was right! "Truly this man was the Son of God." But what is the song in your soul? I pray that it will be wiser and more personal than that of the centurion. Let yours be a song with a marked difference: "Truly this man is the Son of God—my God and beloved Savior."

CHAPTER 8

The Glory of Christ's Victorious Death

Albert N. Martin

In order to draw the reader's mind and heart into this wonderful subject of biblical revelation, consider the obvious thrust of the following Scripture texts:

- "For the preaching of the cross is to them that perish foolishness; but unto us which are saved it is the power of God" (1 Cor. 1:18).

- "And I, brethren, when I came to you, came not with excellency of speech or of wisdom, declaring unto you the testimony of God. For I determined not to know anything among you, save Jesus Christ, and him crucified" (1 Cor. 2:1–2).

- "Moreover, brethren, I declare unto you the gospel which I preached unto you, which also ye have received, and wherein ye stand; by which also ye are saved, if ye keep in memory what I preached to you, unless ye have believed in vain. For I delivered unto you first of all that which I also received, how that Christ died for our sins according to the scriptures" (1 Cor. 15:1–3).

- "But God forbid that I should glory, save in the cross of our Lord Jesus Christ, by whom the world is crucified unto me, and I unto the world" (Gal. 6:14).

In the light of these texts and a host of others with a similar emphasis, I doubt that anyone reading his Bible with Spirit-enlightened eyes would question the validity of the assertion that the death of Jesus Christ upon the cross, in space-time history, and its biblically interpreted significance, is the central fact of biblical revelation. The fact that the God-man, Jesus Christ, actually died outside the city walls of

Jerusalem is the very linchpin that holds together the entire structure of true and saving religion as revealed in the Bible. All of its doctrines, duties, privileges, motives, joys, and hopes have their roots, in one way or another, in the fact and significance of Jesus' death.

When I assert that the death of Jesus Christ is the central fact of biblical revelation, I am assuming that we view that fact as it is presented to us in the Bible—namely, as it is intimately and organically related to three other categories of fact concerning our Lord Jesus Christ. In order to explain what I mean by this assertion, I want to use the analogy of a stage in a theater. On that stage are three objects. Above the front of the stage hangs a large banner, like a valance, extending across the whole width of the stage. Each object has a specific place assigned to it on the stage. I shall identify each of those objects.

In the front and center part of the stage there is a cross. It receives the greatest concentration of the floodlights that illuminate the stage, thereby underscoring the cross's centrality in biblical revelation. Then, placed on the left middle part of the stage, there is a manger. The manger represents the reality of the incarnation. It is only because Jesus is who He is as the God-man that He is able to do what He does as Redeemer and Savior. Everything the Scriptures teach us concerning that which He accomplished on the cross assumes the reality of what occurred in Mary's womb by the supernatural agency of the Holy Spirit and the true identity of the One who was laid in the manger of Bethlehem—Emmanuel, God with us.

Question 21 of the Westminster Shorter Catechism asks, "Who is the Redeemer of God's elect?" The biblically framed answer is, "The only Redeemer of God's elect is the Lord Jesus Christ who, being the eternal Son of God, became man, and so was and continues to be both God and man, in two distinct natures and one person, forever." If we take away the fact and significance of the constitution of the theanthropic person, it utterly neuters the power and effectiveness of the cross of Christ. Hence, all biblical thinking concerning Christ's victorious death assumes the reality of Christ's unique person.

Then, on the right middle part of the stage, there is an empty tomb. Everything that the Scriptures teach us concerning the fact, nature, and benefits procured by Jesus' death assumes that He is no longer lying in Joseph's borrowed tomb. Rather, the Scriptures assert with unmistakable and repeated insistence that the Jesus of

Nazareth who was crucified was raised from the dead—the first stage of His ultimate exaltation to the right hand of the Majesty on high. The vacated tomb validates that which our Lord accomplished on the cross.

Hanging down from the ceiling at the front of the stage is the wide, valance-like banner. Embroidered in large letters into the very fabric of that banner are the words "The Covenant of Grace." That banner announces to all who seek to understand the significance of the manger, the cross, and the empty tomb, that everything transpiring on the stage of redemptive history is rooted in, and is an unfolding of, the covenant of grace. There was a pretemporal and eternal arrangement within the triune Godhead concerning the salvation of men. Everything that transpires on the stage of the history of redemption is a transcript of those inter-Trinitarian counsels, commitments, and designs for our salvation. As we enter upon our study of "Christ's victorious death," it is absolutely vital to remember that all He did, He did as the covenant Head and representative of those who had been given to Him by the Father within the framework of that covenant.

Hugh Martin, a nineteenth-century Scottish theologian, has addressed this principle in a succinct and compelling manner in the opening chapter of his profound book *The Atonement*. He writes,

> It will not be denied or doubted that the doctrine of the Covenant of Grace is a larger category than the doctrine of the atonement. It is wider; comprehending the atonement within its provisions; affording to it also both explanation and support. Now it surely is extremely injudicious and impolitic [unwise] for defenders of the faith to discuss any scriptural doctrine, and particularly to profess to do so fully and exhaustively outside of any greater category to which the doctrine properly and natively belongs. For by doing so they place it in a position of unnecessary danger, and assign to themselves a greater difficulty in defending it than Scripture assigns to them. They rob it of the illustration, and they rob it of the protection, which the higher category affords. They deprive it of the benefit of scriptural considerations in the light of which their defense might be comparatively easy, and would be found, indeed, presented to their hand; and, by the isolated position to which they have

consigned it, they give advantages to the enemy which the abler
and more acute of their number are not slow to seize.[1]

While the significance of this "banner" warrants a much fuller treatment, it is crucial to remember that everything that will be set before
the reader concerning the glory of our Lord Jesus Christ's victorious
death assumes that His death and all of its benefits are effected within
the framework of this larger category of the covenant of grace. In
other words, Christ is able to do what He did on the cross, not only
because of who He is (the significance of the manger), and not only
because of the fact of His resurrection (the significance of the empty
tomb), but also because of the position He occupies as the Head, the
Surety, the Representative, and Substitute of His people, bound to
them and acting for them, within the terms of the covenant of grace.

Assuming that all of our thinking concerning Christ's triumphant death will be conditioned by the biblical significance of the
manger, the empty tomb, and the covenant of grace, I will attempt
to open up this wonderful theme in two major categories: Christ's
victorious death in its manifold accomplishments and in its accomplishment as propitiation.

The Glory of Christ's Victorious Death in Its
Manifold Accomplishments

God's multifaceted rescue mission that we call salvation, a salvation
centered in the cross of Christ, has no "extras." Every cross-secured
redemptive privilege answers to a specific facet of sin's tragic effects
upon the human race. In other words, Christ's work on the cross
is what it is because we are what we are: sinners. When we begin
to meditate on the various categories within which the accomplishments of Jesus' death are set before us, we find that each one of those
categories answers a very specific aspect of sin's tragic influence in
and upon us and also upon God's relationship to us as sinners.

I will seek to illustrate this truth by focusing the reader's attention upon five of the specific categories within which the Scriptures
set before us Christ's work on the cross, each category being God's
gracious answer to a specific aspect of the sinful human condition.

---

1. Hugh Martin, *The Atonement* (Edinburgh: Knox Press, 1976), 9–10.

1. Sin produces guilt. This is real guilt—that is, legal culpability and liability to God's punishment on account of our sin. Romans 3:19 clearly asserts this fact. Here the apostle states that "now we know that what things soever the law saith, it saith to them who are under the law: that every mouth may be stopped, and all the world may become guilty before God." But with equal clarity the Scriptures tell us that our Lord Jesus Christ's death on the cross was a real sacrifice to remove guilt and to cover sin. Many texts clearly assert this, such as Hebrews 9:26b, where we read, "But now, once in the end of the world has he appeared to put away sin by the sacrifice of himself." Hence, Christ's death described as a sacrifice answers specifically to our need as guilty sinners.

2. Sin provokes the wrath of God. This is real, just, and holy wrath against the sinner. Paul's affirmation of this fact is patent in Romans 1:18: "For the wrath of God is revealed from heaven against all ungodliness and unrighteousness of men, who hold the truth in unrighteousness." The apostle bluntly states in Ephesians 2:4 that we are all "by nature children of wrath, even as others." Again, with equal clarity the Scriptures affirm that the death of our Lord Jesus Christ was a propitiation—a sacrifice that turns away and appeases God's just and holy wrath on behalf of those for whom Christ died. John explains in 1 John 4:10 that "herein is love, not that we loved God, but that he loved us, and sent his son to be the propitiation for our sins."

3. Sin creates real alienation. This is an alienation in which God is righteously against us because of our sin. Yes, it is true that we have the disposition of enmity towards God as is clearly stated in Romans 8:7. However, the apostle Paul describes our native condition with the words found in Romans 5:10: "For if, when we were enemies...." Not only do we by nature regard God as our enemy, but He regards us as His enemies. However, the Scriptures set before us Christ's work on the cross as a work of reconciliation that removes God's enmity towards us. This could not be more plainly stated than it is in Romans 5:10, where the apostle writes that "we were reconciled to God by the death of his Son."

4. Sin brings us into a state of bondage and slavery. Jesus said in John 8:34, "Whosoever committeth sin is the servant [slave] of sin." Paul describes the preconversion condition of the Romans with the

words, "Ye were the servants [slaves] of sin." One of the major categories within which Christ's death on the cross is set before us is
the category of redemption. This redemption often has the nuance of
securing release from bondage by means of a ransom. For this reason, Paul can write to the Corinthians and say to them, "For ye are
bought with a price" (1 Cor. 6:20). Again, Peter can write to the Christians in Asia Minor, reminding them that they have been redeemed
not with corruptible things such as silver and gold, but with "the
precious blood of Christ, as of a lamb without blemish and without
spot" (1 Peter 1:19). Jesus Himself said that, as the Son of Man, He
came in order "to give his life a ransom for many" (Matt. 20:28).

5. Sin has brought us under the control of sinister, evil powers.
That all of us by nature are under the control of such powers is a
truth that passages such as Ephesians 2:1–2 vividly affirm: "You hath
he quickened, who were dead in trespasses and sins; wherein in time
past ye walked according to the course of this world, according to
the prince of the power of the air, the spirit that now worketh in the
children of disobedience." Scripture affirms that by nature we are
the very "children of the devil"(1 John 3:9). But, blessed be God, our
Bibles teach us that when Jesus died upon the cross, He was accomplishing a work of massive destruction of the sinister, evil powers. In
fact, the initial gospel promise, spoken to the devil himself in Genesis
3:15, announces that the seed of the woman would eventually crush
the head of the serpent. The writer to the Hebrews affirms that the
Son of God took to Himself true humanity in order that "through
death he might destroy him that had the power of death, that is, the
devil" (Heb. 2:14). This reality is the ancient *Christus Victor* motif,
a dimension of Christ's work that some of the early church fathers
greatly emphasized.

These five categories display something of the glory of Christ's
victorious death in its manifold accomplishments. Surely, the contemplation of the riches of the redemptive activity of our Lord Jesus
Christ on our behalf should cause us to exclaim "Hallelujah, what
a Savior!"[2]

---

2. For any preachers who desire to trace out and expound one or more of these
five categories, the following works may prove to be of help in your preparation:
John Murray, *Redemption Accomplished and Applied* (Grand Rapids: Eerdmans, 1989),
especially chapters 2–4; Robert Reymond, *A New Systematic Theology of the Christian*

The Glory of Christ's Victorious Death in Its
Accomplishment as Propitiation

I have chosen to focus on this aspect of Christ's death for two distinct reasons. First, because propitiation is central to the biblical teaching concerning the significance of Christ's death. From Romans 1:18 all the way through to Romans 3:20, the apostle Paul has skillfully and devastatingly indicted the entire human race as being in a state of sin and condemnation. Then, in Romans 3:21, beginning with wonderful words of transition, "But now," he begins to open up the details concerning God's sovereign and gracious provision for sinners centered in the person and work of our Lord Jesus Christ. In the very condensed statement of this salvation found in chapter 3:21–26, he places "propitiation" at the very center of that provision when he writes, "Whom God hath set forth to be a propitiation...." If God has made propitiation a centerpiece in His gracious saving work, we must not remain willfully ignorant of its significance or indulge in the kind of spiritual arrogance that would marginalize its importance. First John 4:10 informs us that the focal point of God's love to us is to be understood in relationship to His sending His Son "to be the propitiation for our sins."

My second reason for focusing upon propitiation is this. The biblical teaching concerning propitiation has been and is presently a truth that many of God's people often little understand and often misunderstand, while others wickedly caricature or flatly deny it, even mocking it as a silly notion which they describe as a form of "celestial child abuse." In light of this reality, we must not forget Luther's famous words that "where the battle rages, there the loyalty of the soldier is put to the test." Given the battle that rages over this aspect of the redemptive provisions of the cross of Christ, loyal soldiers must draw the "sword of the Spirit" and do battle with ignorance and error concerning propitiation. Further, one of the indictments against the watchmen in Israel was this: "They are all ignorant, they are all dumb dogs, they cannot bark" (Isa. 56:10). As new-covenant watchmen, may we not be found disloyal on the field

---

Faith (Nashville: T. Nelson, 1988), especially pages 629–63; James Denney, *The Death of Christ* (New Canaan, Conn.: Keats Pub., 1981); Leon Morris, *The Atonement* (Downers Grove, Ill.: InterVarsity Press, 1983), especially chapters 2, 5–7.

of battle or be placed in the category of tame and silent canines that ought to be barking loudly!

If I were addressing this subject of propitiation in a seminary classroom, the only responsible approach would be to begin by carefully collating the various word families by which both Testaments set before us the truth of propitiation. Since God has communicated to us the precious truth concerning Christ's saving work in "words which the Holy Spirit teaches" (1 Cor. 2:13), careful biblical study and responsible exposition must necessarily wrestle with the meaning of the Spirit-inspired words. However, since I am not writing for seminary students, I will not ask you to obtain a lexicon of biblical words or a Bible dictionary defining biblical terms. Rather, I am going to ask you to come with me to two very significant places. It is in these two places that I want you to see in your mind's eye the events recorded and to hear with the ears of your heart what the biblical writers record of the words spoken in these two places. In these two places we will, with the Spirit's help, see the great and glorious but utterly sobering reality of propitiation. Those two places are Gethsemane and Golgotha. We shall consider the biblical witness connected with these two places.

Gethsemane: The Presentation and Preview of the Cup of Propitiation
In Mark 14:32–36, we read the following:

> And they came to a place which was called Gethsemane: and he saith to his disciples, Sit ye here, while I shall pray. And he taketh with him Peter and James and John, and began to be sore amazed, and to be very heavy; and saith unto them, My soul is exceeding sorrowful unto death: tarry ye here and watch. And he went forward a little, and fell on the ground, and prayed that, if it were possible, the hour might pass from him. And he said, Abba, Father, all things are possible unto thee; take away this cup from me: nevertheless not what I will, but what thou wilt.

In his account of the Gethsemane experience, Luke adds these words: "And being in an agony he prayed more earnestly: and his sweat was as it were great drops of blood falling down to the ground" (Luke 22:44).

Mark uses unusually vigorous language when describing the fact that our Lord "began to be sore amazed, and to be very heavy."

Something was obviously beginning to cause new dimensions of the deepest kinds of mental and spiritual trauma to our Lord Jesus' sensitive soul. What was it? Our Lord Himself gives us the answer as His prayer focuses upon "the cup." In each account of Gethsemane, the trauma and "the cup" were inseparable. This leads us to ask what there was about the cup that caused such trauma. When we read passages such as Psalm 75:8; Isaiah 51:17, 22; Jeremiah 25:15–17; and Revelation 16:19, it becomes clear that the cup is the symbol of God's stored-up wrath and anger about to be poured out upon deserving men and women. In receiving that outpoured wrath, men are said to drink the contents of the cup and drain it.

That He would drink the cup of God's wrath against the sins of those for whom He was the appointed substitute was not an entirely new revelation to our Lord. Early in Jesus' public ministry, John identified Him as "the Lamb of God which taketh away the sin of the world." Subsequent to Peter's great confession (Matt. 16), our Lord repeatedly announced to His disciples that He was on His way to Jerusalem, where He would be handed over to the Gentiles, condemned, spat upon, mocked, scourged, and ultimately crucified. But as our Lord enters what we commonly call the Passion Week, it would seem that this more intensified and expanded revelation of what lay before Him began unfolding. John tells us that at the beginning of that week, our Lord said, "Now is my soul troubled; and what shall I say? Father, save me from this hour: but for this cause came I unto this hour. Father, glorify thy name" (John 12:27–28).

In Matthew 20:22, our Lord even uses the language of "the cup" that He was prepared to drink. What was new in Gethsemane was the degree to which the Father was making clear to Him what drinking that cup would entail in all of its horrific soul-crushing reality. John Murray has captured the heart of what transpired in Gethsemane in a sermon entitled "The Obedience of Christ." He writes,

> The only explanation is that at this time there was some unprecedented enlargement of knowledge in reference to what was entailed in his sufferings, particularly his suffering unto death upon the accursed tree. Mark tells us that "he began to be amazed" (Mark 14:33). The inference is inevitable. There now invaded his consciousness such increased understanding and experience of the involvements of his commitment, that amazement filled his soul. Our Lord was now looking into the abyss

already beginning to inundate his soul, the abyss that he was to swallow up in himself. The recoil of his whole soul was inevitable. If he had not recoiled from the incomparable ordeal, it would have been unnatural in the deepest sense. We must reckon with the enormity of his agony and the reality of his human nature. Here was the unrelieved, unmitigated judgment of God against sin. It filled him with horror and dread. The recoil evidenced in the prayer is the proof of the ordeal and of the necessary sensibilities and sensitivities of his human nature.[3]

Had the Father given such an expanded revelation of the implications of "the cup" prior to these hours just preceding the event of Golgotha, that revelation would have so swallowed up our Lord as to prevent His finishing the work that the Father had given Him to do. As it was, Luke informs us that the shock of this new revelation was so traumatic that God had to send "an angel to him from heaven, strengthening him"(Luke 22:43). There is a strong hint in Hebrews 5:7 that our Lord may have even felt that this new awareness would crush Him to death there in the garden. We must never forget that a proper doctrine of our Lord's humanity includes the fact that as surely as He grew in wisdom and stature as a youth, He also continued to grow in His human knowledge and understanding of His Father, His Father's will, and what doing that will would involve for Him.

Luke adds another mysterious detail when He informs us that "being in an agony he prayed more earnestly: and his sweat was as it were great drops of blood falling down to the ground" (Luke 22:44). In a night so chilly that, in a couple of hours, soldiers will build fires to warm their hands, the intensity of our Lord's agony causes Him to sweat. But it was not ordinary perspiration. Rather, so torturously intense was the agony of His soul, now spilling its agitation into His physical frame, that some of His capillaries burst, mingling His blood with the sweat.[4]

However, in spite of all of this natural recoil from "the cup," our Lord resolutely commits Himself to the active embrace of the will of

---

3. John Murray, *Collected Writings* (Edinburgh: The Banner of Truth, 1977), 2:154–55.

4. This is a known medical condition designated as hematidrosis or hematohidrosis, technically defined as "a secretion of sweat containing blood."

God. When He said, "Nevertheless, not my will, but thine, be done," He was not saying words of reluctant or even passive submission to a will that was not fully His own. Those words did not mean, "May Thy will be done upon or towards me"; rather, He was declaring that the Father's will would be followed with the same total engagement of His heart and will that marked every other aspect of His life of perfect obedience. He had said earlier in His earthly ministry, "My meat is to do the will of him that sent me, and to finish his work" (John 4:34). Reluctance at the point of performing an act of obedience is less than perfect obedience. Remember the child of the Quaker mother who, in the midst of a Quaker meeting, was told to sit down and not to stand in the pew. The little child reluctantly sat down, but leaned over and whispered in his mother's ear, "Mother, me sitteth on the outside, but me standeth on the inside." Our Lord did not embrace "the cup" on the outside while experiencing a reluctance of will on the inside. Once again, Murray succinctly expresses this principle when he writes, "To be an act of obedience, the whole dispositional complex of motive, direction, and purpose must be in conformity to the divine will."[5]

Once the issue was settled in the deepest springs of His being, our Lord could then say just a few minutes later, when Peter sought to come to His defense when the authorities came to arrest him, "Put up thy sword into the sheath: the cup which my father hath given me, shall I not drink it?" (John 18:11). Again, Murray's words are most helpful in our effort to understand this scene: "The figure Jesus used bespeaks voluntary action on his part. The Father, indeed, gave the cup; gave it, as it were, into our Lord's hand. But he must drink it. He must drink it to its dregs. Any attempt to deny or tone down the reality of his recoil and revulsion betrays our failure to appreciate the bitterness of the cup and the intensity of his commitment to the Father's will. It was the cup of damnation voluntarily taken, vicariously borne, and to be finished in his agony."[6]

If the cup of Gethsemane, in its presentation and preview, was filled with anything less or anything other than the impending unleashed fury of the holy, righteous, and perfectly just wrath of God against the sins of God's elect, then Gethsemane becomes a

5. Murray, *Collected Writings*, 152.
6. Murray, *Collected Writings*, 155.

travesty of overblown histrionics on the part of the staggering, mentally and emotionally traumatized, blood-sweating, and agonizing Son of God. Profoundly and accurately, God teaches us the reality of propitiation when we visit that place named Gethsemane. Let us now make our way to the second place where God teaches us the biblical doctrine of propitiation.

Golgotha: The Drinking and the Draining of the Cup of Propitiation
In Matthew 27:33–35, we read the following: "And when they were come unto a place called Golgotha, that is to say, a place of a skull, they gave him vinegar to drink mingled with gall: and when he had tasted thereof, he would not drink. And they crucified him...." Further on in that same chapter, we are told "Now from the sixth hour there was darkness over all the land until the ninth hour. And about the ninth hour Jesus cried with a loud voice, saying, Eli, Eli, lama sabacthani? that is to say, My God, my God, why hast thou forsaken me?" (vv. 45–46) Matthew informs us that "Jesus, when he had cried again with a loud voice, yielded up the ghost. And, behold, the veil of the temple was rent in twain from the top to the bottom; and the earth did quake, and the rocks rent; and the graves were opened; and many bodies of the saints which slept arose" (vv. 50–52).

Subsequent to His arrest in Gethsemane, our Lord was brought before Caiaphas the high priest, before the Sanhedrin, before Pilate, off to Herod, then back again to Pilate. By comparing the four gospel writers, we know that during this time He was insulted and verbally assaulted by false witnesses and brutalized by the soldiers who put the purple robe on Him, placed the mock scepter in His hand, and pressed the crown of thorns upon His brow as part of their tawdry fun. Brought back before Pilate, He was tied to the whipping post and brutally scourged. However, much to the amazement of the religious and pagan magistrates, He never opened His mouth in a word of complaint towards God or man throughout the entire ordeal. Nor did He say anything in His own defense. In the words of the old Negro spiritual, in response to this unconscionable treatment, "He never said a mumbling word—not a word, not a word, and He never said a mumbling word."

Then, when He was actually brought to Golgotha, He refused to partake of the drugged wine offered to Him. In Gethsemane, He had consented to drink the cup that His Father presented to Him. That cup was full of the undiluted wrath of God against the sins of those for whom He would die as substitute, surety, and covenant head. Determined that He would drink into His soul the full measure of this undiluted wine of the fury of God's wrath against the sins of His people, He refused to dull His physical and mental sensibilities with drugged wine. Since there will be no jugs of drugged wine resting on the lip of hell for the descending wicked, our Lord resolutely refused to take the narcotic. He determined that He would take upon Himself our damnation, body and soul, as He vicariously entered our hell for the next six hours.

Crucified about nine o'clock in the morning, for the following three hours He hung between earth and heaven, constantly mocked by the religious leaders, rudely gaped at by curious onlookers, and taunted by the two criminals crucified on either side of him. During all this time, the only words that came from His mouth were words of grace.

Then, at high noon, the land was suddenly plunged into an eerie and total darkness—a darkness like Egypt's when God afflicted that nation with His judgments. It was a darkness that people could feel by its heavy oppressiveness. There is no record that anyone in the crowds milling around the cross had anything to say then. They were all silent. Jesus was silent. The three hours of supernatural darkness were wedded to three hours of total silence. Then, according to Matthew's testimony, towards the end of those three hours, that silence was suddenly, dramatically broken by the loud and piercing cry emanating from Jesus' lips: "My God, my God, why hast thou forsaken me?"

It is reported that on one occasion, Martin Luther had been sitting at his desk, pondering for some three hours these mysterious words uttered by our Lord. At the end of that time, he pushed himself back from the desk and threw up his hands, exclaiming, "God forsaken by God—who can understand that?" Yes, who can understand that? Eternity will be too short for any of us ever to feel that we have plumbed the depths or scaled the heights of the meaning of those words wrung from our Lord Jesus' tortured soul. Had the Father chosen to answer Jesus' question with His own words now recorded in Scripture, surely the following texts would have been part of his answer: "Christ hath redeemed us from the curse of the law, being made a curse for us: for it is written, cursed is every one that hangeth on a tree" (Gal. 3:13); "for he hath made him to be sin for us, who knew no sin; that we might be made the righteousness of God in him" (2 Cor. 5:21); "and the Lord hath laid on him the iniquity of us all.... Yet it pleased the Lord to bruise him; he hath put him to grief" (Isa. 53:6, 10).

In Romans 8:32, we read, "He that spared not his own son, but delivered him up for us all...." To whom and to what was He delivered up by the Father? He was delivered up into the hands of wicked men (Acts 2:23). The one time God allowed mere men to have Deity in their hands, they impaled Him on a cruel and shameful instrument of execution. But not only was He delivered into the hands of wicked men, the Scriptures affirm that He was also delivered over to the powers of darkness (Matt. 22:53). In some mysterious but real way, our Lord was handed over to an intensified engagement with the powers of darkness when the Father delivered Him up. But, supremely, He was delivered up to nothing less than the full measure of divine wrath and punishment that the sins of those for whom He died deserved. In the rich language of proven and historic orthodoxy, Christ's death as propitiation was nothing less than a penal substitutionary satisfaction to the sanctions of God's holy and immutable law.

God's own character holds Him captive. He cannot and will not, in any of His actions, deny Himself (2 Tim. 2:13). The God who is love, and who exercised that love by sovereignly and freely choosing a people unto life and salvation, is also the God who said of Himself that "he will by no means clear the guilty" (Num. 14:18b). Even the mighty impulses of divine love will not move God to compromise His own integrity. Therefore, the curses precipitated by the broken law must be meted out, either upon the sinner himself or upon a divinely provided substitute. In the death of our Lord Jesus designated as propitiation, this is precisely what God has done. In a marvelous but little known hymn, Annie Cousin captures the concept of propitiation by likening the work of Christ upon the cross to a substitutionary burden bearing; a substitutionary endurance of death; a substitutionary infliction of a rod; a substitutionary enduring of a fearful tempest; and the substitutionary piercing of the sword of divine justice:

> Death and the curse were in our cup:
> O Christ, 'twas full for Thee!
> But Thou hast drained the last dark drop,
> 'Tis empty now for me.
> That bitter cup, love drank it all up,
> Now blessing's draught for me.[7]

Shortly after that cry of dereliction and abandonment, the Father conveyed to His well-beloved Son that the last drop in the cup of His wrath had been fully drained. The cup was now totally empty. It is then that the events recorded in John 19:28–30 transpired. "After this, Jesus knowing that all things were now accomplished, that the scripture might be fulfilled, saith, I thirst. Now there was set a vessel full of vinegar: and they filled a sponge with vinegar, and put it upon hyssop, and put it to his mouth. When Jesus therefore had received the vinegar, he said, It is finished: and he bowed his head, and gave up the ghost."

It is a well-established fact that among the manifold cruelties of crucifixion, one of them was acute dehydration. After six hours upon the cross, it is no wonder that the psalmist predicts that Messiah would say while on the cross, "And my tongue cleaveth to my jaws"(Ps. 22:15) Therefore, in fulfillment of the prophecy of Psalm 69:21, Jesus makes known His thirst. I am persuaded that He desired His thirst to be assuaged not only because of His condition of dehydration, but also because He wanted His tongue loosed from His jaws so that bystanders would distinctly and clearly understand His next words. It was then that He spoke with a loud voice those words of majestic triumph: "It is finished." Our Lord was proclaiming that the work He came to accomplish for His people had now been brought to its full and irreversible completion. He was declaring, "Having voluntarily placed Myself under the preceptual demands of the law on behalf of My people, I have kept that law in the full length and breadth of its demands. Now, in complete obedience to My Father's will, I have taken to Myself all the penal sanctions directed to My

---

7. Annie Cousin, "O Christ, What Burdens Bowed Thy Head," in *Gospel Hymns Consolidated* (Chicago and New York: Biglow and Main, and John Church and Co., 1883), no. 57, stanza 2.

people who have broken that law and have fully exhausted every last righteous infliction of divine wrath upon their sins." My dear reader, this is propitiation.

Summary and Final Applications

Do you now see why I asserted that it is in Gethsemane and at Golgotha that we learn the wonderful, redemptive provision of pro-pitiation? Gethsemane, with its amazement, deep trouble of soul, and bloody sweat, was indeed a real and traumatic presentation and preview of the cup of the deeper agony of the actual forsaken-ness of Golgotha. On the other hand, the piercing cry of dereliction from Golgotha, precipitated by the actual drinking and draining of the cup, constitutes a justification for the extent of the trauma expe-rienced by our Lord in Gethsemane. Together they bear eloquent testimony to the wonderful truth that Christ's death was indeed pro-pitiation—the turning away of God's pure, holy, righteous anger and fury against the sins of His people which were borne by their federal head, surety, and substitute: our blessed Lord Jesus Christ.

How can we ever begin to appreciate the mystery surrounding these realities? Think of it. At the point of being abandoned by the Father, in His position as covenant head and representative of His people, our Lord was never more loved in His person. John 10:17–18 makes this truth clear: "Therefore doth my Father love me because I lay down my life, that I might take it again. No man taketh it from me, but I lay it down of myself. I have power to lay it down, and I have power to take it again. This commandment have I received of my Father." These words make it plain that the Father's love of delight for and complacency toward His Son increased with every single act of His Son's obedience. Therefore, when that obedience reached its zenith in our Lord's death upon the cross, the Father never loved Him more than at the very time when the Father abandoned Him. While being utterly abandoned judicially in His position as covenant head and representative of His people, He was never more upheld and supported according to the covenantal commitments between the Father and Son as stated by the prophet Isaiah, where God says to us, "Behold my servant, whom I uphold; mine elect, in whom my soul delighteth" (Isa. 42:1).

Christ's death as a propitiation is not a theological abstraction or a mere theory concerning what transpired on the cross. It constitutes the solid basis for confidence in God's promise to His people: "I will never leave thee, nor forsake thee" (Heb. 13:5b). Because God forsook His Son, He can make this promise to us. Every sin in itself, even the sins of God's children, deserves the wrath and curse of God. However, we have the wonderful promise of 1 John 2:1–2, that when we sin, even at the very point of our sin, "we have an advocate with the father, Jesus Christ the righteous: and he is the propitiation for our sins." Sitting at the right hand of the Father, He "embodies in himself for ever, all the propitiatory efficacy of the propitiation once for all accomplished."[8]

Many of us are familiar with the words of Charles Wesley's hymn "Arise, My Soul, Arise." In the third stanza, Wesley writes, "Five bleeding wounds he bears, received on Calvary." I have never felt comfortable singing those words. Our Lord's bleeding ceased when He cried, "It is finished." We should alter those words as follows: "Five vivid scars he bears." Those scars constantly remind the Father that Christ is indeed "the propitiation for our sins." The Father's cup of wrath was put to our blessed Savior's lips, and He drained the last dark drop! It is this wonderful truth woven into the texture of the mind and soul of Augustus Toplady that caused him to pen the following hymn. Dear child of God, may the Holy Spirit weave the same truth into the texture of your mind and soul, that your soul would bask in the light and warmth of the truth and glory of Christ as our propitiation in His victorious death.

> Payment God cannot twice demand—
> First at my bleeding Surety's hand,
> And then again at mine.
>
> Complete atonement Thou hast made,
> And to the utmost farthing paid
> What e'er Thy people owed.
>
> How then can wrath on me take place
> If sheltered in Thy righteousness
> And sprinkled with Thy blood?

---

8. Murray, *Redemption Accomplished and Applied*, 33.

Turn, then, my soul, unto thy rest!
The merits of thy Great High Priest
Speak peace and liberty.

Trust in His efficacious blood,
Nor fear thy banishment from God,
Since Jesus died for thee.

But you may be reading these pages as one who has never repented of your sin and abandoned yourself to Jesus Christ and to His salvation, as He is so freely and sincerely offered to you in the gospel. What does all of this say to you? No doubt one of the reasons why you have not "closed with Christ" is that you have no deep sense of dread and fear of the wrath of God that hangs over your head at this very moment as an unbeliever. The hymn writer Thomas Kelly made the following assertion, urging men and women to a serious consideration of Christ's cross: "You who think of sin but lightly, nor suppose the evil great, here [at Golgotha] may view its nature rightly, here its guilt may estimate."[9] If God were ever to relax the strict demands of His law in avenging His holy and righteous wrath upon human sin, would He not have done so when His own well-beloved Son was the sin-bearer? But, the Scripture tells us that "he spared not his own Son" (Rom. 8:32a).

My unconverted reader, what makes you think that God will in any way relax the same fiery indignation when the time comes to pour it out upon you? Scripture tells us just the opposite. God declares that "the Lord Jesus shall be revealed from heaven with his mighty angels, in flaming fire taking vengeance on them that know not God, and that obey not the gospel of our Lord Jesus Christ: who shall be punished with everlasting destruction from the presence of the Lord, and from the glory of his power" (2 Thess. 1:7–9). May you be wooed and won into the arms of an inviting Savior through this contemplation of the glory of Christ's victorious death.

9. Thomas Kelly, "Stricken, Smitten, and Afflicted," in *Trinity Hymnal* (Suwanee, Ga.: Great Commisssion Publications, 2008), no. 257.

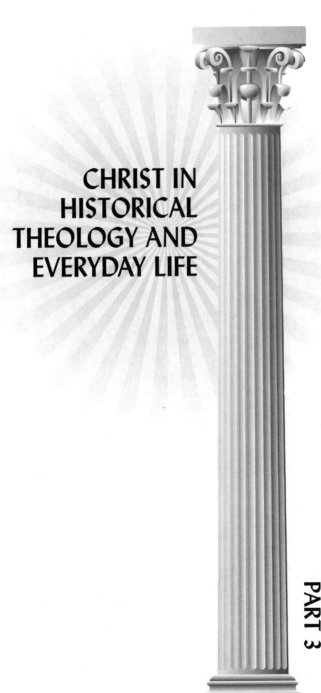

CHRIST IN HISTORICAL THEOLOGY AND EVERYDAY LIFE

PART 3

CHAPTER 9

Glorying in the Imputed Righteousness of Christ

Richard D. Phillips

> *But to him that worketh not, but believeth on him that justifieth the ungodly, his faith is counted for righteousness.*
> —Romans 4:5

Scholars should always be able to explain theological controversies in terms that regular Christians can understand. With this in mind, a pastor friend of mine was explaining to his mother the recent controversies regarding the doctrine of justification. He explained how some are denying the bicovenantal system of the covenant of works and the covenant of grace, redefining faith as faithfulness, and casting other important matters into dispute. His mother followed this all perfectly well. But she reacted particularly strongly, as all Christians should, when my friend explained how purportedly Reformed theologians are denying the doctrine of Christ's imputed righteousness. To this, the godly matriarch reacted with a shocked and pained expression. "You know, son," she said, "I have been rather counting on that being true."

My friend's mother is not the only Christian who has been counting on the imputation of Christ's righteousness. J. Gresham Machen expressed his reliance upon it when he sent a cable to his friend John Murray, on January 1, 1937, the day of Machen's death: "I'm so thankful for active obedience of Christ. No hope without it."[1] Machen was referring to Jesus' perfect, lived obedience to God's law throughout His earthly life. Jesus lived the life that we should have lived, and He did so on behalf of His people. As Machen sent those final words

---

1. Ned B. Stonehouse, *J. Gresham Machen: A Biographical Memoir* (Edinburgh: 1955; repr. Banner of Truth, 1987), 508.

before he passed into the presence of God, he was relying on Christ not only to pay the penalty for his sins but also to provide a perfect righteousness on his behalf. In a radio address given just weeks previous to his death, Machen explained how he expected to enter into heaven: "I have not merited eternal life by my own perfect obedience," he confessed. "God knows and my own conscience knows that even after I became a Christian I have sinned in thought, word, and deed. But although I have not merited eternal life by any obedience of my own, Christ has merited it for me by His perfect obedience.... I have no righteousness of my own, but clad in Christ's perfect righteousness, imputed to me and received by faith alone, I can glory in the fact that...there awaits me the glorious reward which Christ thus earned for me."[2] This is a confession that every Christian should rejoice to make, so that with my friend's mother and J. Gresham Machen, every Christian should say of imputed righteousness, "This is what I am counting on in the presence of God."

Imputed Righteousness Defended

The doctrine of imputation concerns our understanding of *how* Christ justifies sinners who believe in Him. The Reformed faith teaches that a double imputation occurs through Christ's death on the cross. First, our sins are imputed—that is, credited or reckoned—to the crucified Lord Jesus. The Greek verb most frequently used is *logizomai,* which gives us our English words *logistics* and *logarithm,* and means "to account or credit." God records our sins under our names and we have to answer for them. But God takes our debt and reckons it to Christ's account, so that He will answer for it. This is imputation. Christ did not commit the sins, but God reckons our sins to His account. Martyn Lloyd-Jones explained: "He died to bear my punishment. That is what killed Him. So my guilt has been imputed to Him and it has been taken away from me and therefore I am freely forgiven."[3]

Evangelicals all affirm the imputation of our sins to Jesus, since we believe that He died for us while He was Himself perfectly sinless. What some deny is that a double imputation takes place in our

---

2. J. Gresham Machen, *God Transcendent* (Edinburgh: Banner of Truth, 1949), 189–90.

3. D. Martyn Lloyd-Jones, *The Kingdom of God* (Wheaton, Ill.: Crossway, 1992), 80.

justification: first, the imputation of our sins to Christ and, second, the imputation of His righteousness to those who believe. The Westminster Confession of Faith states that God justifies believers "not by infusing righteousness into them…not for anything wrought in them, or done by them…nor by imputing faith itself, the act of believing, or any other evangelical obedience to them, as their righteousness; but by imputing the obedience and satisfaction of Christ unto them, they receiving and resting on him and his righteousness, by faith" (XI.1). Lloyd-Jones explains: "Out of my ledger goes my sin, put to His account; then His goodness, His righteousness, His purity are put into my account under my name!… God sees me in Him clothed with His righteousness."[4] This is what opponents of imputed righteousness reject, both evangelicals who deny any need for a positive righteousness — considering simple forgiveness to exhaust the meaning of justification or finding some other ground for our righteousness — and liberal scholars, who configure salvation in wholly different terms.

When waging a war it is best to avoid fighting on both flanks. Germany's standing policy for generations was to avoid a two-front war; the neglect of this policy led to defeat in two world wars. The United States showed its strength in the Second World War by fighting massive conflicts on both sides, and it remains the military policy of our nation always to be strong enough to fight two wars simultaneously if needed. Reformed theology finds itself in just such a position today, fighting a heated war on numerous important doctrines — none more important than imputed righteousness — against opponents on both flanks, from both evangelicalism and liberalism.

One way that some evangelicals deny imputed righteousness is by substituting faith for works in attaining righteousness. Reformed theology teaches that faith is the instrument by which the believer receives justification, including imputed righteousness. In opposition, many Arminians teach that faith, the act of believing, is imputed for our righteousness. The supposed biblical basis for this teaching is Genesis 15:6, which Paul cites as proving the doctrine of justification: "Abraham believed God, and it was counted to him for righteousness." According to Robert Gundry, who has used this text to argue against imputed righteousness, Paul taught that "what God counts

---

4. Lloyd-Jones, *The Kingdom of God*, 80.

as righteousness consists in faith."[5] Faith, he means, takes the place of righteousness; whereas Adam failed to be justified by his perfect obedience, faith is something that man can do to receive credit for righteousness.

To assess this argument, consider Paul's teaching in Romans 4:1–6. Here, Paul appeals to the example of Abraham to prove the doctrine of justification, which he introduced in chapter 3. The question, Paul says, is whether Abraham was justified by his works or through faith alone: "For if Abraham were justified by works, he hath whereof to glory" (Rom. 4:2). It is at this point that Paul cites Genesis 15:6, writing, "For what saith the scripture? Abraham believed God, and it was counted unto him for righteousness" (Rom. 4:3).

Paul considers Abraham's justification in terms of two possibilities. Abraham's faith justified him either as a work that merited his status of righteousness, or as a gift of grace through which righteousness was imputed to him. Verse 4 considers both options. "Now to him that worketh is the reward...reckoned...of debt." This is the Arminian approach that Gundry advocates: Abraham deserved to be justified because he believed God's promise. God owed justification to Abraham because he had believed. Note, however, that Paul insists that this is not how Abraham was justified. Paul says that in being justified, Abraham gained something he did not deserve and had not merited. Even after he believed, righteousness was not Abraham's due. In Paul's doctrine, justification is a gift of grace by imputation; justification is "reckoned of grace" (Rom. 4:4). Paul asserts that Abraham did not deserve to be justified; his justification through faith was unmerited, as Paul states in verse 5: "But to him that worketh not, but believeth on him that justifieth the ungodly, his faith is counted for righteousness."

Some argue that Paul here teaches the opposite of imputation. After all, he says that Abraham's "faith is counted for righteousness" (Rom. 4:5). Does that not plainly state the doctrine that faith merits justification? Consider what Paul is saying about Abraham, however, to see that this is not what he is teaching. First, Paul insists that, in being justified, Abraham has nothing to boast about before

---

5. Robert H. Gundry, "The Nonimputation of Christ's Righteousness," in *Justification: What's at Stake in the Current Debates*, ed. Mark Husbands and Daniel J. Treier (Downers Grove, Ill.: InterVarsity, 2004), 25.

God (Rom. 4:2). Moreover, he states that Abraham's justification is an example of an ungodly person being justified: "to him that worketh not, but believeth on him that justifieth the ungodly" (Rom. 4:5). So Abraham did not become godly by believing; he was justified not on the basis of meriting the status of righteous, for he still "worketh not."

Most importantly, consider that parallel that Paul constructs when he adds in the example of David in Romans 4:6. Paul comments, "Even as David also describeth the blessedness of the man, unto whom God imputeth righteousness without works." Notice the parallel between Romans 4:5 and 4:6, comparing Abraham's justification to David's. Verse 5 says that God "justifieth the ungodly." Verse 6 states, "God imputeth righteousness without works." The subject in both these sentences is God. The object in verse 5 is "the ungodly," and verse 6 describes this same person as "without works." Most important are Paul's verbs in these parallel clauses. Verse 5 says that God "justifieth." Verse 6 says that God "imputeth righteousness." Here, "justifies" is equated with "imputing righteousness." Thus, the apostle teaches that "ungodly" people are "justified" in that God "imputes righteousness" to them "apart from works." D. A. Carson asserts: "We perceive that justification of the ungodly *means* the imputation of righteousness."[6] This careful study of Paul's teaching in Romans 4:6 shows that Paul by the Holy Spirit did not teach that faith justifies us by meriting righteousness in the place of works. Instead, he wrote that ungodly persons like Abraham and Paul, while they remain unrighteous in their persons, are nonetheless justified through faith by the imputing to them of what Martin Luther commonly referred to as an alien righteousness. Moreover, this imputed righteousness can be none other than the righteousness of Christ.

The Arminian objection, answered by Romans 4:1–6, presents one front in the battle for justification and imputation today. The other front pits Reformed theology against a popularized liberalism in the writings of Anglican scholar N. T. Wright. Wright is widely acclaimed as an evangelical scholar—some even consider him the leading evangelical scholar—yet his hermeneutic commitments

---

6. D. A. Carson, "The Vindication of Imputation: On Fields of Discourse and Semantic Fields," in *Justification: What's at Stake in the Current Debates*, ed. Mark Husbands and Daniel J. Treier (Downers Grove, Ill.: InterVarsity, 2004), 63.

involve straightforward higher critical interpretation of the Bible.[7] In his reformulation of the Protestant doctrine of justification, Wright has no place for the imputation of Christ's righteousness, alleging that imputed righteousness "is…not actually found stated as such anywhere in Paul."[8] We have already answered this claim by showing that Paul teaches justification as the imputation of righteousness in Romans 4:5–6: "God imputeth righteousness without works." This is just one of many places where not only Paul but the Scriptures as a whole teach justification through faith alone in the form of the imputation of Christ's righteousness. In fact, imputation is not merely a Pauline doctrine but a doctrine taught consistently and decisively throughout the Scriptures in their teaching of salvation.

Biblical Affirmations of Imputed Righteousness

The place to begin a tour of the Bible's teaching of imputed righteousness is the scene of the crime itself: Genesis 3 and the fall of mankind into sin. Adam and Eve had broken God's commandment and come under His curse. He had said that disobedience would receive the penalty of death (Gen. 2:17). Adam and Eve would die, being barred from the Tree of Life and thus kept from living forever (Gen. 3:22). But, at the same time, God announced His gracious purpose to achieve their salvation, and to each of the players in the drama of the Fall God foretold a Savior. First, God warned the serpent that a seed from the woman would crush his head (Gen. 3:15). In Genesis 3:21, God proclaimed Christ to Adam and Eve in a wholly wonderful way: "Unto Adam also and to his wife did the LORD God make coats of skins, and clothed them."

We remember that sin had contaminated the first couple's nakedness with shame, so God covered their sin and guilt with the skins of an innocent substitute. On the one hand, it was a spotless creature who had not participated in our first parents' sin but who nonetheless paid sin's penalty of death, in this way depicting penal substitutionary atonement. On the other hand, Adam and Eve, not participating in the sacrifice's righteousness, are clothed by it so as

---

7. See, for instance, N. T. Wright, *The New Testament and the People of God* (Minneapolis: Fortress, 1992), 3–28, where Wright rejects the hermeneutical principles historically associated with evangelical theology.

8. N. T. Wright, *Justification: God's Plan and Paul's Vision* (London: SPCK, 2009), 29.

to stand justified before God. The great evangelist George Whitefield explained the significance of this twofold provision of saving grace:

> What were the coats that God made to put on our first parents, but types of the application of the merits of righteousness of Jesus Christ to believers' hearts? We are told…that those beasts were slain in sacrifice, in commemoration of the great sacrifice, Jesus Christ, thereafter to be offered. And the skins of the beasts thus slain, being put on Adam and Eve, they were hereby taught how their nakedness was to be covered with the righteousness of the Lamb of God.[9]

What a testimony this bears, not merely to the truth of imputed righteousness but also to its central place in the salvation that God offers to us. God responded to the Fall with an immediate typological enacting of penal substitutionary atonement and the imputation of Christ's righteousness as His first redemptive act of grace towards fallen mankind.

Another bold Old Testament depiction of this doctrine is found in the vision of Zechariah 3. Joshua, the high priest, representing all of Israel in their return from punishment in the exile, stood before the Lord in filthy clothes. How loathsome Joshua must have felt, representing the entire nation that had been condemned for sin, judged, and sent into the hell of the Babylonian exile. Now, having returned with the remnant to Jerusalem, he stood still dirty and with Satan at his side to accuse him of his guilt. In a marvelous display of what Martin Luther called the "great exchange" of Christian salvation, the Angel of the Lord (who most Reformed exegetes believe to have been the preincarnate Christ) rebuked the devil, reminding Satan of His cleansing blood and imputed righteousness: "Now Joshua was clothed with filthy garments, and stood before the angel. And he answered and spake unto those that stood before him, saying, Take away the filthy garments from him. And unto him he said, Behold, I have caused thine iniquity to pass from thee, and I will clothe thee with change of raiment" (Zech. 3:3–4). What a glorious depiction of what the Lord Jesus offers to us by His cross: He takes our sins onto Himself and places His own righteousness on us.

---

9. George Whitefield, *Select Sermons of George Whitefield* (Edinburgh: Banner of Truth, 1958), 117.

A third passage comes from Jesus' parable of the wedding feast. The king sent his servants out to bring in the people for his son's wedding feast. But after they were gathered, "he saw there a man which had not on a wedding garment: and he saith unto him, Friend, how camest thou in hither not having a wedding garment? And he was speechless. Then said the king to the servants, Bind him hand and foot, and take him away, and cast him into outer darkness; there shall be weeping and gnashing of teeth" (Matt. 22:11–13). This passage refutes those who teach that we need only be forgiven to enter into heaven and have no need of any positive garment of righteousness. John Owen comments on this:

> It is not enough to say that we are not guilty. We must also be perfectly righteous. The law must be fulfilled by perfect obedience if we would enter into eternal life. And this is found only in Jesus (Rom. 5:10). His death reconciled us to God. Now we are saved by his life. The perfect actual obedience that Christ rendered on earth is that righteousness by which we are saved. His righteousness is imputed to me so that I am counted as having perfectly obeyed the law myself. This must be my righteousness if I would be found in Christ, not having my own righteousness which is of the law, but the righteousness which is of God by faith (Phil. 3:9).[10]

N. T. Wright has challenged Reformed theologians to show where Paul teaches imputed righteousness. We have already considered Romans 4:5–6, in which the expression "God justifieth the ungodly" parallels the matching statement, "God imputeth righteousness without works." Another decisive passage is 2 Corinthians 5:21, which states that God "hath made [Christ] to be sin for us, who knew no sin; that we might be made the righteousness of God in him." Wright argues that this verse teaches the opposite of imputation, since it says that believers are "made the righteousness of God" in Christ. Wright asserts that this language "does not sit comfortably with the normal interpretation, according to which 'God's righteousness' is 'imputed' or 'reckoned' to believers," since in that case "the one thing he ought not to have said is that we 'become' that righteousness."[11] Careful

---

10. John Owen, *The Works of John Owen* (Edinburgh: Banner of Truth, 1991), 2:94–95.

11. Wright, *Justification*, 141.

consideration will show to the contrary that Paul's teaching is justly beloved to Reformed Christians as teaching imputed righteousness in the form of the great exchange, whereby our sin and Christ's righteousness are exchanged at the cross.

Let us consider the context of this verse. Verse 19 says, "God was in Christ, reconciling the world unto himself, not imputing their trespasses unto them; and hath committed unto us the word of reconciliation." In other words, God acted to save sinners by the death of His Son and through the apostolic preaching of the gospel. Paul continues in verse 20, "Now then we are ambassadors for Christ, as though God did beseech you by us: we pray you in Christ's stead, be ye reconciled to God." Then, in verse 21, Paul offers the substance of his gospel message about what God has done to reconcile sinners: "For he hath made him to be sin for us, who knew no sin; that we might be made the righteousness of God in him." Notice the central place Paul gives to the doctrine of imputed righteousness: he makes it the very essence of his ambassadorial message to sinners for reconciliation and salvation.

Verse 21 presents a parallel structure. Paul says that God "made him to be sin for us who knew no sin." When Paul says that Christ was "made sin," he cannot mean that Jesus personally *became* a sinner. Instead, Jesus received our sins *by imputation*. Our sins were not *infused* into Christ, nor did he receive them by *participation*. In Paul's parallel construction, in the same manner that Christ was "made to be sin," believers are "made the righteousness of God" —namely, by imputation. In Paul's admittedly provocative language, we receive Christ's righteousness in the same manner that He received our sin. This can only be by imputation: Christ receiving what He did not deserve by His gracious will, and we receiving by that same gracious will what we do not deserve—that is, the credit of His righteousness—so that we might enter into the blessing of eternal life.

Wright counters again, noting that Paul speaks of "the righteousness of God," not the righteousness of Christ. But all this is "in Christ." Paul had said, "God was in Christ, reconciling the world unto himself" (2 Cor. 5:19). Just as only God the Son, not God the Father, could suffer humiliation and death upon the cross, so also only the Son was born into this world under the law to fulfill it for us. Yes, it is God's righteousness "in Christ" that He imputes to believers for reconciliation with Himself.

Another vital passage is Romans 5:12–21, which we can consider only briefly. Here, Paul compares and contrasts Adam and Christ as our covenant heads. Speaking of Adam's fall, Paul explains, "by one man sin entered into the world, and death by sin" (Rom. 5:12). We are so fully identified with our first father and covenant representative that when he sinned we sinned in him: "so death passed upon all men, for that all have sinned" (Rom. 5:12). But Adam was also a type of Christ, a "figure of him that was to come" (Rom. 5:14), since both were federal representatives for their people. Jesus is different from Adam, however, because of His perfect obedience and the salvation it brings. Paul writes, "Therefore as by the offence of one judgment came upon all men to condemnation; even so by the righteousness of one the free gift came upon all men unto justification of life. For as by one man's disobedience many were made sinners, so by the obedience of one shall many be made righteous" (Rom. 5:18–19).

A couple of observations are important. First, notice the structure of justification as Paul presents it here. In verse 18, he establishes the progression: "righteousness" leads to "justification" and "life." This is the way of salvation found all through the Bible. If we want to enjoy salvation *life*, with all the fullness this speaks of, then we must be *justified*. But in order to be justified, we must possess *righteousness*: only the righteous can be justified. Verse 19 completes the progression by adding "by the obedience of one shall many be made righteous." Now we insert "obedience" at the beginning of the progression. Working backwards, *life* requires *justification*, which relies upon perfect *righteousness*, and that righteousness in turn is based on *obedience* to God's commands. The forward progression is this: obedience—righteousness—justification—life.

Second, observe that our problem in Adam is that we have not obeyed, either federally via Adam or personally in our own lives. Having disobeyed, we do not possess righteousness, so we will be not justified but condemned. Instead of life, we partake of death. The good news is what Christ has done: "By the obedience of one shall many be made righteous" (Rom. 5:19). Does this mean we need a moral change or a spiritual transformation so that we will become righteous? No, for our corrupt Adamic natures are incapable of that kind of reform and our prior sins cry out for condemnation. When Paul writes that in Christ many are "made righteous," he does not mean that we should be "transformed" into righteous persons but rather "appointed" or "established" righteous [Greek, *katastatheson-tai*] (Rom. 5:19). This word for "made" or "established" is a legal term that is a synonym for "imputed."

This, then, is Paul's way of explaining how God makes it possible for us to enter into eternal life. Having disobeyed, we are unrighteous. But Christ has obeyed in our place, meriting righteousness. The good news is that when we believe in Jesus, God transfers us from Adam's covenant headship to Christ's, and imputes Christ's righteousness to us in the place of Adam's condemnation. Thus justified, we enter into life. Now we have the clean garments of which the Angel of the Lord spoke to the high priest Joshua in Zechariah 3:4: "Behold, I have caused thine iniquity to pass from thee, and I will clothe thee with change of raiment."

Thy Blood and Righteousness

I have noted the difficulty of fighting a two-front war. You can succeed on one hand, but failure on the other destroys you. This is the sinner's plight before God. We have two requirements necessary for entering into the blessings of eternal life, neither of which we have the ability to fulfill. On the one hand is our need to deal with the problem of our sins. What can we do to remove the black stain of our well-earned guilt before God? On the other hand, the holy God requires a perfect righteousness that we have not attained and do not possess. How can ungodly people like we are gain the righteousness without which we must be cast into outer darkness?

The answer is given in the title of the great hymn of Count Zinzendorf: "Jesus, Thy Blood and Righteousness." These are resources equal to the sinner's need. What can wash away my sin? The blood of Jesus can do it, making me "white as snow" (Isa. 1:18). But what robe shall I wear in God's presence? John Murray answers, "The righteousness of Christ is the righteousness of his perfect obedience, a righteousness undefiled and undefilable, a righteousness which not only warrants the justification of the ungodly but one that necessarily elicits and constrains such justification. God cannot but accept into his favor those who are invested with the righteousness of his own Son."[12]

Based on our study, we see that the church must uphold the doctrine of Christ's imputed righteousness because of its biblical affirmations. Believers should also treasure it because of the assurance it gives of an entrance into God's glory, an assurance held up by the joint appeals of God's mercy and justice: mercy pleads pardon and justice affirms imputed righteousness. But there is another consideration, for which this great doctrine must be demanded with great zeal and defended at great cost, namely, the honor and glory of the Lord Jesus Christ. To this end, let me repeat the words of John Piper:

> Alongside the pastoral preciousness of the doctrine of the imputed righteousness of Christ is the great truth that this doctrine bestows on Jesus Christ the fullest honor that he deserves. Not only should he be honored as the one who died to pardon us, and not only should he be honored as the one who sovereignly works faith and obedience in us, but he should also be honored as the one who provided a perfect righteousness for us as the ground of our full acceptance and endorsement by God. I pray that the "newer" ways of understanding justification, which deny the reality of the imputation of divine righteousness to sinners by faith alone, will not flourish, and that the fullest glory of Christ and the fullest pastoral help for souls will not be diminished.[13]

This, it turns out, is the very line of thinking to which the Holy Spirit directed the apostle Paul in thoughts of the righteousness that comes from Christ. In Philippians 3, he specifically repudiated anything in and of himself that might stand for righteousness before God—not his faith as something that itself merited righteousness, and certainly not his status as a covenant member, of which faith was a badge of honor (as N. T. Wright would have it[14]). Instead, Paul says, "what things were gain to me, those I counted loss for Christ" (Phil. 3:7). Instead of any righteousness of his own, Paul clings only to "the righteousness which is of God by faith" in Christ

---

12. John Murray, *Redemption Accomplished and Applied* (Grand Rapids: Eerdmans, 1955), 124.

13. John Piper, *Counted Righteous in Christ* (Wheaton, Ill.: Crossway, 2002), 125.

14. N. T. Wright, *What Saint Paul Really Said* (Grand Rapids: Eerdmans, 1997), 129.

(Phil. 3:8–9). Likewise, this was Paul's thinking in 1 Corinthians 1:30–31, where the inspired apostle rejoiced that Christ is "made unto us...righteousness" (1 Cor. 1:30), and then hastened to the application that should most animate our hearts: "He that glorieth, let him glory in the Lord" (1 Cor. 1:31).

Therefore, let us defend and promote this great doctrine of Christ's imputed righteousness, glorifying in God alone for His righteousness in Christ. And let us go on to follow the example of Esther in the court of her husband, the Persian king. Let us by faith put on the royal robe granted to us at so great a cost by our Savior. Let us approach our royal Lord, kneeling before Him in adoration, and draw near to Christ with joyful confidence to pray, worship, and serve.

CHAPTER 10

Thomas Goodwin on Christ's Beautiful Heart

Joel R. Beeke

• *Read Hebrews 4:14–5:10*

> *O the deep, deep love of Jesus! Vast, unmeasured, boundless free:*
> *Rolling as a mighty ocean in its fullness over me.*
> *Underneath me, all around me, is the current of Thy love;*
> *Leading onward, leading homeward, to Thy glorious rest above!*[1]

Today we will contemplate the loving tenderness of Jesus Christ. In particular, we will meditate on the heart of Christ's glorified human nature that He shows to His people here on earth. Though we do not see Jesus in the flesh today, we can, by faith, rejoice in Him and His compassionate heart. Our guide for these insights is Thomas Goodwin, a seventeenth-century English Puritan, who wrote with peculiar unction and liberty about Christ's heart.

In presenting Goodwin's teachings on Christ's heart, I will speak first of the Puritan preacher; second, a problem; third, the promises; and fourth, the proof of Christ's compassionate heart. Prior to that I will briefly define what it meant to be a Puritan and say a few words about Thomas Goodwin.

The Definition of Puritanism
Tom Webster suggests that there are three elements of being a Puritan. First, Puritans had a dynamic fellowship with God that shaped their minds, affected their emotions, and penetrated their souls. They were grounded in Someone outside of themselves: the triune

---

1. Samuel Trevor Francis, "O the Deep, Deep Love of Jesus," stanza 1 (1875). http://songsandhymns.org/pdf/sheet_music/o-the-deep-deep-love-of-jesus.pdf (accessed August 9, 2010). I thank Paul Smalley for his assistance on this chapter.

God of the Scriptures. Second, Puritans embraced a shared system of beliefs grounded in the Scriptures. Today we refer to this system as Reformed orthodoxy. Third, out of this spiritually dynamic world-view, the Puritans established a network of relationships among believers and ministers.[2]

Puritans were committed to search the Scriptures, organize their findings, and then apply them to all areas of life. This created a confessional, theological, and Trinitarian approach. It sought personal conversion and communion with God, family, church, and national life.[3] So, in labeling Thomas Goodwin a Puritan, we mean that he was part of a spiritual brotherhood[4] driven by Reformed beliefs and experiential fellowship with God. He worked with other Puritans for Bible-based reformation and Spirit-empowered revival on personal, familial, ecclesiastical, and national levels.

Goodwin's Life and Works

Thomas Goodwin was born in 1600[5] and raised by God-fearing parents. Shortly before his twentieth birthday, God deeply convicted

---

2. "It has proved possible to trace a network of godly divines in early Stuart England, similar to William Haller's 'spiritual brotherhood,' but going far beyond the great names of Sibbes, Gouge, Preston, and Dod to draw in the humblest of the painful preachers and the most junior of the aspirant ministers coming out of Oxford and Cambridge.... It was rooted in what Peter Lake called a 'certain evangelical protestant world-view' predicated upon the 'potentially transforming effects of the gospel on both individuals and on the social order as a whole.' It is Lake's contention that if Puritanism is to be defined at all it must be in terms of this 'spiritual dynamic'...the nature of that spiritual dynamic [being] a sense of communion with God, Scripturally informed, deeply emotional, and yet aspiring to something beyond the subjective" (Tom Webster, *Godly Clergy in Early Stuart England: The Caroline Puritan Movement, c. 1620–1643* [Cambridge: Cambridge University Press, 1997], 333). Webster cites William Haller, *The Rise of Puritanism* (New York: Columbia University Press, 1938), chap. 1, and Peter Lake, *Moderate Puritans and the Elizabethan Church* (Cambridge: Cambridge University Press, 1982), 279, 282–83.

3. Joel R. Beeke and Randall J. Pederson, *Meet the Puritans* (Grand Rapids: Reformation Heritage Books, 2006), xvii.

4. On Goodwin's participation in social networks and conferences of the godly, cf. Webster, *Godly Clergy in Early Stuart England*, 57–58, 79–80.

5. For a succinct treatment of his biography, see Joel R. Beeke, introduction to *The Works of Thomas Goodwin* by Thomas Goodwin (Nichol's edition, 1861–1866; repr., Grand Rapids: Reformation Heritage Books, 2006), 1:[2–10, 22] and James Reid, "Life of Thomas Goodwin," in *Memoirs of the Westminster Divines* (1811; repr., Edinburgh: Banner of Truth Trust, 1982), 319–43. See also Brian Freer, "Thomas Goodwin, the Peaceable Puritan," and Graham Harrison, "Thomas Goodwin and

him of his sins, and by grace he became a believer. Resolving to deny his personal ambitions for fame, he aspired to preach the Word of God plainly to bring Christ to the lost and to build up believers' souls.

In the 1620s and early 1630s, Goodwin taught and preached at Cambridge University until Archbishop Laud drove the Puritans out of Cambridge in 1634. Goodwin left to serve as a minister in London, but that did not stop the persecution; five years later Goodwin fled to the Netherlands. He returned to London in 1641 when the Puritans rose in power. He was a leading figure in the Westminster Assembly, though he was an Independent and not part of the Presbyterian majority.[6] In 1650, Goodwin became president of Magdalen College at Oxford University, serving with John Owen. After King Charles II returned to England in 1660, Goodwin led the Independent Christians in London through persecution, plague, and the Great Fire of London, which consumed half of Goodwin's massive theological library.

Goodwin died in 1680. After his death, other Puritans collected and published his writings. They are now available in the twelve-

---

Independency," and Paul E. G. Cook, "Thomas Goodwin—Mystic?" in *Diversities of Gifts*, Westminster Conference Reports, 1980 (London: The Westminster Conference, 1981), 7–56. For a more lengthy treatment, see Mark Jones, "Why Heaven Kissed Earth: The Christology of Thomas Goodwin (1600–1680)" (Ph.D. dissertation, University of Leiden, 2009), 34–83.

6. Wayne Spear asserts that Goodwin gave more addresses at the assembly than any other divine ("Covenanted Uniformity in Religion: The Influence of the Scottish Commissioners upon the Ecclesiology of the Westminster Assembly" (Ph.D. dissertation, University of Pittsburgh, 1976), 362. Cf. Chad van Dixhoorn, "Reforming the Reformation: Theological Debate at the Westminster Assembly 1643–1652," 7 vols. (Ph.D. dissertation, Cambridge University, 2004). For Goodwin's role in the Presbyterian-Independent controversy, see Stanley Fienberg, "Thomas Goodwin, Puritan Pastor and Independent Divine" (Ph.D. dissertation, University of Chicago, 1974), 80–265; idem, "Thomas Goodwin's Scriptural Hermeneutics and the Dissolution of Puritan Unity," *Journal of Religious History* 10 (1978): 32–49; Berndt Gustafsson, *The Five Dissenting Brethren: A Study of the Dutch Background of Their Independentism* (London: C. W. K. Gloerup, 1955); R. B. Carter, "The Presbyterian-Independent Controversy with Special Reference to Dr. Thomas Goodwin and the Years 1640 to 1660" (Ph.D. dissertation, Edinburgh, 1961); David R. Ehalt, "The Development of Early Congregational Theory of the Church with Special Reference to the Five `Dissenting Brethren' at the Westminster Assembly" (Ph.D. dissertation, Claremont, 1969); J. R. De Witt, *Jus Divinum: The Westminster Assembly and the Divine Right of Church Government* (Kampen: Kok, 1969); Gordon D. Crompton, "The Life and Theology of Thomas Goodwin, D.D." (Th.M. thesis, Greenville Presbyterian Theological Seminary, 1997), 180–224; D. J. Walker, "Thomas Goodwin and the Debate on Church Government," *Journal of Ecclesiastical History* 34 (1983): 85–99.

volume set of his *Works,* which I highly recommend to you.[7] For an introduction to Goodwin in a little collection of readings, consult *"A Habitual Sight of Him": The Christ-Centered Piety of Thomas Goodwin.*[8]

The Scotsman Alexander Whyte said of Goodwin, "Full as Goodwin always is of the ripest scriptural and Reformation scholarship; full as he always is of the best theological and philosophical learning of his own day and of all foregoing days; full, also, as he always is of the deepest spiritual experience—all the same, he is always so simple, so clear, so direct, and un-technical, so personal, and so pastoral."[9]

Preacher of the Compassionate Christ

Goodwin's writings are a shining example of Christ-centered Puritanism. Before examining Goodwin's teaching on the heart of Christ in heaven, we must begin with his teaching on Christ crucified on earth.

Goodwin loved to preach the good news of reconciliation between God and man. He stressed that God created all mankind in friendship with Him. But man rebelled against God, greatly offending God's justice. God the Father, being infinite in love and rich in mercy, made an eternal covenant of peace with His Son before time began.[10] The Father determined to send His Son to serve as Mediator between sinful man and holy God. Christ took on the task of satisfying the Father for all the wrong done against God; He took on Himself the guilt and sin of His chosen people, dying under the curse of God's law against sinners. The Father was so satisfied with Christ's work that He not only forgives everyone who trusts

---

7. Reprinted, Grand Rapids: Reformation Heritage Books, 2006. For guidance on how to read Goodwin, see Beeke, introduction to *Works of Goodwin,* 1:[11–14].

8. Joel R. Beeke and Mark Jones, eds., *"A Habitual Sight of Him": The Christ-Centered Piety of Thomas Goodwin* (Grand Rapids: Reformation Heritage Books, 2009).

9. Alexander Whyte, *Thirteen Appreciations* (Edinburgh: Oliphant, Anderson, and Ferrier, 1913), 170–71. Cf. J. C. Philpot, *Reviews by the late Mr. J. C. Philpot* (London: Frederick Kirby, 1901), 2:479ff., who comments: "Being a man of choice experience, Goodwin so blends with [his sound expositions of Scripture] the work of the Spirit, in all its various branches, as to enrich his exposition with a heavenly savour and unction which carries with it great force, and commends itself in a very sensible and profitable manner to the conscience."

10. For Goodwin on the covenant of grace, see Paul Edward Brown, "The Principle of the Covenant in the Theology of Thomas Goodwin" (Ph.D. dissertation, Drew University, 1950).

in Christ alone for salvation but counts believers righteous through Jesus' very righteousness. On the basis of Christ's work, preachers may call the world to be reconciled to God.[11] Goodwin thus says to us, "Rest on Christ alone, especially as crucified."[12]

Gordon Crompton says that Goodwin defined faith as the spiritual sight and knowledge of Christ. In Goodwin, "we see Christ's spiritual excellencies and His glory, and our heart is taken with them."[13] Michael Horton asserts that Goodwin's favorite definition of faith was this: "Now this Spirit, when he comes down thus into the heart, works eyes, and feet, and hands, and all to look upon Christ, and to come to Christ, and to lay hold upon Christ.... And faith is eyes, and hands, and feet, yea, and mouth, and stomach, and all; for we eat his flesh and drink his blood by faith."[14]

Goodwin also loved to preach on Christ's resurrection from the dead and ascension to heaven. He had a beautiful view of Christ's intimate ministry in glory to His children. He wrote a helpful book on this subject titled *The Heart of Christ in Heaven towards Sinners on Earth* (1645).[15] Its subtitle is *A Treatise Demonstrating the Glorious Disposition and Tender Affection of Christ, in His Human Nature Now in Glory, unto His Members, under all sorts of Infirmities, either of Sin or Misery.* The immediate purpose of the treatise was to reject the popular idea that Christians in the post-apostolic age were at a disadvantage to Christians who knew Christ on earth because Christ was now glorified and less affected by humanity. Goodwin asserted from the Holy Scriptures that Christ feels strong affections, deep compassion, and emotional sympathy towards His suffering people even while seated

---

11. Goodwin, *Works*, 5:3–5.

12. Goodwin, *Works*, 5:292.

13. Crompton, "The Life and Theology of Thomas Goodwin," 139, 142.

14. Michael S. Horton, "Thomas Goodwin and the Puritan Doctrine of Assurance: Continuity and Discontinuity in the Reformed Tradition, 1600–1680" (Ph.D. dissertation, Wycliffe Hall, Oxford, and Coventry University, 1995), 182. He quotes Goodwin, *Works*, 8:147. For additional studies on Goodwin's views of faith and assurance, see Alexander McNally, "Some Aspects of Thomas Goodwin's Doctrine of Assurance" (Th.M. thesis, Westminster Theological Seminary, 1972) and Joel R. Beeke, *The Quest for Full Assurance: The Legacy of Calvin and His Successors* (Edinburgh: Banner of Truth Trust, 1999), 245–68.

15. Goodwin, *Works*, 4:93–150. For a summary of this book, see Cook, "Goodwin—Mystic?," 49–56, and Crompton, "The Life and Theology of Thomas Goodwin," 289–308.

at God's right hand. This treatise was one of Goodwin's most popular works, reprinted several times in England and translated into German.[16]

"Goodwin wishes to express that Christ's exaltation has not diminished His emotions, but rather, has caused them to increase," Crompton writes. "Christ is still the compassionate One that He was while on earth."[17] Many Reformed theologians have written on Christ's exaltation and intercession, but writing about Christ's emotions in heaven towards us on earth, Paul Cook observes, was "an unusual theme."[18]

Goodwin did not write with the false colors of human speculation. Instead, he looked to the Scriptures, which, he said, "open a window into Christ's heart."[19] Scripture alone is our authority.[20] How else can our minds grasp what Christ is thinking and feeling in heaven?[21] Goodwin said that the Bible "doth, as it were, take our hands and lay them upon Christ's breast, and let us feel how his heart beats...toward us, even now [when] he is in glory."[22]

Goodwin was a Puritan preacher of the compassionate Christ. Before examining what this great preacher-theologian taught about the tender mercies of our Savior, we must consider a practical problem created by our Savior's exaltation.

The Problem of the Compassionate Christ

Thomas Goodwin centered his discussion of Christ's heavenly heart of compassion upon Hebrews 4:14–15: "Seeing then that we have a great

---

16. Crompton, "The Life and Theology of Thomas Goodwin," 289.

17. Crompton, "The Life and Theology of Thomas Goodwin," 290.

18. Cook, "Goodwin—Mystic?," 45.

19. Goodwin, *Works*, 4:96.

20. Goodwin writes, "First, that the holy Scripture is that rule of knowing God, and living unto him, which who so doth not believe, but betakes himself to any other way of discovering truth, and the mind of God instead thereof, cannot be saved" (Thomas Goodwin, et al., *The Principles of Faith* [London, 1654], quoted in Jones, "Why Heaven Kissed Earth," 101.

21. Commenting on how Christ suffers with His people (Heb. 4:15), Goodwin wrote, "Now, concerning this affection, as here thus expressed, how far it extends, and how deep it may reach, I think no man in this life can fathom. If *cor regis*, the heart of a king, be inscrutable, as Solomon speaks [Prov. 25:3], the heart of the King of kings now in glory is much more. I will not take upon me to 'intrude into things which I have not seen,' but shall endeavor to speak safely, and therefore warily, so far as the light of Scripture and right reason shall warrant my way" (*Works*, 4:143).

22. Goodwin, *Works*, 4:111.

high priest, that is passed into the heavens, Jesus the Son of God, let us hold fast our profession. For we have not an high priest which cannot be touched with the feeling of our infirmities; but was in all points tempted like as we are, yet without sin." This Scripture, as Goodwin saw it, contains both a problem and a solution for our faith in Christ.

The Problem: Our Great High Priest Passed into the Heavens
Goodwin recognized that sinful men might be put off by the words, "a *great* high priest that is passed into the *heavens*." We might think that the greatness of the exalted Christ might cause Him to forget us. Think of a boy from a small town who graduates from college, then finds a high-paying job in a big city. He puts his friends and family behind him, thinking them inferior to his new associates. Likewise, Goodwin wrote that we might think that, if Christ remembered us in heaven, "having cast off the frailties of his flesh which he had here, and having clothed his human nature with so great a glory, ...he cannot now pity us, as he did when he dwelt among us here below, nor be so feelingly affected and touched with our miseries." Surely He has left behind Him all memories of weakness and pain.[23]

Goodwin saw this thinking as a "great stone of stumbling which we meet with (and yet lieth unseen) in the thoughts of men in the way to faith." Christ is absent from us on earth. Surely it would be better for us if we could talk with Him as Mary and Peter did on earth. He was so gentle with them. "But now He has gone into a far country, where He has put on glory and immortality," Goodwin points out.[24] He sits as King at God's right hand in heaven. His human nature is aflame with glory. How can we boldly approach such a King? How can we expect Him, in exalted power and holiness, to bear patiently with us when we are so weak, foolish, and sinful? But Goodwin says that the same Scripture that speaks of Christ's exaltation also reveals His compassion.

Still Touched with Compassion
Goodwin wielded the sword of the Spirit—the Word of God—against this obstacle. He taught that Christ's mercy is so certain that Scripture uses a double negative to forcefully declare the positive

---

23. Goodwin, *Works,* 4:112.
24. Goodwin, *Works,* 4:95.

truth: "We have *not* a high priest which *cannot* be touched with the feeling of our infirmities."

Our infirmities stir Christ's compassion; Goodwin argues from Hebrews that "infirmities" include both our troubles and our sins. The letter to the Hebrews addressed people facing pressure and persecution. So "infirmities" must be our earthly troubles. But our sin is also an infirmity. Hebrews 5:2 declares that a high priest "could have compassion on the ignorant, and those that were out of the way." Even our foolishness and sinful choices awaken Christ's compassion.[25]

Goodwin drives his point home with a bold comparison. He writes to believers: "Your very sins move him to pity more than to anger...even as the heart of a father is to a child that hath some loathsome disease, or as one is to a member of his body that hath the leprosy, he hates not the member, for it is his flesh, but the disease, and that provokes him to pity the part affected the more."[26] If your child becomes very sick, you do not kick the child out; you weep with him and tend to his needs. Christ responds to our sins with compassion despite His abhorrence of them.

Christ's compassion flows out of His personal human experience. Hebrews 4:15 says that He "was in all points tempted like as we are, yet without sin." Earlier, Hebrews 2:18 says, "For in that he himself hath suffered being tempted, he is able to succour [help] them that are tempted." Goodwin explains how this works: In His days on earth, "Christ took to heart all that befell him as deeply as might be; he slighted no cross, either from God or men, but had and felt the utmost load of it. Yea, his heart was made more tender in all sorts of affections than any of ours, even as it was in love and pity; and this made him 'a man of sorrows,' and that more than any other man was or shall be."[27]

Today in heaven, Jesus in His human nature knows everything that happens to believers on earth. Jesus says to His church in Revelation 2:2, "I know thy works, and thy labour, and thy patience." This is possible because Christ's human nature is filled with the Holy Spirit beyond measure, and the Spirit is like Christ's eyes in all the earth (Rev. 5:6). Knowing our distress, He remembers how He felt

---

25. Goodwin, *Works*, 4:111–12.
26. Goodwin, *Works*, 4:149.
27. Goodwin, *Works*, 4:141.

when facing similar miseries.[28] Christ even knows the experience of sin's guilt and the horror of facing God's wrath against sin. Although personally sinless, Christ bore all the sins of His people.[29] His knowledge of our pain along with the memory of His pain moves His heart to overflow with compassion.

Glorious Human Tenderness

Christ sympathizes with us. That is not to say that Christ is still suffering in heaven; always a careful theologian, Goodwin clearly taught that Christ's humiliation was completed at the cross and tomb. In His exaltation, His human nature is glorified and free from all pain.

How then can Christ be touched with the feeling of our infirmities? Goodwin said this is not an act of weakness but of the power of heavenly love. He writes, "And whereas it may be objected, that this were a weakness, the apostle affirms that this is his power, and a perfection and strength of love surely, in him, as the word [*able*] importeth; that is, that makes him thus able and powerful to take our miseries into his heart, though glorified, and so to be affected with them, as if he suffered with us."[30]

On one hand, we should not think of Jesus suffering in heaven as He did on earth. He is no longer subject to any frailty, weariness, tears, exhaustion, or fear. On the other hand, He remains a person with human emotions and a human body. He is not a spirit or a ghost. And His frailty is replaced with a vastly expanded capacity for the affections of love. Christ is God and man. As God, Christ is infinite, eternal, and unchanging. But, as a man, He has been lifted up to a new level of glory. Goodwin said, "For it is certain that as his knowledge was enlarged upon his entering into glory, so his human affections of love and pity are enlarged in solidity, strength, and reality…Eph. 3:19, 'The love of Christ,' God-man, 'passeth knowledge.'"[31] So Christ is not hurt by our sufferings, but His human soul responds to our sufferings with glorious, beautiful tenderness.

Crompton summarized Goodwin's teachings, saying, "Christ, as our High Priest, was not just touched with the feelings of our

---

28. Goodwin, *Works*, 4:141–42.
29. Goodwin, *Works*, 4:149.
30. Goodwin, *Works*, 4:112–13.
31. Goodwin, *Works*, 4:143–46.

infirmities during His time on earth, taking only the memory of it to heaven. But now in heaven, in a glorified state, He is touched in His very feelings for us. This is by no means a weakness of any sort. Rather, this ability to feel for us is part of His power. It is a perfection and strength of love and grace."[32]

Let us now look at the promises in Scripture that reassure us of Christ's tender thoughts toward us. These promises are amazingly comprehensive and comforting.

The Promises of the Compassionate Christ

Hebrews 4:14 says, "Seeing then that we have a great high priest, that is passed into the heavens, Jesus the Son of God, let us hold fast to our profession." Let us cling to our profession of the doctrines of Christ, which stands upon the promises of Christ. Later, Hebrews 10:23 says, "Let us hold fast the profession of our faith without wavering; (for he is faithful that promised)." As Goodwin said, God's promises are like coins held out in mercy's hands for God's children to take.[33]

Our text in Hebrews 4 speaks of Christ as the One who has "passed into the heavens." When did Christ promise that His heart would remain full of mercy while He was in heaven?

Promises before His Death

Goodwin focuses here on John 13 to 17. He reminds us of these opening words in John 13:1: "Now before the feast of the passover, when Jesus knew that his hour was come that he should depart out of this world unto the Father, having loved his own which were in the world, he loved them unto the end." Even when Jesus' mind was set on His imminent exaltation to supreme glory, Goodwin said, "his heart ran out in love towards, and was set upon, 'his own:'…his own, a word denoting the greatest nearness, dearness, and intimacy founded upon propriety [or ownership]."[34] At that precise time, Jesus washed the feet of His disciples, demonstrating that Christ's

---

32. Crompton, "The Life and Theology of Thomas Goodwin," 299.
33. Goodwin, *Works*, 8:5–6. Cf. Horton, "Thomas Goodwin and the Puritan Doctrine of Assurance," 177.
34. Goodwin, *Works*, 4:96–97.

glorification would not diminish but rather increase His love and grace service to His people.

Jesus said in John 14 to 16 that He would ascend to heaven to secure our happiness as believers. He would prepare a place for us, He said. And He would return like a bridegroom to bring us to our eternal home. Goodwin wrote, "It is as if [Jesus] had said, 'The truth is, I cannot live without you, I shall never be quiet till I have you where I am, that so we may never part again; that is the reason of it. Heaven shall not hold me, nor my Father's company, if I have not you with me, my heart is set upon you; and if I have any glory, you shall have part of it.'"[35]

Meanwhile, Christ would not orphan or abandon His bride but would commit her to the care of His "dearest friend," the Comforter. In Goodwin's words, Jesus said the Holy Spirit would comfort us with "nothing but stories of my love," for He would not speak of Himself but as one sent from Christ. Meanwhile, Christ promised to pray for us in heaven, and to send answers like love letters from a bridegroom to his beloved. He demonstrated His commitment to pray for us by interceding even then, as seen in John 17.[36]

Assurances after His Resurrection
Goodwin asked, "Now when Christ came first out of the other world, from the dead, clothed with that heart and body which he was to wear in heaven, what message sends he first to them?" The answer is in John 20:17, where Jesus called His disciples "my brethren" and said, "I ascend to my Father, and your Father." What sweet words of grace to the men who had denied Christ and abandoned Him in His darkest hour! Christ, who promises to intercede for us as a brother, also intercedes with His Father for the rest of the family. When Jesus appeared to the disciples later, His first words were, "Peace be to you" (John 20:19, 21). Even after His resurrection, Christ's heart remained full of mercy and concern for sinners.[37]

To be sure, Christ rebuked His disciples. But for what? Luke 24:25 tells us: "He said unto them, O fools, and slow of heart to believe all that the prophets have spoken." Goodwin says that He gave this rep-

---

35. Goodwin, *Works,* 4:100.
36. Goodwin, *Works,* 4:98–103.
37. Goodwin, *Works,* 4:104–105.

rimand "only because they would not believe on him.... He desires nothing more than to have men believe in him; and this now when glorified." When Jesus restored Peter after his denials, He reinstated Peter by commanding him, "Feed my lambs." Christ asked Peter to feed His lambs to show his love for Christ. Goodwin observes that "His heart runs altogether upon his lambs, upon souls to be converted."[38] Christ's glorified heart still beats today for sinners.

Pledges with His Ascension

Goodwin stresses that when Jesus ascended to heaven, His last earthly act was to pronounce a blessing on His disciples (Luke 24:50–51). His first official act as the enthroned King was to pour out the Holy Spirit upon His church (Acts 2:33)—all the works of the Holy Spirit testify of Christ's present love for His church. Does a minister preach the gospel by the Holy Spirit? It is because of Christ's heart for sinners. Does the Spirit move you to pray? It is because Christ is praying for you. Does the New Testament express Christ's love for sinners? It was all written "since Christ's being in heaven, by his Spirit."[39]

Goodwin offers another pledge to sinners in Christ's glorious appearance to Paul on the road to Damascus. In 1 Timothy 1:15–16, Paul writes, "This is a faithful saying, and worthy of all acceptation, that Christ Jesus came into the world to save sinners; of whom I am chief. Howbeit for this cause I obtained mercy, that in me first Jesus Christ might shew forth all longsuffering, for a pattern to them which should hereafter believe on him to life everlasting." Goodwin comments that Paul is expressly stating that his own salvation is meant "to assure all sinners, unto the end of the world, of Christ's heart towards them."[40]

Goodwin's final pledge of Christ's compassion comes from Christ's last recorded words. When the Spirit and the bride call out for Christ to come back to earth, Revelation 22:17 gives Jesus' answer: "And let him that is athirst come. And whosoever will, let him take the water of life freely." Goodwin comments, "They cannot desire

---

38. Goodwin, *Works,* 4:106.
39. Goodwin, *Works,* 4:107–108.
40. Goodwin, *Works,* 4:108.

his coming to them, so much as he desires their coming to him...
hereby expressing how much his heart now longs after them."[41]

Christ gave us promises and pledges before and after His exaltation to help us trust that His heart is tender toward sinners. Let us
now consider the proof of this compassion.

The Proof of the Compassionate Christ

Goodwin explained that Christ is compassionate because of the
influence of the Trinity on the ministry of Christ. The doctrine of
the Trinity profoundly shaped Goodwin's theology.[42] He believed
the ancient doctrine that "the external works of the Trinity are undi-
vided"—that is, everything God does in creation, providence, and
redemption is the work of all three persons in cooperation with each
other, each acting in His own distinct manner.[43] Christ's ministry of
compassion flows from the Father, the Son, and the Holy Spirit.

Christ's Mission from the Father

Hebrews 4:14–15 describes Christ as our "high priest." Christ did
not take this office by His own initiative but was appointed to it by
His Father: "And no man taketh this honour unto himself, but he that
is called of God, as was Aaron. So also Christ glorified not himself to
be made an high priest; but he that said unto him, Thou art my Son,
to day have I begotten thee. As he saith also in another place, Thou
art a priest for ever after the order of Melchizedek" (Heb. 5:4–6).
Goodwin argues that "God therefore called him to it...and therefore
Christ calls it his 'Father's business.'"[44]

---

41. Goodwin, *Works*, 4:109.
42. Mark Jones writes, "Thomas Goodwin wrote a great deal on the Trinity,
and his work, *The Knowledge of God the Father, and His Son Jesus Christ*, represents
one of the most detailed expositions of the doctrine of the Trinity in the seventeenth
century.... His defense of the Trinity is exegetically rigorous and his emphasis
on the union and communion of the three persons among themselves, and the
practical implications this had for how Christians commune with God, figures
prominently.... The triunity of God constitutes the necessary ground for Goodwin's
theology, particularly in terms of the soteric role of the Trinity in the redemption and
restoration of fallen humanity.... The Trinity represents the necessary ontological
framework for Goodwin's soteriology" ("Why Heaven Kissed Earth," 116–17).
43. Jones, "Why Heaven Kissed Earth," 128–29.
44. Goodwin, *Works*, 5:23.

God the Father gave Christ the office of high priesthood to exhibit mercy and compassion. Goodwin says that the priesthood "requires of him all mercifulness and graciousness towards sinners that do come unto him.... As his kingly office is an office of power and dominion, and his prophetical office an office of knowledge and wisdom, so his priestly office is an office of grace and mercy." He proved this from Hebrews 5:2 and 2:18, which say that a high priest must have an inward ability to show compassion.[45] God the Father commanded God the Son to welcome and save to the end sinners who come to Him. Jesus Himself taught us this in John 6:37–40, where He says that He cannot fail to do His Father's will. Indeed, as Psalm 40:6–8 says, God wrote His law of mercy upon His Son's human heart.[46]

Everything the Father sent Christ to do, He has done for us. As Goodwin said in his treatise *Christ Set Forth*, Christ died for us; He rose for us; He ascended into heaven for us; He sits at the right hand of God for us; He intercedes for us. From beginning to end, our High Priest acts as the Father's appointed surety and representative of His elect people.[47]

So we look through Christ to see the Father's love. The ultimate object of faith is our covenant Father, for it is He who justifies (Rom. 8:33). We rest upon God through Christ because God sent Christ according to His covenant of grace.[48] In seeing the Father's heart, the believer knows the love that God has had for him before time began. All of redemption aims, as Stanley Fienberg puts it, "to reveal the fullness of God's love."[49]

Goodwin writes, "All that Christ doth for us is but the expression of that love which was taken up originally in God's own heart.... Christ adds not one drop of love to God's heart, [but] only draws it out."[50] The Son's beautiful heart is a manifestation of the Father's beautiful heart. So Goodwin invites us, "Come first to Christ, and he will take thee by the hand, and go along with thee, and lead thee to

---

45. Goodwin, *Works*, 4:127–28.
46. Goodwin, *Works*, 4:113–14.
47. Goodwin, *Works*, 4:1–91.
48. Horton, "Thomas Goodwin and the Puritan Doctrine of Assurance," 183. Cf. Goodwin, *Works*, 8:133–34.
49. Fienberg, "Thomas Goodwin, Puritan Pastor and Independent Divine," 16.
50. Goodwin, *Works*, 4:86. He cited John 3:16 and Romans 5:8.

his Father."[51] In seeing the Father's loving heart, we are assured that His obedient Son will love us forever. This is one important proof of Christ's compassion.

Christ's Divine Nature as the Son

Hebrews 4:14 says that our great High Priest is "the Son of God." On the basis of Christ's sonship, Goodwin concluded that Christ's love is not a forced love that He performs just because His Father commanded it. Christ has a "free and natural" disposition to love us because He is the natural Son of the "Father of mercies."[52] Whatever the Father wills, the Son wills, for they are one; they share one will and one power (John 5:19; 10:30). Therefore, Christ's heart in heaven as He intercedes for His people is the Father's heart.[53] The doctrine of the Trinity is so practical and comforting!

Goodwin also cites Matthew 11:28–29, which reveals Jesus as God's exalted Son. But Jesus also says in these verses, "Come unto me, all ye that labour and are heavy laden, and I will give you rest. Take my yoke upon you, and learn of me; for I am meek and lowly in heart: and ye shall find rest unto your souls." Goodwin says, "We are apt to think that he, being so holy, is therefore of a severe and sour disposition against sinners, and not able to bear them. No, says, he; 'I am meek,' gentleness is my nature and temper.... Yea, but (may we think) he being the Son of God and heir of heaven, and especially now filled with glory, and sitting at God's right hand, he may now despise the lowliness of us here below.... No, says Christ; 'I am lowly' also, willing to bestow my love and favour upon the poorest." Therefore, Goodwin said, we are to take the sweetest thoughts we ever had of a dear friend and raise them up infinitely higher in our thoughts of the sweetness of Jesus.[54]

What a friend we have in Jesus! His divine nature as the Son of God proves that He will have compassion on every sinner who comes to Him.

---

51. Goodwin, *Works*, 4:89.
52. Goodwin, *Works*, 4:115.
53. Goodwin, *Works*, 4:71, 81.
54. Goodwin, *Works*, 4:116–17.

Christ's Humanity from the Holy Spirit

Hebrews 4:14 says that our great High Priest is not only the eternal Son of God, but also "Jesus." How did the second person of the Trinity become human like us? Luke 1:35 says that the Holy Spirit worked a miracle in the womb of a virgin. Goodwin writes, "It was the Spirit who overshadowed his mother, and, in the meanwhile, knit that indissoluble knot between our nature and the second person, and that also knit his heart unto us."[55]

But Goodwin says that the Spirit did more. All the "excellencies" or graces that filled Christ's human nature were a result of the Spirit's work in Him. Goodwin's comforting and cogent argument here is that "if the same Spirit that was upon him, and in him, when he was on earth, doth but still rest upon him now he is in heaven, then those dispositions must needs still rest entirely upon him."[56]

Goodwin said that the Spirit's work in Christ is evident in nearly all the major events of Christ's life, from His incarnation to His ascension.[57] At His baptism, the Holy Spirit descended on Christ as a dove, an image of meekness and tenderness.[58] He sanctified Christ's human nature and constituted Him as the Christ.[59]

Entering His ministry thus filled with the Spirit, Jesus declared in Luke 4:18 that the Spirit of the Lord had anointed Him to preach good news to the poor. Jesus was the servant on whom the Lord had set His Spirit, as Isaiah prophesied; He would not break the bruised reed. Now that Christ is glorified, Goodwin wrote, "Christ hath the Spirit in the utmost measure that human nature is capable of."[60]

The Holy Spirit empowered Christ's human nature to be a channel of God's mercy to us. Christ's human heart has a greater capacity for kindness than the hearts of all men and angels.[61] God is infinitely merciful. Christ's humanity does not make Him more merciful, but

55. Goodwin, *Works*, 4:118. Cf. Paul Blackham, "The Pneumatology of Thomas Goodwin" (Ph.D. dissertation, University of London, 1995), 55–61.

56. Goodwin, *Works*, 4:118.

57. Goodwin, *Works*, 5:9–10. Cf. Jones, "Why Heaven Kissed Earth," 205–206. Jones points out (207) that Goodwin's emphasis here is reminiscent of Richard Sibbes's statement that "whatsoever Christ did as man he did by the Spirit" (*The Works of Richard Sibbes* [repr., Edinburgh: Banner of Truth Trust, 2004], 3:162).

58. Goodwin, *Works*, 4:118.

59. Goodwin, *Works*, 5:43.

60. Goodwin, *Works*, 4:119–21.

61. Goodwin, *Works*, 4:116.

makes Him merciful in a way suited to our needs. The incarnation does not increase God's mercy, but brings His mercy near to us.[62] Goodwin wrote, "'God is love,' as John says, and Christ is love covered over with flesh, yea, our flesh."[63] Jesus is mercy in the flesh.

> *O the deep, deep love of Jesus! Spread His praise from shore to shore;*
> *How He loveth, ever loveth, changeth never, nevermore;*
> *How He watches o'er His loved ones, died to call them all His own;*
> *How for them He intercedeth, watcheth o'er them from the throne!*[64]

The Wonder of Christ's Compassionate Heart

Goodwin concluded his masterful *The Heart of Christ in Heaven towards Sinners on Earth* with four applications to believers:

- Christ's heart of compassion affords us the strongest encouragements against sin. We know that Christ is not at rest in His heart until our sins are removed. Those sins move Him more to pity than to anger even though He hates them.

- Whatever trial, temptation, or misery we may suffer, we know that Christ also endured it and that His heart moves to relieve us in our distress.

- The thought of how much we grieve Christ's heart by sin and disobedience is the strongest incentive we have against sinning.

- In all our miseries and distresses, though every human comforter fails, we know that we have a Friend who will help, pity, and succor us: Christ in heaven.[65]

Dear believers, how full of compassion Christ is for us as He sits upon His throne of glory. Surely, reflecting on this truth should help us rejoice in Christ and set our hearts on things above, where Christ is seated at the right hand of God.[66] Goodwin writes, "What is it to have Christ thus dwell in the heart by faith?... It is to have Jesus Christ continually in one's eye, an habitual sight of him."[67] As people live and walk in the light of the sun, we must learn to live and walk in the light

---

62. Goodwin, *Works*, 4:135–36, 139.
63. Goodwin, *Works*, 4:116.
64. Francis, "O the Deep, Deep Love of Jesus," stanza 2.
65. Goodwin, *Works*, 4:149–50. Cf. Cook, "Goodwin—Mystic?," 55–56.
66. Cf. Paul Ling-Ji Chang, "Thomas Goodwin on the Christian Life" (Ph.D. dissertation, Westminster Theological Seminary, 2001).
67. Goodwin, *Works*, 2:411.

of God's Son. May God focus Christ's glory upon us so that our hearts ignite and burn for Him until our dying day.

Goodwin experienced Christ's beautiful heart to the end of his life. His son wrote that on his deathbed, Goodwin said, "I could not have imagined I should ever have had such a measure of faith in this hour.... Christ cannot love me better than he doth; I think I cannot love Christ better than I do."[68] What a way to die—and then to embrace and be united to Christ forever in glory![69]

In his book *Heaven Help Us*, Steve Lawson tells of a young aristocrat, William Montague, who was stricken with blindness at the age of ten. In graduate school, he met the beautiful daughter of a British admiral. The courtship flamed into romance, leading to engagement. Shortly before the wedding, William agreed to submit to a new eye surgery. With no assurance that it would restore sight, the doctors operated. William wanted his first sight to be his bride on their wedding day. So, hoping against hope, he asked that the bandages be removed from his eyes just as the bride came up the aisle. As she approached, William's father began removing the gauze from his son's eyes. When the last bandage was unwrapped, William's eyes opened, light flooded in, and he saw his bride's radiant face. Tears flowed from his eyes as he looked into her beautiful face and whispered, "You are more beautiful than I ever imagined."[70]

Something like that will happen to us when glorification takes the veil from our eyes and we see Jesus no longer in part but in full as our Savior, Lover, Interceder, and Friend. We will behold His great love and beautiful heart. We will experience what Rutherford wrote of:

> The king there in His beauty,
> Without a veil is seen:
> It were a well-spent journey,
> Though seven deaths lay between:
> The Lamb with His fair army,
> Doth on Mount Zion stand,

---

68. Goodwin, *Works*, 2:lxxv.

69. Goodwin, *Works*, 2:411–12. For Goodwin's rather unique millennial views for a Puritan, see A. R. Dallison, "The Latter-Day Glory in the Thought of Thomas Goodwin," *Evangelical Quarterly* 58 (1986): 53–68.

70. Steven J. Lawson, *Heaven Help Us!: Truths about Eternity That Will Help You Live Today* (Colorado Springs: NavPress, 1995), 168–69.

And glory, glory dwelleth
In Emmanuel's land.

O Christ, He is the fountain,
The deep, sweet well of love!
The streams on earth I've tasted
More deep I'll drink above:
There to an ocean fullness
His mercy doth expand,
And glory, glory dwelleth
In Emmanuel's land.

The bride eyes not her garment,
But her dear Bridegroom's face;
I will not gaze at glory
But on my King of grace.
Not at the crown He giveth
But on His pierced hand;
The Lamb is all the glory
Of Emmanuel's land.[71]

Does your heart warm at the thought of being with Christ forever and increasingly knowing His beautiful heart? A true child of God can identify with this. If you cannot, you are not a child of God. You are still unconverted and dead to God. You will not enter heaven unless God's Spirit teaches you to hate sin, to repent of it, to forsake it, and to turn to Christ, believing in Him alone for salvation and loving Him above all.

Rejoice, dear believer! In glory, we will know the Bridegroom's beautiful heart, even as He knows ours, and both of our hearts will be perfect. Oh, to be sinless in the presence of our sinless Savior and Bridegroom! Forever we will experience Christ's high priestly heart—the heart of the Lamb of God, the Prince of Peace and Love. In glory we will be ravished with His love, even as He rejoices over us with singing (Zeph. 3:17).

Psalm 45:11 says of the anticipated marriage between Christ and His bride, "So shall the king greatly desire thy beauty." Dear believer, the King of kings will make us His queen of heaven, and

---

71. A. R. Cousin, "The Sands of Time Are Sinking," based on Samuel Rutherford's *Letters*. http://www.igracemusic.com/hymnbook/hymns/t05.html (accessed August 10, 2010).

we will be beautiful in His sight. The angels will be our servants, and the King will take us by hand into His garden of paradise and show us His estate.

> To that love, we will respond with singing and praise:
> O the deep, deep love of Jesus! Love of ev'ry love the best;
> 'Tis an ocean vast of blessing, 'tis a haven sweet of rest.
> O the deep, deep love of Jesus! 'Tis a heav'n of heav'ns to me;
> And it lifts me up to glory, for it lifts me up to Thee.[72]

---

72. Francis, "O the Deep, Deep Love of Jesus," stanza 3.

CHAPTER 11

"The True Knowledge of Jesus Christ and Him Crucified": Christology in Marrow Theology

William VanDoodewaard

The Marrow of Modern Divinity was first published in London, England, in two parts in 1645 and 1648. Its author, known in his writings only as E. F., was Edward Fisher (c. 1590–1650).[1] Fisher was not the sort of man that you might think would write a significant work of theology. By vocation he was a barber, which then included being a surgeon, and he belonged to the guild of barber-surgeons in London. We know that Fisher was also a bookseller: legal records indicate that his sale of Puritan books attracted Archbishop William Laud's attention as persecution of Puritans began in the 1620s. As a bookseller and lay-theologian, Fisher had contact with a wide range of Puritans. He wrote that he was converted under the ministry of Thomas Hooker, who was criticized for a legalistic preparationism in his preaching. Fisher also befriended believers towards the other end of the Puritan spectrum: John Eaton, a strong critic of real or perceived legalism, tended to antinomianism. Authoring a number of works published during the 1640s when restrictions on Puritan publications eased, Fisher's writings show a concern over tendencies to either legalism or lawlessness within the church of his day and a passionate desire to promote a biblical understanding of both the gospel and the Christian life.

---

1. For an expanded discussion of the author and context of *The Marrow of Modern Divinity*, see William VanDoodewaard, "'To Walk According to the Gospel': The Origin and History of *The Marrow of Modern Divinity*" in *Puritan Reformed Journal* 1 (July 2009) 2:96–114, and "A Journey into the Past: The Story of *The Marrow of Modern Divinity*" in Edward Fisher, *The Marrow of Modern Divinity* (Fearn, Rosshire: Christian Focus Publications, 2009), 21–32.

Among his works, *The Marrow of Modern Divinity* was Fisher's most significant. Quickly rising in popularity, the work was frequently republished (in both English and Welsh) during the decades after its initial release. What caught the attention of so many readers? Likely it was the profoundly relevant conversation Fisher created between his four characters: Evangelista, an evangelical pastor; Neophytus, a young believer; Nomista, a legalist friend of Neophytus; and Antinomista, an antinomian friend of Neophytus. In Fisher's dialogue, Evangelista shepherds both the group and the reader through animated discussions to a right understanding of the relationship of the law and the gospel—"a true knowledge of Jesus Christ and Him Crucified."[2] Through Evangelista, Fisher also instructs believers in a holy life of thankfulness to God for salvation. *The Marrow* gained commendation from a number of Puritan ministers: Joseph Caryl, Jeremiah Burroughs, and William Strong. Though many of the early commenders were Independents or Congregationalists, Fisher was a convicted Presbyterian by the mid 1640s, connected with significant Presbyterian figures. Despite the publication's early popularity, in the years following Fisher's death, *The Marrow of Modern Divinity* seemed to fade to obscurity. It would not have the current stature it does if, in God's providence, a young Presbyterian minister had not discovered it in Scotland.

With the 1688 accession of Protestant William I and Mary to the English throne, a significant change took place on the British religious scene. Because of the new royals, the Presbyterian Church of Scotland suddenly gained the opportunity to reestablish as a freely operating, confessional Reformed church. While enjoying the blessings of renewed freedom, many in the Church of Scotland in the late seventeenth and early eighteenth century developed a tendency of adding conditions to the gospel. Hyper-Calvinism and legalism began to dominate the church in a variety of forms. Some ministers preached a legal preparation—offering Christ only to those who they deemed had shown enough conviction of sin or pursuit of holiness as a mark of potential election. Men's additions dimmed and encumbered the gospel offer of the all-sufficient Christ.

Though legalism was influential in the Church of Scotland at this point, there were also those who loved the gospel of Jesus

---

2. E[dward] F[isher], *The Marrow of Modern Divinity* (London: Printed by R.W. for G. Calvert, 1645), 14.

Christ, were evangelical at heart, and were deeply concerned by these developments. Increasing friction over the differences came to a flashpoint when the evangelically minded Auchterarder Presbytery decided to add a vow to the Church of Scotland's ordination requirements, unilaterally adding "the Auchterarder Creed" to their ordination requirements: "I believe it is not sound and orthodox to teach that we must forsake sin in order to our coming to Christ, and instating us in Covenant to God."[3] The goal was to keep the Presbytery from ordaining legalistic preachers. The Auchterarder men sought to emphasize that while coming to Christ included a forsaking of sin, forsaking sin without coming to Christ was impossible. Problems arose when one candidate appealed the newly required vow to the Church of Scotland General Assembly of 1717, which then overturned the Auchterarder Presbytery's "creed." Influenced by legalist, hyper-Calvinist theology, the Assembly declared the statement to be "unsound and detestable."[4] The decision created deep dismay among the men troubled by the denomination's increasingly legalistic tendencies.

Thomas Boston, one of the ministers sympathetic to the Presbytery's concerns at the 1717 Synod, had struggled with aspects of hyper-Calvinism and assurance of his salvation in Christ early on in his ministry. Visiting a parishioner and veteran of the English Civil War, he found and borrowed a copy of *The Marrow of Modern Divinity*. Reading it, Boston gained scriptural clarity on the doctrines of grace, finding liberation from his own struggles through Fisher's simple, clear application of the Word. The person and work of Jesus Christ in fulfilling all the requirements of the law, as well as the role of the law both to convict of sin and as a rule of thankful holiness, were now clear to him. Sitting in the 1717 Assembly meeting, Boston mentioned *The Marrow* to a friend, Thomas Drummond, as an antidote to "the public actings of this church, against the doctrine of grace."[5] Drummond searched for and found a copy in an Edinburgh

---

3. *Register of the Acts and Proceedings of the General Assembly of the Church of Scotland, Held and Begun in the Year 1717...in Register of the General Assembly annes 1712, 1713, 1714, 1715, and 1717* (MSS 232, Special Libraries and Archives, King's College, Aberdeen), 839–40.

4. *Register of the Acts and Proceedings of the General Assembly of the Church of Scotland...1717*, 840.

5. Thomas Boston, *Memoirs of Mr. Thomas Boston...in The Complete Works of the*

bookshop; he read it and then passed it on to another Church of Scotland pastor, who in turn passed it along to fellow pastor James Hog.

James Hog (1658–1734) was a Luther-like firebrand, bold and blunt. Realizing that *The Marrow* addressed the Church of Scotland's situation, he republished part 1 with a daring foreword, declaring that the book addressed "the errors and darkening of the gospel in our day in the Church of Scotland by those who profess to be preachers of the gospel but are not."[6] By 1719, Church of Scotland ministers upset with Hog brought formal complaints regarding antinomianism in *The Marrow* to the General Assembly.[7] A number of ministers, including Thomas Boston, James Hog, Ebenezer Erskine (1680–1754), Ralph Erskine (1685–1752), and Robert Riccaltoun (1691–1769), banded together in defense of the book and the doctrine it promoted. They became known as the Marrow men. The Marrow controversy continued to 1722 in the Church of Scotland with the Assembly condemning the book but not requiring repentance from the Marrow men for fear of deepening denominational division. In 1726, Thomas Boston republished *The Marrow* with extensive footnotes, defending and explaining the text and creating a valuable work of theology.[8]

The Doctrine of Christ in *The Marrow of Modern Divinity* and Marrow Theology

What did Edward Fisher in *The Marrow of Modern Divinity* and the Scottish Marrow men believe and teach on the doctrine of Christ? How did they understand His atoning work and its implications for their ministries? How did they answer the questions What has Jesus done? and How does Jesus' work reflect who Jesus is?

Late Reverend Thomas Boston, ed. Samuel M'Millan (London: William Tegg and Co., 1854), 7:317.

6. James Hog, preface to *The Marrow of Modern Divinity* by Edward Fisher (Edinburgh: John Mosman and William Brown, 1718), 1.

7. *Register of the Acts and Proceedings of the General Assembly of the Church of Scotland…1719*, 177–342.

8. Fisher, *The Marrow of Modern Divinity…with notes*, in *The Complete Works of the Late Reverend Thomas Boston*, ed. Samuel M'Millan (London: William Tegg and Co., 1854), 7:143–489. All subsequent citations of Fisher's *The Marrow* are from the recent reprint of *The Marrow of Modern Divinity*, by Edward Fisher (Fearn, Rosshire: Christian Focus Publications, 2009).

When reading *The Marrow of Modern Divinity* and works by Marrow men, it is quickly evident that they frame the nature of Christ's sacrificial work in terms of covenant, or federal, theology. Understanding Scripture not only in its particulars but also in its grand, overarching themes, these men wrote of the covenant of works made with and broken by Adam as enacting the necessity of the atonement for salvation. Jesus Christ, as the second Adam, is the only one who could and did fulfill the broken covenant of works, establishing a new covenant—the covenant of grace, promised in Eden the day man fell into his state of sin and misery. These grand themes of covenant theology framed the thinking of these men as they preached and wrote about what Jesus has done. Edward Fisher, describing the necessity of Christ's atoning work, said that because man broke the covenant of works, "he was now become liable for the payment of a double debt, viz. the debt of satisfaction for his sin committed in time past, and the debt of perfect and perpetual obedience for the time to come; and he was utterly unable to pay for either of them.... His sin... was committed against an infinite and eternal God, and therefore merited an infinite and eternal satisfaction."[9] Hog proclaimed that "the obligation both to the obedience and penal sanction remains inviolable."[10] Under the reality of the covenant of works violated by man but still in force towards him, man remains in a state of "utter inability to recover himself," Boston explained.[11] Ebenezer Erskine wrote, "Man who has broken the law, is utterly incapable to repair its honor, or to satisfy justice."[12]

This theme of man's desperate condition runs through Fisher's *The Marrow of Modern Divinity* and the Scottish Marrow theologians. Man cannot repay the double debt. The covenant of works is still in force—but unattainable because man violated it and willfully placed himself under the dominion of sin. Man justly deserves eternity in

---

9. Fisher, *The Marrow*, 58–59.

10. James Hog, *A Vindication of the Doctrine of Grace from the Charge of Antinomianism: Contained in a Letter to a Minister of the Gospel* (Edinburgh: Robert Brown, 1718), 8–12.

11. Thomas Boston, *Man's Fourfold State*, in *The Complete Works of the Late Reverend Thomas Boston*, ed. Samuel M'Millan (London: William Tegg and Co., 1854), 8:27, 97, 124.

12. Ebenezer Erskine, "The Assurance of Faith, Opened and Applied. Being the Substance of Several Sermons on Heb. x. 22," in *The Whole Works of Ebenezer Erskine* (Glasgow: Free Presbyterian Publications, 2004), 1:207.

hell, forever satisfying the justice of God, who is infinite and perfect in holiness. This is the indispensable context of the doctrine of Christ in Marrow theology. Marrow theologians describe how God gloriously and beautifully meets this profound need by the covenant of grace established in Jesus Christ. Christ and the gospel stand at the center of their covenant theology. Boston declares, "Our Lord Jesus Christ became surety for the elect in the second covenant…[putting] himself in the room [place] of the principle debtors."[13] The Marrow men taught Scripture's strong, covenant emphasis on Jesus' fulfillment of every aspect of the covenant of works in the place of His elect people. Through His incarnate suffering and penal, substitutionary atonement on the cross, He fully paid the penalty for the violation of the covenant of works, the law of God, by bearing the full weight of the just wrath of God against the sin of His people. Fisher proclaims, "[Christ] yield[ed] in man's flesh the price of the satisfaction of the just judgment of God, and, in the same flesh…suffer[ed] the punishment that man had deserved…and thus was justice satisfied."[14] "[Who] can fully describe the wrath of an angry God?" asked Boston. "Consider how God dealt with his own Son, whom he spared not. The wrath of God seized on his soul and body both, and brought him into the dust of death. That his sufferings were not eternal, flowed from the quality of the Sufferer, who was infinite; and therefore able to bear, at once, the whole load of wrath; and upon that account his sufferings were of infinite value."[15] Ralph Erskine agreed: "[Christ] met with…that which sin deserves, viz. death and the curse; the hiding of his Father's face…the wrath of God; the awakened sword of the justice of God smiting him…[the] eternal Son bearing the stroke of vengeance in the room of elect sinners."[16]

---

13. Boston, "Notes on *The Marrow of Modern Divinity*," 185. Boston presents further description of the atoning work of Christ in terms of federal theology in his works *The Covenant of Grace* and *Covenant of Works*, both published after the days of the Marrow controversy.

14. Fisher, *The Marrow*, 65.

15. Boston, *Man's Fourfold State*, 111.

16. Ralph Erskine, "The Sword of Justice Awakened against God's Fellow," in *The Sermons and Other Practical Works of Ralph Erskine* (Aberdeen: George and Robert King, 1862), 1:28–56; "The Rent Vail of the Temple…," in *The Sermons and Other Practical Works of Ralph Erskine* (Aberdeen: George and Robert King, 1862), 1:75–109; reprint, vols. 1–6 (Edmonton: Still Waters Revival Books, n.d.).

Christ paying the debt of penalty overflows from Marrow writings. While this is essential and common to Reformed theology, the Marrow theologians were distinct in their strong stress on Jesus Christ's positive fulfillment of all righteousness. Both Christ's passive obedience and His active obedience are part of His atoning work. The dual aspect of Jesus Christ's atoning work is essential, because not only did Adam sin and deserve judgment for it, but in sin he also failed to do what was righteous. Further, in a post-lapse world and fallen state, man remains incapable of performing the required righteousness and obedience. Even in a state of grace man will not live in full righteousness and obedience. This is a crucial part of the "Marrow" understanding of what Jesus has done: Christ fulfilled the demands of obedience under the covenant of works, for His people. He bore the penalty for sin, making His sacrifice the perfect and complete sacrifice, and also fulfilled all righteousness, securing the imputation of His righteousness and obedience to His people through the covenant of grace. Edward Fisher elaborates: "God did, as it were, say to Christ, what they owe me I require all at thy hands. Then said Christ, 'Lo, I come to do thy will! In the volume of the book it is written of me, I delight to do thy will, O my God! Yea, thy law is in my heart' (Ps. 40:7–8). Thus Christ assented, and from everlasting struck hands with God, to put upon him man's person, and to take upon him his name, and to enter in his stead in obeying his Father, and to do all for man that he should require."[17] Thomas Boston said that "Christ made satisfaction of God's justice, by payment of the double debt...namely the debt of punishment, and the debt of perfect obedience.... Man being as unable to sanctify himself, as to satisfy justice...the Savior behooved, not only to obey and suffer in his stead, but also to have a fullness of the Spirit of holiness in him communicated to the sinner."[18] Jesus Christ, for the believer, "is made unto us holiness, righteousness and justification: he hath clothed us in all his merits and taken to himself all our sin—so that, if any should be now condemned for that same, it must needs be Jesus Christ, who hath taken them upon him."[19] "Christ did everything that the law required," Ebenezer Erskine writes, "he

---

17. Fisher, *The Marrow*, 64–65.
18. Boston, "Notes on *The Marrow*...," 184.
19. Boston, "Notes on *The Marrow*...," 169.

fulfilled all righteousness…in his own person, by an active and passive obedience, and in all his members by imputation."[20]

The Marrow theologians proclaimed a Jesus Christ who fulfills everything that the covenant of works requires and establishes the new covenant of grace so that the Christian, justified by faith and united to Christ his federal head, is both forgiven and accepted as righteous in God's sight. So when answering the question What has Jesus done? as described by the Marrow theologians from their study of Scripture, we see that Jesus was and is the perfect, all-sufficient sacrifice and our perfect, all-sufficient obedience.

It is important to note that in terms of the work of Jesus Christ, both Fisher and Boston, along with the other Marrow theologians, were very clear in the delineation between the scriptural connection of covenant and election. They firmly believed Scripture's teaching that atonement is limited in extent and particular in application. Jesus Christ, through His perfect, all-sufficient work of atonement, establishes the covenant of grace only with the elect. Theologian Louis Berkhof reflects:

> The Marrow men of Scotland were perfectly orthodox in maintaining that Christ died for the purpose of saving only the elect, though some of them used expressions which also pointed to a more general reference of the atonement. They said that Christ did not die for all men, but that He is dead, that is, available, for all. God's giving love, which is universal, led Him to make a deed of gift and grant to all men; and this is the foundation for the universal offer of salvation. His electing love, however, which is special, results in the salvation of the elect only.[21]

Having explored the Marrow answer to the question of what Jesus has done, we come to examine the Marrow answer to the second question: How does the atoning work of Christ reflect who Jesus is? Surveying the writings of the Marrow theologians, we see them

---

20. Ebenezer Erksine, "The Broken Law Magnified and Made Honourable," in *The Whole Works of Ebenezer Erskine* (Glasgow: Free Presbyterian Publications, 2004), 3:174. Erskine goes on in this sermon to warn against "the error of those who deny Christ's active obedience to the law to be any part of our justifying righteousness; alleging, that it is only his passive obedience, or his suffering the penalty, that is imputed to us for justification." Erskine, "The Broken Law Magnified…," 175. This was a clear rebuttal to the theological view of the leading opponents of Marrow theology.

21. Louis Berkhof, *Systematic Theology* (Grand Rapids: Eerdmans, 1999), 394.

articulate that the Lord Jesus Christ, the mediator of the new covenant, the covenant of grace, is fully God, the only begotten Son of God, fully man, God incarnate, the second Adam. As such, He is the perfect, all-sufficient Savior and Redeemer; He is the perfect and eternal High Priest. Christ's three offices are prominent in Edward Fisher's work and the Marrow theologians' sermons. As Priest, Christ offers Himself as the sacrifice and intercedes for His people. As Prophet, He teaches and proclaims the offer of Himself and what He has done in substitutionary atonement. As King, Christ extends the free offer of complete salvation, fully sufficient for any, to all mankind. This is what the Marrow men called "the deed of gift and grant": the idea that the gospel offer was like a royal letter emblazoned with the seal of the king freely offering a sure promise. The promise is to be proclaimed throughout Christ's dominion, declaring that anyone who comes to Christ will receive full, free, and complete pardon—everything necessary for full salvation. The Marrow men saw that throughout the Scriptures King Jesus calls His ministers, ambassadors, and angels to preach the gospel, this royal deed of gift and grant, to every man. By the work of His Spirit, Christ's word does not return void, but effectively brings His elect to saving faith and sincere repentance, delivering them from sin and its punishment and subduing all His and their enemies.

What was the impact of the doctrine of Christ in Marrow theology? What was the impact of their understanding of what Jesus has done and who He is? The writings and sermons of Edward Fisher and the Marrow men beautifully, powerfully, and clearly present the gospel offer as universal, free, and full. Time and again, they root the gospel offer in the person and work of Jesus Christ and His promises. In *The Marrow of Modern Divinity*, Fisher preaches through his character Evangelista, proclaiming the gospel to his generation in London:

> I beseech you consider, that God the Father, as he is in his Son Jesus Christ, moved with nothing but his free love to mankind lost, hath made a deed of gift and grant unto them all, that whosoever of them all shall believe in this his Son, shall not perish, but have eternal life. And hence it was, that Jesus Christ himself said unto his disciples, 'Go and preach the gospel to every creature under heaven: that is Go and tell every man without exception, that here is good news for him; Christ is dead for

him; and if he will take him, and accept of his righteousness, he shall have him.[22]

Thomas Boston's notes on this section of *The Marrow* make clear his understanding that when Fisher declares that Christ is dead for every man, He is not referring to or advocating universal atonement, but rather sending the gospel out as universally as Christ did. Fisher passionately and directly applies the doctrine of Christ's complete work through many of the conversations in *The Marrow*:

> Nomista: "But sir, suppose he hath not as yet truly repented for his many and great sins, hath he any warrant to come unto Christ, by believing, till he has done so?" Evangelista: "I tell you truly, that whatsoever a man is, or whatsoever he hath done or not done, he hath warrant enough to come to Christ by believing.... Christ makes a general proclamation... 'Ho every one that thirsteth, come ye to the waters, come buy and eat; yea, come buy wine and milk without money, and without price.' This you see is the condition 'buy wine and milk without money' that is without any sufficiency of your own."[23]

Fisher leaves those who claim they cannot come to Christ without excuse: they can confess their coldness to Christ; tell their spiritual dullness to Him; go to Him with their problems, their impossibilities, and everything they lack, and be filled. Christ is the all-sufficient Savior.

In their sermons and writings, the Scottish Marrow men offer Christ perhaps even more passionately and directly than Fisher does. Like Fisher, they hold out the gospel as universal, free, and full. They do not hesitate to preach that He is freely offered to all without condition and fully sufficient for any condition. In his sermon *The Everlasting Espousals*, Thomas Boston compares the offer of the gospel to a marriage contract, "drawn up already and signed by the Bridegroom, bearing his consent to match with the captive daughter of Zion."[24] Boston goes on to exhort his hearers:

22. Fisher, *The Marrow*, 144.
23. Fisher, *The Marrow*, 151.
24. Thomas Boston, *The Everlasting Espousals* in *The Complete Works of the Late Reverend Thomas Boston*, ed. Samuel M'Millan (London: William Tegg and Co., 1854), 7:498.

The Royal Bridegroom has signed this, and it is incumbent upon you to sign it likewise, consenting to take Christ as he is offered to you in the gospel…. It is indorsed and directed to you, every one of you: therefore you have a sufficient warrant to sign it for yourselves. What is your name?…thirsty sinners? Then read your name, and see how it is directed to you, Isaiah 55:1, "Ho everyone that thirsts, come…. Will you answer to the name willing sinner? Then it is directed to you, Rev. 22:17, "Whosoever will, let him take of the water of life freely." Are you called heavy laden sinner? Arise then, the Master calls you, Matth. 11:28, "Come to me, all ye that labor and are heavy laden and I will give you rest." Is your name whorish backslider? "You have played the harlot with many lovers, yet return again unto me says the Lord," Jer. 3:1. Are you a lost sinner? The son of man is come to seek and to save that which was lost, Luke 19:10. Are you the chief of sinners? Even to you the word of this salvation is sent, Christ Jesus came into the world to save sinners, of whom I am chief, 1 Tim. 1:15. But whatsoever artifice ye may use to disown these, or any of these to be your name; surely you are men, sons of men; you cannot deny that to be your name: therefore it is directed to you, and every one of you: "unto you O men I call, my voice is to the sons of men" Prov. 8:4…. O the riches and the freedom of grace!… This offer is made unto all of you without exception, Christ is willing to be yours.[25]

A similar gospel passion with the same freeness and sufficiency in Christ comes from a sermon by Ralph Erskine, who proclaims:

O happy are believers! All things are yours; for ye are Christ's and Christ is God's: you have wisdom, righteousness, sanctification, and redemption, and all things in Christ; it is easy with Christ to supply all your needs, and to give you all sufficiency in all things…. There is an overflowing ocean of all good in Christ for sinners…. Hence we see the duty of all poor and needy sinners, and where they ought to go for supply, and for a share in all things they need: and what a broad foundation for faith is here. God in Christ is the fountain of living waters. God the Father hath all things; but how shall we come at them? Why says Christ, come to me; for they are all mine; mine to give out, mine to distribute.[26]

---

25. Boston, *The Everlasting Espousals*, 499.
26. Ralph Erskine, "Christ's Treasures Opened by Himself," in *The Sermons and*

James Fisher, Ebenezer Erskine's son-in-law, preached a communion sermon in the summer of 1745 that called the congregation to "come to [Christ] with all your sins, that they may be pardoned, because he hath paid the ransom; with all your wants, that they may be supplied.... Come to him with your doubts, that they may be solved.... Come to him for all that you need."[27] Transformed and gripped by new personal understanding of the gospel of Jesus Christ, the Scottish Marrow theologians stood as faithful preachers and ministers of their all-sufficient Savior.[28]

Conclusion

The impact of *The Marrow* understanding of Jesus Christ as the second Adam, the one who fulfilled all righteousness and bore the complete penalty, establishing the covenant of grace and fulfilling the covenant of works, is written across their sermons and through their correspondence. Again and again, they point us to Jesus Christ. Many of them had, at points in their lives and ministries, wrestled with a right understanding of the gospel, how to live in faith, how to preach, and how to minister. They found the answer in not merely reading the works of previous theologians, but ultimately in turning to the living Word—in knowing Christ, His rich grace, and His precious promises more fully. As they grew in knowing Christ and

---

Other Practical Works of Ralph Erskine (Aberdeen: George and Robert King, 1862), 6:213.

27. James Fisher, *Christ the Sole and Wonderful Doer in the Work of Man's Redemption. An Action Sermon Preached Immediately before Dispensing the Sacrament of the Lord's Supper, in the Associate Congregation of Glasgow, June 23d. 1745* (Glasgow: James Oliphant, 1755), 22. Several unpublished sermons of James Fisher exist in manuscript form; they indicate a continuity of the same understanding of the atonement in his preaching. See MS 3245 *Handwritten Volume of Sermons by James Fisher, Ralph Erskine, Ebenezer Erskine, Boston, Swanston, All at Sacramental Occasions* (Special Libraries and Archives, King's College, Aberdeen), which includes the following sermons: *A Sermon Preached at Dunfermline Sacrament July 10 by Mr. James Fisher Minister of the Gospel at Glasgow on a Sabbath Day. On Song 6:16—Yea He Is Altogether Lovely*, 1–14; *A Sermon at the Opening of the Associate Synod, at Dunfermline Septr. 1st 1747 on Isaiah xxi, 11, 12.—Watchman What of the Night?*, 1–34; *A Sermon Preached at the Sacrament of Dunfermline on Monday July 17th 1749 on Ephes. 1:14—That Holy Spirit of Promise, Which Is the Earnest of Our Inheritance*, 35–48.

28. Cf. William VanDoodewaard, "The Marrow Controversy and Seceder Tradition: Marrow Theology in the Associate Presbytery and Associate Synod Churches of Scotland (1718–1799)" (Ph.D. dissertation, University of Aberdeen, 2009).

His complete, perfect work, as well as increased understanding of what they as covenant breakers deserved, these men were filled with an overflowing delight in Christ and His self-revelation to them. It became their passion to freely proclaim the gospel to others, without setting conditions or hurdles or expectations that would add law to the gospel. This is the value of their example: they loved and proclaimed Jesus Christ universally, fully, and freely, as He is and as He called them to. This passion filled their hearts because they understood it; the Lord Jesus Christ had brought them from darkness to light, from wrath to love, from bondage to freedom and liberty. They, with their friend William Wilson, were impelled to proclaim,

> O sirs, the market of grace is a rare market, the wares that are therein proclaimed are all given freely. Ho, everyone that thirsteth, come ye to the waters; and he that hath no money let him come, and buy wine and milk without money and without price! Whosoever will, let him take the waters of life freely. O come and take freely! O come and enjoy! O come and share of the unsearchable riches of Christ Jesus, the worthy Lamb![29]

---

29. William Wilson, *The Lamb's Retinue Attending Him whithersoever He Goeth. Being the Substance of Two Sermons, Preached... At the Celebration of the Sacrament of the Lord's Supper at Orwell, August 6. 1738* (Edinburgh: David Duncan, 1747), 71–72.

CHAPTER 12

Christology:
Calvin, Kuyper, and Politics

Ray Pennings

It is a matter of historical record that those who take Reformed theology seriously have almost always connected God's sovereignty with the nation's political life as a matter of confession and practice. Romans 13:1–7 establishes that civil rulers, including ungodly ones, are "ministers of God," bearing the power of the sword to punish wrongdoers and are owed respect and obedience. Civil leaders possess a delegated authority for which they will give account to God. One day, every knee, including presidents' and prime ministers', will bow and every tongue confess that Jesus Christ is Lord (Phil. 2:8–11). Political life takes place within the context of God's providential reign and His unfolding of history. It is God who directs randomly shot arrows to the chink of the king's armor, bringing an evil regime like Ahab's to an end (1 Kings 22:34–35). The truth that Isaiah confessed—"The man that executeth my counsel from a far country; yea I have spoken it, I will also bring it to pass" (Isa. 46:11)—was not only true in Israel's day, but also remains true in our times.

In cataloging the biblical data that is crucial for understanding the church-state relationship, the difference between Old Testament Israel, where church and nation overlapped, and the New Testament era, where the church is universal, is obvious. Joseph's service in Egypt and Daniel's service in both the Babylonian and Persian governments seems a more relevant Old Testament example for our times. Jeremiah's injunction to "seek the peace of the city... and pray to the Lord for it; for in the peace thereof ye shall have peace" (Jer. 29:7) is appropriate as we sojourn in a modern Babylon. In all things, including political matters, we are to pray, work, and be good stewards of the opportunities that God provides—and the political opportunities afforded early twenty-first-century North Americans are significant. Thus, understanding that there is a significant connection between biblical discipleship and participating in contemporary political life should not be difficult among those who call themselves Reformed.

Establishing a connection and agreeing on how these principles should be applied are, however, two very different projects. The approaches that Calvinist, Anabaptist, Lutheran, and Roman Catholic political theorists take are clearly distinguishable. However, even if we consider North American, Calvinist approaches over the past century, very different streams of thinking emerge. The late nineteenth-century Dutch Prime Minister Abraham Kuyper's influence is widely acknowledged but controversial. While the debates surrounding the Doleantie of 1886 and the Church Union of 1892 were more theological and ecclesiastical in nature, they were not without political consequences. In 1932, Klaas Schilder wrote a book titled *Christ and Culture*,[1] arguing that Kuyper's emphasis on common grace moved away from Reformed orthodoxy and promoted a disproportionate emphasis on creation at the expense of redemption. A few decades ago, a movement known as Reconstructionism, advocated by authors such as R. J. Rushdoony and Gary North, provided a very different approach as to how Christians should apply Calvinist and Reformed thinking to our present context. While the influence of those advocating Reconstructionist interpretations seems to be on the decline, in recent years a new interpretation of Calvin has come in the Two Kingdoms perspective, advanced by some faculty at Westminster Seminary (California). David VanDrunen's recent book, *Natural Law and the Two Kingdoms: A Study in Development of Reformed Social Thought*,[2] is an extensive, scholarly work arguing that we need to rediscover the "forgotten story of the place of natural law and the two kingdoms in the Reformed tradition."[3] Dealing with this multifaceted discussion and its implications is beyond the scope of this chapter, but everyone would acknowledge that the questions it

---

1. Klaas Schilder, *Christ and Culture*, trans. G. van Rongen and W. Helder (Winnipeg: Premier, 1977). http://reformed.org/webfiles/cc/christ_and_culture.pdf.
2. David VanDrunen, *Natural Law and the Two Kingdoms: A Study in Development of Reformed Social Thought* (Grand Rapids: Eerdmans, 2010).
3. VanDrunen, *Natural Law and the Two Kingdoms*, 3.

raises are significant, challenging our thinking at both theological and political theory levels.

This discussion in the Reformed community occurs in the context of another involved discussion in the broader evangelical community. Sixty years ago, Richard Niebuhr developed five categories of cultural engagement in *Christ and Culture*,[4] which have generally been referenced as the working taxonomy for these conversations.[5] In recent times, our society's increasing secularization and pluralism have led many to question Niebuhr's assumptions. In 2006, Craig Carter, approaching the subject from a perspective that would have been traditionally aligned with Anabaptism, proposed a new paradigm in his *Rethinking Christ and Culture: A Post-Christendom Perspective*.[6] In *Christ and Culture Revisited*, Donald Carson provides an extended critique of both Niebuhr and Carter, arguing that Niebuhr does not adequately integrate various aspects of biblical theology into his categories and dismissing Carter's framework as "sadly reductionistic."[7]

While acknowledging the significance of these discussions, my own positions do not neatly fit within any established category. I recognize that there are questions for which I do not have ready answers. I come to the table as a practitioner, not a theoretician. Although theory is necessary and important, faithful political service must proceed, not always waiting until theorists work out satisfactory, comprehensive answers to the questions of the day. Hence, what follows in this chapter is not a perfected road map but a field report from the front lines. I have organized my reflections around four ruts that seem to trip up many who try to navigate this terrain, regardless of which map they use.

Faithful Politics Requires Discerning the Spirits of the Age

Sometimes we fail to adequately think about the contextualized nature of Christian political obedience. Our calling and the imperatives demanding our attention are different in early twenty-first-century

---

4. H. Richard Niebuhr, *Christ and Culture* (New York: Harper Collins, 2001) .

5. Donald Carson, *Christ and Culture Revisited* (Grand Rapids: Eerdmans, 2008), 29–30.

6. Craig Carter, *Rethinking Christ and Culture: A Post-Christendom Perspective* (Grand Rapids: Brazos Press, 2006).

7. Carson, *Christ and Culture Revisited*, 222.

North America than they were in twentieth-century Netherlands or sixteenth-century Scotland. That statement might sound like relativism, as though God's law is not permanent and as though we are seeking to fit into the spirit of our age. Often it seems that when Christians reflect on political issues, they speak as if the Scriptures provide us with insights and a formula providing easy answers to today's issues. Every challenge faced is a consequence of disobedience, and "if our leaders would only listen to the Bible, all would be well." Some Christians propose the imperatives of Christian political obedience in formulaic terms; they cite biblical texts along with a nostalgic recollection of particular historic expressions of Christian politics as keys to solving contemporary problems. We celebrate the successes of certain eras and try to recreate them, but are silent to the darker pages of the same era.

But Christian political obedience is not formulaic. David's era was a time of war and consolidating the nation's security. Solomon's rule was one of relative peace, stability, and building infrastructure. God called both to be kings but gave them very different tasks. Similarly, we might compare the examples of Joseph and Daniel, whom God called to serve in foreign governments. Each circumstance has its own questions, and the challenge of providing biblically informed answers is not a simple matter of formula.

John Calvin acknowledged different laws for different times and circumstance in the *Institutes*:

> Equity, as it is natural, cannot be the same in all, and therefore ought to be proposed by all laws, according to the nature of the thing enacted. As constitutions have some circumstances on which they partly depend, there is nothing to prevent their diversity, provided they all alike aim at equity as their end.... Hence [the law of God] alone ought to be the aim, the rule, and the end of all laws. Wherever laws are formed after this rule, directed to this aim, and restricted to this end, there is no reason why they should be disapproved by us, however much they may differ from the Jewish law, or from each other.[8]

Even on such basic issues as laws regarding murder and theft, Calvin made clear that "the Lord did not deliver [laws regarding murder]

---

8. John Calvin, *Institutes of the Christian Religion*, trans. Henry Beveridge (Grand Rapids: Eerdmans, 1981), 4.20.16.

by the hand of Moses to be promulgated in all countries, and to be everywhere enforced; but having taken the Jewish nation under his special care, patronage, and guardianship, he was pleased to be specially its legislator, and as became a wise legislator, he had special regard to it in enacting laws."[9]

An essential prerequisite for political obedience is to wisely discern the times. This is not a plea for historical illiteracy and short-term thinking—quite the opposite! Political obedience in our day requires learning history's lessons, both positive and negative. Not only does this provide a wiser approach to the immediate issues confronting us, but it also provides a stabilizing perspective. Short-term approaches exaggerate the importance of immediate campaigns and issues, making our political engagement an emotional roller-coaster ride; they expect too much of any realized success while prone to despair at every failure. For North American Christians living at the beginning of the twenty-first century, there are significant factors to consider. We are transitioning from a society that lived with Constantinian assumptions to a post-Constantinian age. While Christians often discuss and observe this fact with laments about the loss of our Christian heritage, we do not frequently consider the import of this for the public square.

We need to come to grips with the reality that the church suffers a plausibility crisis in society.[10] Many neighbors question the effectiveness of our witness and the distinctiveness of our lives. Apart from certain religious practices (which pluralist generosity is prepared to grant us—"if it works for you"), most North Americans do not see individual Christians as being that different from the rest of society. We pursue our materialistic appetites, career ambitions, and vacations in a way that makes us fit in quite well. They see churches that resemble social clubs: eager to protect our rights, keep the nosy eyes of state and media out of our affairs, and serve the needs of our own members. Already in 1965, Canadian author Pierre Berton—hardly a leading defender for the importance of the church's prophetic voice—observed, "Christianity has, in the past, always been at its

9. Calvin, *Institutes*, 4.20.16.

10. Ray Pennings, "Public Religion in a Privatized Society: The Role of Christianity in Secular Society," delivered on May 4, 2010, Ottawa, Canada. Audio available at http://www.arpacanada.ca/index.php/bookstore/arpa-audio-mp3/973-update-on-ottawa-meetingsevents.

most vigorous when it has been in a state of tension with the society around it. That is no longer the case.... In the great issues of our time, the voice of the Church, when it has been heard at all, has been weak, tardy, equivocal, and irrelevant."[11]

I fear that Christian churches in North America bear a significant responsibility for the church's public irrelevance. We have catered to a religious consumerism, serving up what our congregants are looking for as we compete with other churches for our share of the religious market, often at the expense of our prophetic witness. We have raised the walls and tried to hide our dirty laundry, arguing that what was happening within the church was a matter of private concern. Instead of admitting that it should be no surprise that the church has to deal with adulterers, tax evaders, and sex abusers—the gospel is for sinners, after all—we have tried to hide the facts and protect our image. The church should be known for dealing with these matters in a way that shows mercy and justice coming together. Those outside of the church should be able to look at the church as an example of an institution that deals with difficult matters in a way that deserves emulation.

Lest I be misinterpreted, I am not indicting the entire Christian church as if there are no positive examples. There are clearly many good and wonderful examples. My point is simply this: the North American church, broadly understood, needs to understand that the church's role is not that of a private institution serving her members, but that of a public witness, a light set on a hill providing a witness not only through the gospel she preaches, but also in the way she conducts her affairs. Let us candidly ask ourselves: Can we point to our individual churches as model communities in which people deal with life's difficult issues in a manner that embodies the love, forgiveness, and healing that is to be found in Christ Jesus? The next time a public scandal hits, can we take those involved into our own churches and show them how to biblically respond to such matters? Is that what the church is known for publicly in our day?

---

11. Cited in Pierre Berton in Mark Noll, *Whatever Happened to Christian Canada?* (Vancouver: Regent College Publishing, 2007), 27.

Faithful Politics Requires Understanding That Scripture Has Something to Say to Institutions, Not Just to Individuals

Where do rights and authority come from? This is a significant political question, and we need to make a few basic points. The prevalent view today is a social contract theory in which rights proceed from the individual, and the state has authority through the consent of the governed.[12] The practical implications of this are perhaps best illustrated by a recent statement of Michael Ignatieff, Canada's current Opposition leader. In defense of human rights, Mr. Ignatieff went so far as to argue that rights must always belong to individuals, not groups. The very language of rights "cannot be translated into a non-individualistic, communitarian framework. It presumes moral individualism and is nonsensical outside that assumption." Rights have meaning "only if they can be enforced against institutions like the family, the state, and the church." They function furthermore to defend the autonomy of the individual "against the *oppression* of religion, state, family, and group" (emphasis added).[13]

This modern understanding of rights is very different from Calvin's, who, even the secular academy acknowledges, laid much of the groundwork for the development of human rights in his work as a religious reformer. In his early years in Geneva, Calvin echoed Luther's earlier calls for Christian liberty; he later worked out a much fuller theory of law, religion, and human rights. It was foundational for the ensuing development of Calvinist theories of religious rights.[14] This discussion is important because many Christians are attracted to political movements, on either the political left or right, whose intellectual roots regarding rights owe much more to Rousseau than to Calvin. I have found Abraham Kuyper's concept of sphere sovereignty most helpful in thinking through these issues in an alternative

---

12. The origins of this come from Jean Jacques Rousseau's 1762 treatise *The Social Contract*, a strong influence on the United States' Declaration of Independence. In more recent years, John Rawls's work has been most influential in North American political theory.

13. Cited in David Koyzis, "The Oppressiveness of Civil Society," *Comment Online*, August 20, 2010. Available at http://www.cardus.ca/comment/article/2136/.

14. Cf. John Witte, *The Reformation of Rights: Law, Religion, and Human Rights in Early Modern Calvinism* (Cambridge: Cambridge University Press, 2007). For a helpful review of Witte's book by Greg Bereiter, see http://symposia.library.utoronto.ca/index.php/symposia/article/viewFile/8471/7852 (accessed Jan. 24, 2011).

manner.[15] Kuyper could not attribute to any human institution an absolute authority—not even an absolute temporal authority. To do so, he argued, would be idolatrous. Placing limitations on the government's power was a simple acknowledgment that only God has the right to absolute, sovereign rule. The timeless truth of God's rule was balanced by the organic, unfolding nature of human society. Kuyper thought that human social structures are latent in creation; as a culture develops, its people discover organizational principles and structures to meet developing needs. These structures are not artificial creations; they reflect something about what it means to be human and in society. Each also has a unique purpose, a mission distinct from every other social structure. So business, science, art, and educational institutions derive their authority directly from God Himself rather than from the state or the individual. This perspective can be contrasted with the basic presumptions undergirding mainline political thinking from the left and right of today's political spectrum.

Although Kuyper first presented his sphere sovereignty concept at the opening of the Free University of Amsterdam in 1900,[16] his Stone Lectures, delivered at Princeton in 1898, provide the most convenient English language source for his views. In the third lecture, "Calvinism and Politics," Kuyper pointed out that

> There exists, side by side with this personal sovereignty the sovereignty of *the sphere*. The University exercises scientific dominion; the Academy of fine arts is possessed of art power; the guild exercised a technical dominion; the trades-union rules over labor—and each of these spheres or corporations is conscious of the power of exclusive independent judgment and authoritative action, within its proper sphere of operation. Behind these organic spheres, with intellectual, aesthetical and technical sovereignty, the sphere of the family opens itself, with its right of marriage, domestic peace, education and possession; and in this sphere also the natural head is conscious of

15. This section on sphere sovereignty borrows heavily from Ray Pennings, "Kuyper's Sphere Sovereignty and Modern Economic Institutions," delivered at Baylor University's Christian Economics Conference, April 2001.

16. A "slightly earlier but less developed exposition of Kuyper's idea of sphere sovereignty can be found in *Ons program,* 2nd edition: 20–25." Peter Heslam, *Creating a Christian Worldview: Abraham Kuyper's Lectures on Calvinism* (Grand Rapids: Eerdmans, 1998), 154.

exercising an inherent authority,—not because the government allows it, but because God has imposed it.[17]

Within the sphere sovereignty framework, the sphere of government has a unique place:

> Bound by its own mandate, therefore, the government may neither ignore nor modify nor disrupt the divine mandate, under which these social spheres stand. The sovereignty, by the grace of God, of the government is here set aside and limited, for God's sake, by another sovereignty, which is equally divine in origin. Neither the life of science nor of art, nor of agriculture, nor of industry, nor of commerce, nor of navigation, nor of the family, nor of human relationship may be coerced to suit itself to the grace of the government. The State may never become an octopus, which stifles the whole of life. It must occupy its own place, on its own root, among all the other trees of the forest, and thus it has to honor and maintain every form of life which grows independently in its own sacred autonomy.[18]

Kuyper saw sphere sovereignty as a third way between popular sovereignty and state sovereignty.[19] Does this mean that government has no right of interference in these autonomous spheres of life? Not at all.

> It possesses the threefold right and duty: 1. Whenever different spheres clash, to compel mutual regard for the boundary-lines of each; 2. To defend individuals and the weak ones, in those spheres, against the abuse of power of the rest; and 3. To coerce all together to bear *personal* and *financial* burdens for the maintenance of the natural unity of the State. The decision cannot, however, in these cases, *unilaterally* rest with the magistrate. The Law here has to indicate the rights of each, and the rights of the citizens over their own purses must remain the invincible bulwark against the abuse of power on the part of the government.[20]

---

17. Abraham Kuyper, "Stone Lectures," http://www.kuyper.org/stone/lecture3.html (accessed Jan. 24, 2011).

18. Kuyper, "Stone Lectures."

19. Peter Heslam, "Prophet of the Third Way in Markets and Morality," http://www.acton.org/pub/journal-markets-morality/volume-5-number-1 (accessed Jan. 24, 2011).

20. Kuyper, "Stone Lectures."

There are obvious and controversial questions arising from this that go beyond our present purposes. My point is simple, but needs emphasis. A Christian perspective on political life must be informed by a biblical view of institutions and human rights that is fundamentally different from those views undergirding most secular politics, both on the right and the left. Institutions have a place in the created order; we ought to think about our politics in a way that respects their God-created place, not subsuming them under the state's purview or seeing them as an extension of the individual.

Faith Politics Is Significantly Shaped by a Diaconal Heart

In our day, one cannot go far in public conversation on the interface between politics and faith without facing the accusation that Christians have a subversive agenda motivating their political engagement. While these accusations are generally ahistorical, hypocritical, and impose a narrow, secularist worldview, politically engaged Christians are wise to consider how most winsomely to pursue involvement in this context.

Faithful political involvement ought to be characterized by a love for God. Piety, it has been said, is faith put into flesh. It is in life's brokenness that gospel grace often sparkles most. The Scriptures speak numerous times of our Savior being moved with compassion (Matt. 14:14; 15:32; 20:34; Mark 1:41; 6:34; 8:2; Luke 7:13–15). Giving expression to this compassion is an underemphasized theme in contemporary Christian political involvement.

It has not always been so. We can look at the historical examples of both John Calvin and Abraham Kuyper and see that social issues occupied a significant proportion of their political attention and energies. In Calvin's case, this contrasted with the Roman Catholic view of the office of deacon, where men served as assistant priests in largely sacramental duties. Calvin developed a much more robust understanding of our responsibilities to the poor. In a 1557 letter to churches in Geneva, Calvin wrote, "Let us raise in each member of the Christian community the spiritual problem of his material life, of his goods, of his time, and of his capabilities, at the view of freely putting them at the service of God and his neighbour."[21] But he did not leave it simply to the individual responsibilities of individual

---

21. Cited in David S. Apple, "The Role of the Deacon," 5, Google Docs, http://tinyurl.com/role-of-deacon (accessed May 25, 2011).

believers. Calvin established the *Bourse Francaise*, which provided housing and care for over sixty thousand orphans, the elderly, refugees, and people who were physically or mentally handicapped. Reading the Ecclesiastical Ordinances, one is struck with the detailed regulations and policies that were put into place; it reads like a modern policy manual. Calvin developed a systematic approach to poverty amelioration.[22]

Concern for poverty and its alleviation was one of the defining characteristics of Abraham Kuyper's political career. Although his keynote address to the 1891 Christian Social Congress is usually referenced as his signature pronouncement on the subject,[23] James Bratt observes that Kuyper "deemed the very existence of the social question, the accumulation of titanic wealth, on the one hand, over against hunger and homelessness on the other, as the Church's greatest shame, an open invitation to its enemies, an index of how little the Gospel had been taken to heart. 'How entirely different things would be in Christendom if the preaching of Jesus were also *our* preaching, and if the basic principles of his Kingdom had not been cut off and cast away from our social life by virtue of over-spiritualization.'"[24]

It is difficult simply to transpose political arguments from one era, whether Calvin's or Kuyper's, into another. It is anachronistic to suggest that either of these men would have advocated for or against any specific policy measures that are being debated in our present context. It is fair, however, to make the point that poverty and social issues have not been in the forefront of Christian political activism, especially on the political right, over the past few decades. I understand that a legitimate debate regarding the appropriate role of government in welfare and often-exemplary work led by Christian NGOs and churches mitigates this neglect. Many individuals show generosity to organizations; but in general, with exceptions, conservative Reformed and Presbyterian communities are not known for leadership in dealing with local social issues, neither individually nor corporately.

---

22. Jennine Olsen, cited in David Hall, *Calvin and Commerce: The Transforming Power of Calvinism in Market Economics* (Philadelphia: P&R, 2009), 123.

23. James Bratt, *The Problem of Poverty* (Grand Rapids: Baker, 1991).

24. James Bratt, "Passionate About the Poor: The Social Attitudes of Abraham Kuyper" in *Journal of Markets and Morality*, 5, 1 (Spring 2002). Available online at http://www.acton.org/sites/v4.acton.org/files/pdf/mm-v5n1-bratt.pdf.

Emerging voices within the broader Reformed community are focusing on differing priorities motivating our political engagement, however. Two emphases in particular are receiving increased focus from voices that have been identified with the "young, restless and Reformed" movement:[25] a political philosophy that is rooted in a love response to the challenges of our time and an emphasis on rediscovering transcendence, even in the midst of the mundane.

Albert Mohler Jr. suggests that "love of neighbor for the sake of loving God is a profound political philosophy that strikes a balance between the disobedience of political disengagement and the idolatry of politics as our main priority."[26] As we live in our communities, we are salt and light with a view to bringing our unbelieving neighbor into God's kingdom: "Love of neighbor—grounded in our love for God—requires us to work for good in the City of Man, even as we set as our first priority the preaching of the gospel—the only means of bringing citizens of the City of Man into citizenship of the City of God."[27] Cultural engagement is not only a matter of obedience that brings glory to God—it also serves as a means of pre-evangelism.

It is not surprising that an approach based on love of neighbor finds its priorities set by the issues of the day. Whether the issues are abortion, euthanasia, poverty, civil rights, or the environment, many of the arguments for engagement come in very personal terms proceeding from empathy with the victims. Typically, there are appeals to worldview, reaching back through history to Calvin and Augustine, but the promoted response is primarily diaconal. Ministries of mercy that seek to alleviate human suffering and provide the opportunity for the preached gospel are a common emphasis in this "Neopuritan" literature, which emphasizes affections as well as intellect. "My whole project theologically," John Piper writes, "is to say that God is more God-centered than any other being in the universe, and then to back that up with dozens of texts that say God does everything for his glory. God is most glorified when we're most

---

25. In the chapter "Calvin the Revolutionary," in Joel Beeke and Garry Williams, eds., *Calvin, Theologian and Reformer* (Grand Rapids: Reformation Heritage Books, 2010), Joel Beeke and I describe four categories of current Reformed political voices. The voices I describe here belong to the group labeled "Neopuritans" in that essay.

26. Albert J. Mohler Jr., *Culture Shift: Engaging Current Issues with Timeless Truth* (Colorado Springs: Multnomah, 2008), 4.

27. Mohler, *Culture Shift*, 3.

satisfied in him. Affections are central—not just marginal—and it's okay to be happy in God."[28]

This relates closely to a second theme of Christian social engagement that echos through Neopuritanism—rediscovering the transcendent in the midst of the mundane. Introducing Tullian Tchividjian's recent book *Unfashionable,* Timothy Keller hears "ringing calls to form a distinct, 'thick' Christian counterculture as perhaps the ultimate witness to the presence of the future, the coming of the kingdom."[29] Tchividjian summarizes his case as having less to do with political engagement or evangelistic strategies than with "living with the people we're trying to reach and showing them what human life and community look like when the gospel is believed and embraced."[30] This demonstration comes in two ways: a spiritual courage to reject dominant cultural trends and live "unfashionably," and, second, living as "transplants looking homeward" for a "new, sin-free physical world with new, sin-free physical bodies...new, sin-free job responsibilities and personal relationships" that will be the inheritance of believers. "The world desperately needs the church to be the church, reflecting the kingdom of God so that those who are lost will know where to turn when their own kingdoms begin to collapse."[31]

These voices provide welcome, albeit challenging, considerations to the way most conservative Reformed and Presbyterian communities have done their politics over the past few decades. There is no denying that, as individuals and churches, we tend to be very generous, especially in response to international needs, especially to Christian relief agencies and mission endeavors, as well as to impoverished members of local congregations. However, when it comes to thinking through dealing with these matters in a political and public arena, our record is generally less impressive. In part, it may be that because we have not been sure regarding policy solutions to these matters, we have instead avoided them. However, if we are to embrace the rich legacy of Christian political influence that has helped shape the Western world for good, we ought to address with a new vigor and seriousness

---

28. John Piper, *Desiring God* (Sister, Ore.: Multnomah, 1996), 15.

29. Timothy Keller, foreword to *Unfashionable: Making a Difference in the World by being Different,* by Tullian Tchividjian (Colorado Springs: Multnomah, 2009), xvii.

30. Tchividjian, *Unfashionable,* 112.

31. Tchividjian, *Unfashionable,* 78–79.

the importance of responding to our neighbor's needs. The parable of the good Samaritan has important lessons that we need to take to heart. We have not only the legacy of Calvin and Kuyper, but also of Thomas Chalmers, whose Glasgow parish has long been regarded as a model of dealing with poverty issues, and not only by those who are theologically sympathetic. Men of faith worked through politics to abolish the slave trade; men whose theological commitments to the doctrine of man as God's image-bearer spurred a passion resulting in social and political upheaval for the good.

Translating this into practical steps is not easy and can rightly be the subject of debate. How does a country at war, such as the United States or Canada, deal with tragedies impacting those who may be aiding our enemies? Do we respond the same way to an earthquake in Pakistan as we do to one in Haiti? What about a tragedy that might befall Afghanistan or Iraq? We cannot reduce these complex questions as if they all had simple answers. We must be challenged to think through the implications of our own rich heritage as it deals both through the diaconal ministry of the church and through the political influence available to us. It is fair to say that when the history of our times is written, if the Lord tarries, the church in our day will be more known for her materialism than for her exemplary care for the poor. More important than what it says about our inheritance and legacy is the fact that we might be accused of not living out of and embodying the compassion of Christ that is expected to be dominant in our political engagement.

Faith Politics Understands Its Limits and Its Place

Christ's lordship over all of life means that political obedience is not optional. Taking every thought captive in obedience to Christ (2 Cor. 10:5) includes our political thoughts. However, it would also be historically irresponsible to ignore the mistakes of many who have elevated kingdoms of this world to a point that they neglected the one to come. We are not building an abiding city here, but we seek one to come (Heb. 13:14).

A recent book by James Davison Hunter explicitly challenges the predominant evangelism, politics, and social reform strategies practiced by Christians today as being "fundamentally flawed" and not living up to their "world-changing" promise.[32] Christian witness in our time has been compromised because, Hunter suggests, we have mistakenly thought that changed individuals will change culture, when the truth is that culture more often shapes us. Christians have mistakenly made culture-change an end when, at best, it should be a secondary consequence of our faithful presence in the culture in which we find ourselves.

Few orthodox believers would argue that obedience, not outcomes, ought to be the impetus for our activities. A robust doctrine of creation and providence makes clear that our daily and social activities are not simply things we do as we put in time waiting for the eschaton, but an essential part of our obedience. Nevertheless, a very different analysis of our present predicament implies different prescriptions. Secularists who dismiss any religious talk in public life as "theocratic imposition" rarely notice the diversity within the Christian community regarding these questions. Perhaps the reason they see Christian public involvement as such a threat is because they evaluate it within the naturally human desires of taking over, fighting, and winning. And perhaps the reason secularists think that Christian involvement is a threat is because Christians have often engaged in the public square in a triumphalist manner, more interested in leading than serving. Acknowledging and lamenting misrepresentations of the gospel is a useful and honest exercise.

But that is not a reason to pack up and go home. Even while we admit the imperfections of Christian living in the public square, we can also point to the good works and applied biblical truths that provide a preserving social salt as Jesus described in the Sermon on the Mount. We ought not to hide the gospel and its life-affirming, society-blessing impacts under a bushel. God's Word has social wisdom to offer, and we should share that good news. To not proclaim this is to proclaim a truncated gospel and disobey the injunction to always be ready to give reason of the hope that is in us.

Are we called to change the world? Yes—just as we are called to be holy. We can no more change the world than we can change

---

32. James Davison Hunter, *To Change the World* (New York: Oxford University Press, 2010). This section of the chapter draws on ideas previously published in "Embracing the Paradox" in *Comment*, June 25, 2010. Available online at http://www.cardus.ca/comment/article/2049.

ourselves. But our inability to change ourselves is not an excuse for unholy living, and neither is our inability to change the world a reason to hide in our privatized bushels. It is precisely because our involvement is faith-inspired that a very different calculation than the world's measures the results of our activity. When the benchmarks for our success link our activities with world-changing consequences, we are almost always on the wrong path.

There are many voices in our day—as there were in the days of Calvin and Kuyper—who provide us with insight regarding how to obey our calling to live faithfully. None is entirely right, nor are any entirely wrong. In a culture that challenges Christians to conform to a "no-truth" paradigm, living culturally engaged lives which by our daily postures and practices proclaim that we bow the knee to God's truth is, in itself, a witness. Wisely choosing tactics and approaches requires a discerning wisdom, humble graciousness, and readiness to listen and learn from others. There are no formulaic answers. The existence of paradoxes of kingdom life in a fallen world reminds us daily of our own finitude and the limitations of our influence in the context of God's eternal plans, even for those who have achieved elite status in central political institutions.

We need not answer, but embrace, the paradox. The result will be a posture of humble confession, prayerful dependence, and thankful living. It will also cause us to seek to understand the world in which we live, recognizing that wise and stewardly strategies are more God-honoring than foolish and self-serving ones. But at the end of the day, it is not about changing the world; Christ has already done that work.

D. Martyn Lloyd-Jones argued a generation ago "that a lack of political and social concern on the part of Christians can very definitely alienate people from the Gospel and the Church."[33] Yet Lloyd-Jones was conscious of the imperfections of politics and warned: "The Christian must act as a citizen, and play his part in politics and other matters in order to get the best possible conditions. But we must always remember that politics is 'the art of the possible': and so the Christian must remember as he begins that he can only get the possible. Because he is

---

33. D. Martyn Lloyd-Jones, "The French Revolution and After" in *The Christian and the State in Revolutionary Times* (London: The Westminster Conference, 1975), 106.

a Christian he must work for the best possible and be content with that which is less than fully Christian."[34]

Our political engagement will quickly bring us face to face with the limits of politics. Even our political successes—and they can seem few and far between—amount to little more than proximate justice. The world remains a broken, sinful place, and no political kingdom can soothe the pains or deal with the fundamental questions of the heart. Even as we work in politics, we are reminded of the difference between political justice and God's perfect justice; in Christ righteousness, justice, and mercy are fully reconciled. Politics is a necessary but unsatisfying activity. Serving in politics can not only reveal the glory of the creation and the impact of the Fall, but also the glory of redemption. Paul says that creation is groaning, awaiting its redemption (Rom. 8:22). We, too, look forward to the day when every knee shall bow and every tongue confess that Jesus Christ is Lord. May our witness show something of His glory, even as we seek to serve Him in our day.

---

34. Lloyd-Jones, "The French Revolution and After," 108.

CHAPTER 13

The Daily Challenge of Christ-Centered Living

Ray Pennings

Reflecting on the beauty and glory of Christ often causes an inner tension. Thinking about who Christ is and what He has done prompts a spiritual sweetness and contentment that floods the soul with an inner peace. It sparks a spirit of worship and adoration and invigorates a confidence in my eternal vocation of glorifying Him. Like Peter on the Mount of Transfiguration, I want to stay there.

But I cannot. I am not called to a life of reflection. My vocation beckons. Ordinary life is busy, and only a small portion of my time is free to consciously reflect on these glorious truths. The work I am engaged in requires concentration. Whether it is providing leadership in my home as a husband and father, tending to the files my employer assigns to me, interacting with co-workers and clients, serving as an elder, attending church meetings, and even in the down-time that I need, a conscious engagement with the beauty and glory of Christ and its accompanying spiritual contentment is often elusive.

The focus of this chapter is finding the glory and beauty of Christ in the events of everyday Christian living. This is hardly a new question. In writing to the Galatians, Paul addressed the tension that believers face in their everyday life when he wrote, "I am crucified with Christ: nevertheless I live; yet not I, but Christ liveth in me: and the life which I now live in the flesh I live by the faith of the Son of God, who loved me, and gave himself for me" (Gal. 2:20). Paul is saying that Christ is in me as I live life in the flesh, yet I am still the one who is doing the living, the thinking, the doing. It is not as though, after his conversion, Paul no longer had daily concerns. As William Hendriksen points out, Paul is not advocating a doctrine in which the believer's personality merges with Christ such that only Christ's personality can be said to exist.[1] How we wish sometimes that could be the case! But Paul is still Paul, living life "in the flesh." with all that entails. "I live," he says, "yet not I but Christ lives in me."

Daily Christ-centered living requires us to look not only at the person and work of Christ, but also to see the circumstances of daily life with spiritual eyes. The psalmist of Psalm 111 was able to do so with his Old Testament perspective. He used the Hebrew alphabet to contemplate the *aleph* to *tav*, the A to Z of reasons to praise God, and left us with a work of inspired poetry that ought to similarly prompt hallelujahs of praise from our hearts. Using the reflections of the inspired psalmist as a roadmap, this chapter will explore ten themes related to Christ-centered living that I pray will be of help in sorting through this tension in our daily lives.

Christ-Centered Living Is Rooted in a Strong Ecclesiology

Praise ye the LORD. *I will praise the* LORD *with my whole heart, in the assembly of the upright, and in the congregation.* —Psalm 111:1

John Calvin notes that praise contains two parts: the first, a personal and wholehearted sentiment, and the second, flowing out of the first, public proclamation. To not proclaim the glory of God publicly is to deprive God "of one half of the honor which is due to him."[2]

The communal nature of the Christian life and the importance of public worship are important points to emphasize in our age. North American evangelicalism has been very influenced by the individualism of our times and generally suffers from a confused ecclesiology. Many understand that faith needs to be *personal* but conclude that it can therefore be *private*. They focus on "Jesus and me," what Christ has done in saving me from my sin, and how that impacts how I think about the various problems that come my way. They evaluate a church based on "what I get out of it" and whether "I am being fed," with church membership and sometimes even attendance at worship services seen as matters of personal preference. While these are sweeping generalizations for which there are many exceptions, an underlying individualistic ethos is shaping behavior even in

---

1. William Hendriksen, *New Testament Commentary Exposition of Galatians, Ephesians, Philippians, Colossians, and Philemon* (Grand Rapids: Baker Book House, 2004), 106.

2. John Calvin, *Calvin's Commentaries* (Grand Rapids: Christian Classics Ethereal Library, 1999-11-24, v1.0), Psalm 111:1–4.

conservative Reformed and Presbyterian churches once known for their strong ecclesiology.

The psalmist provides us with a biblical antidote to this sentiment. The psalmist praised God in the congregation with fellow believers. He saw himself as part of a body and did not content himself with private praise, no matter how wholehearted that may have been. He realized that the congregational voice of praise would have been incomplete without his participation. Hence, we find him in his place as part of "the assembly of the upright."

Daily Christ-centered living begins with how we perceive ourselves in Christ. The Scriptures frequently describe the church as the bride of Christ. That requires not only a personal relationship with Christ, but also a relationship with fellow church members as part of the body. Like the body parts described in 1 Corinthians 12, we must see ourselves connected and reliant on each other, just as we need our eyes and ears and nose for a complete sensory experience. Reminding ourselves that we belong to Christ, who is preparing us together for that great wedding feast, provides a very different framework for daily life. We focus on the Bridegroom and His love for and relationship with the bride. We delight in the corporate worship of the church, where the bride expresses her adoration for the Bridegroom and listens to the wise counsel and instruction of her Beloved. We respect the offices of the church as an embodiment of Christ as Prophet, Priest, and King. We experience the joys and sorrows of our fellow believers, even as the Bridegroom Himself is empathetic to their needs.

A biblical ecclesiology is not simply a theoretical matter involving the marks, government, and offices of the church. It changes how we view ourselves. Instead of "me," the focus turns to "we." The believer lives with fellow believers in anticipation of the great wedding feast where the church as a body will live in eternal communion with her Groom, praising Him for what He has done for her.

Christ-Centered Living Flows from an Awareness of the Greatness of God's Work

The works of the LORD are great. —Psalm 111:2a

A bride delights in the accomplishments of her groom. A Christ-centered daily life has open eyes to see God's work around us. God's work is timeless and comprehensive, yet He carries it out in real time and history. There is much to learn about God from carefully observing the everyday stuff around us. Jesus' parables used very ordinary and regular events of life to teach His audience about God and His ways.

When we think about God's work, we typically use the categories of creation, providence, and redemption. Paul, writing to the Colossians, reminds us that "by [Christ] were all things created, that are in heaven, and that are in earth, visible and invisible, whether they be thrones, or dominions, or principalities, or powers; all things were created by him, and for him: and he is before all things, and by him all things consist" (Col. 1:16–17). Although there was completeness in the creation, as "God saw everything that he had made, and behold, it was very good" (Gen. 1:31), that does not mean that God's creative work ended when He placed Adam and Eve in the garden of Eden. The potential that God placed within the creation required unfolding, and that work continues to this day. Every scientific discovery, technological advance, and new birth needs to be understood in light of God's creative power. Translating this matter from theoretical knowledge to our embedded understanding of the events of day-to-day life can be a challenge. But we gain much when we see in the mathematical patterns on which technology relies, as well as the seasonal weather and bird migration patterns, a reflection of a creator God who is a God of order! How many occasions are there to observe the ongoing work of Christ in creation, each of which gives additional reasons to admire and worship Him who is our bridegroom? Calvin writes, "Wherever you cast your eyes, there is no spot in the universe wherein you cannot discern at least some sparks of his glory."[3]

God's work in providence is something that should similarly permeate our thinking. When we hear a sermon on the providence of God, it reminds us to be "patient in adversity, thankful in prosperity, and that in all things, which may hereafter befall us, we place our firm trust in our faithful God and Father, that nothing shall separate us from His love, since all creatures are so in His hand, that without His will they cannot so much as move."[4] In times of distress, we remember this truth, but it is more difficult to make this

---

3. Calvin, *Institutes*, 1.5.1.
4. Heidelberg Catechism, Q & A 28, Lord's Day 10.

the default framework for daily life. History is unfolding as part of the accomplishment of the divine plan. John Wesley is said to have read his daily newspaper because he wanted "to see how God was governing His world."[5]

I have spent most of my adult life working in the public policy field, which requires reading several newspapers a day. Yet, if you could read my mind as I scan the news, you might justly accuse me of being a practical deist. How easy it is to make our confession of God's eternal decrees, the Son's accomplishment of salvation, and the Holy Spirit's work as something invisible, a matter that we talk about in spiritual settings but far removed from day-to-day reality. What does this have to do with an oil spill, currency decline, or the musings of a political figure in the headlines? Isaiah certainly did not observe the events of his time in such a way: "Remember the former things of old: for I am God, and there is none else; I am God, and there is none like me, declaring the end from the beginning, and from ancient times the things that are not yet done, saying, My counsel shall stand, and I will do all my pleasure: calling a ravenous bird from the east, the man that executeth my counsel from a far country: yea, I have spoken it, I will also bring it to pass; I have purposed it, I will also do it" (Isa. 46:9–11). The pronouncements of a foreign king as well as the flight of a bird in his backyard were occasions for Isaiah to reflect on what God was doing, not just in history, but also today.

God's works of creation and providence provide us with many reasons to see our Bridegroom at work in our times and lives, but there is no doubt that the work of redemption is the brightest jewel in His crown. In Psalm 90:12, Moses counsels us to live with the realization that our days are numbered: "So teach us to number our days, that we may apply our hearts unto wisdom." This text is often read at funerals or on New Year's Eve, occasions when the brevity of life comes into focus. However, the instruction for us to count our days is not only given to make us ready for the time when the last number in the sequence is arrived at, but also to focus us on every number. The reason for counting is not simply that we might die well, but also that we might apply our hearts to wisdom while we live. And that wisdom can only be found in Christ Jesus Himself,

---

5. Cited in Warren Wiersbe, *Old Testament: Prophets*, Bible Exposition Commentary, vol. 6 (Colorado Springs: David C. Cook Publisher, 2004), 372.

who "is made unto us wisdom, and righteousness, and sanctification and redemption" (1 Cor. 1:30). How this wisdom was to be accomplished in the divine plan became plain in the fullness of time when Christ came "to redeem them that were under the law, that we might receive the adoption of sons" (Gal. 4:5). Therefore, we must redeem the time: "Wherefore he saith, Awake thou that sleepest, and arise from the dead, and Christ shall give thee light" (Eph. 5:14). This awareness ought to prepare us for the end of time (Heb. 9:27), causing us to live "circumspectly, not as fools, but as wise, redeeming the time, because the days are evil" (Eph. 5:15–16).

It is helpful to categorize God's work into creation, providence, and redemption, and the interconnectedness of these truths also aids in a daily Christ-centered focus. God's work has a single focus, and there is unity in how all of the pieces work together to accomplish His eternal purpose. The story of Jonah illustrates this.

Jonah had a selfish view of God and His works, wanting judgment, not grace, to come to the Ninevites. Through remarkable providences, God used this unwilling prophet as a gospel preacher, providing an amazing deliverance for the Ninevites. Jonah, who thought he had been sent as a preacher of judgment to Nineveh, was upset at God for this. You know the story. God sent a gourd to grow and then die in order to teach Jonah a lesson. "Then said the LORD, Thou hast had pity on the gourd, for the which thou hast not laboured, neither madest it grow; which came up in a night, and perished in a night: and should not I spare Nineveh, that great city, wherein are more than sixscore thousand persons that cannot discern between their right hand and their left hand; and also much cattle?" (Jonah 4:10–11).

Not only were there 120,000 persons whose plight evoked the Lord's mercy, but there were also many cattle! It was partly out of concern for the cattle of Nineveh that God sent a prophet from Joppa to preach the gospel. If it were not in the Scriptures, this point would seem almost irreverent. We see here how creation, providence, and redemption all work together to accomplish the divine plan. When Jonah disobeyed and went the other way, God used a storm, some sailors, and a great fish to humble this wayward servant. He used Jonah's warnings to convict the Ninevite king, causing him to call a national day of repentance. How do all these things fit into the divine plan? The Lord clearly brought His wayward servant Jonah through a humbling journey in grace, and we may believe that he will be among the saints gathered around the throne of the Lamb, declaring through eternity that "salvation is of the Lord." With him will be many Ninevites, brought out of their pagan darkness, having repented before Jehovah God (Luke 11:32). As we know from subsequent biblical and secular history, the city of Nineveh did not continue to serve the Lord. It became the capital of Assyria, whose ungodly king Sennacherib blasphemously taunted Hezekiah and Israel's God; Nineveh was the subject of Nahum's warnings of judgment, and, in 612 BC, it was razed to the ground and became a desolation as was foretold in Zephaniah 2:13.

How much more is going on in the story of Jonah than meets the eye? We cannot see the divine plan and the particulars of how the works of creation, providence, and redemption work together to achieve God's purposes. And what is that purpose? Paul's doxological expression in Philippians provides a valuable perspective here: "And being found in fashion as a man, he humbled himself, and became obedient unto death, even the death of the cross. Wherefore God also hath highly exalted him, and given him a name which is above every name: that at the name of Jesus every knee should bow, of things in heaven, and things in earth, and things under the earth; and that every tongue should confess that Jesus Christ is Lord, to the glory of God the Father" (2:8–11).

God is active in every detail of history. Our challenge is to be conscious of this in the affairs of everyday life. It is not that we can discern the purposes of God's work in our day with absolute certainty. Jonah certainly could not. He thought that God was preparing the Ninevites for destruction, and that was quite alright to his nationalist mindset. God had different purposes in store. Psalm 111:6 tells us that God's people will receive the "heritage of the heathen." When thinking about the comprehensiveness of God's work, we must with Scripture affirm that all the events of history, including disasters, wars, and other judgments, take place within God's rule.

But in the story of Jonah, supported by other passages of Scripture, there is also a caution. On the one hand, we need to affirm the comprehensiveness of God's work, including His work of justice and punishment. Disasters strike as God's judgment on sin. That ought to humble us and motivate us, like the Ninevites, to repent and seek God's mercy. God's judgment is also a perfect work that glorifies Him. At the same time, Jonah's misinterpretation of God's plan provides an important lesson to us. In his self-righteousness, Jonah followed human logic to conclude that, as God's called one, he deserved the comfort of the gourd while the Ninevites deserved God's judgment. But this conclusion was unwarranted. If the application of God's judgment in time were based on human criteria, then all of us would be destroyed. Jesus made this clear to those who asked him about the tragedies of His day. The Galileans killed in the temple and the victims who died in the collapse of the Siloam tower were not greater sinners than those who were spared. These disasters happened as a warning, for "except ye repent, ye shall all likewise perish" (Luke 13:5).

Christ-centered living in our own day requires an ongoing awareness of God's active work in all that happens. We read the newspapers to see what God is doing in the world today. But we recognize that the reason that the hurricane hit New Orleans instead of Boston, the reason that the war is in Iraq instead of Alberta, is not because one place is more believing or deserving than the other. We see God's hand working and warning us all through the events of history, provoking us to admire the greatness of His work manifested in creation, providence, and redemption.

Do we live with this sense of the active work of God in our own age? Would God's people today not live with a richer sense of Christ's nearness and the reality of His beauty and glory in everyday life and be much more conscious of the unfolding of our lives in the context of God's grand purposes of the world in redemptive history if we had a more robust doctrine of creation and providence?

Christ-Centered Living Requires Diligent Focus

...sought out of all them that have pleasure therein. —Psalm 111:2b

The admiration that the bride has for the work of her bridegroom is not passive observation. The psalmist instructs God's people to seek out His work. It is a matter of diligent focus requiring exertion. The believer is interested in the works of God not only because the works themselves are admirable—although that certainly is the case—but also because of their Author. Just as a parent will expend great energy to be present at a child's performance, or a husband will show interest in a matter that he knows is important to his wife, so there is in the relationship between the heavenly Bridegroom and His earthly bride a mutual interest in each other's work.

God's interest in man's work was evident from creation. God created the earth to glorify Himself and gave Adam the assignment of replenishing and subduing the earth (Gen. 1:28). This presumed that he would develop an understanding of botany, develop technology such as shovels to cultivate the ground, and acquire knowledge that was required for successful horticulture. Adam was not created with all of this knowledge; he presumably began learning in his pre-Fall state, just as Jesus Himself in His human nature "increased in wisdom and stature" (Luke 2:52). Scripture does not provide a detailed account of the communication between God and Adam before the Fall, but it seems consistent with the Genesis account to imagine God coming in the cool of the evening to fellowship with Adam and hear something of Adam's wonder at the richness, diversity, and beauty that he had discovered in the creation that day.

The Scriptures also speak of God's interest in the work of His people. "The LORD looketh from heaven; he beholdeth all the sons of men. From the place of his habitation he looketh upon all the inhabitants of the earth. He fashioneth their hearts alike; he considereth all their works" (Ps. 33:13–15). Although our finite minds cannot fully understand how an omniscient God beholds, looks, and considers the works of men, we need not settle that question. What we must, however, learn from this and many other passages is that God is interested in and attentive to our work. He is not passively sitting on the divine throne, indifferent to the affairs that take place in time. In fact, He is more concerned about the details than we ourselves often are: even the very hairs of our head are numbered (Luke 12:7).

Though God is interested in all that takes place on the earth, it is especially true that Jesus has a special interest in the work of His people. We have the comfort of having in the person of Jesus our great High Priest, who was touched with the feelings of our infirmities (Heb. 4:15), who suffered as He carried out His calling, who "learned obedience" through that suffering (Heb. 5:8). He knows and understands our situation, our work, and our calling. There is comfort in this as we deal with the brokenness of life and the effects of the Fall on our toil. But there is also comfort in this in that He knows and delights in the goodness of the work He calls us to do, those elements of the goodness of creation that still can be experienced in the world today.

There is a mutual delight between God and His people in the work that fulfills the divine purpose and plan. As we go about our daily work and tasks, seeking to love God and neighbor, stewarding our gifts in fulfillment of the creation mandate, we can delight that our Savior understands that calling, thankful that what we do with such incompleteness and brokenness He did perfectly in obedience to the divine law.

Christ-Centered Living Understands Life in the Context of History's Purpose

His work is honourable and glorious: and his righteousness endureth for ever. He hath made his wonderful works to be remembered. —Psalm 111:3–4

The picture of Christ as a Bridegroom to His people, the bride, looking forward to the great wedding feast while experiencing love and fellowship, is a powerful one. It draws our attention not only to the details of His work today, but it also places those details in the context of its great purpose. Christ is active today, preparing a place (John 14:2–3) and carrying out His task as the great intercessor (Rom. 8:34) for His people. The church is active today, preaching the gospel so that unbelievers may be brought to faith (Rom. 10:14–15) and live as a preserving salt in this world (Matt. 5:13).

The psalmist speaks of remembering God's works; it is worth noting that, through eternity, God's people will forever be remembering His great work. The book of Revelation presents Jesus as the Lamb, highlighting that His great work of accomplishing salvation for His people will forever be the subject of contemplation for His bride. We will never forget His work or become tired of remembering it.

This perspective helps us put each day and its challenges into perspective. History has a purpose and direction; "all things work together for good to them that love God" (Rom. 8:28)—not that we experience all things as pleasant, but we can know with confidence that they are accomplishing their purpose. When the Scriptures tell us that the sons of Issachar "understood their times" (1 Chron. 12:32), the implication is that they not only understood matters in their larger spiritual perspective, but also that this gave them insight on the practical next steps that they needed to pursue.

Today, many believers are discouraged, and a superficial observation of the place of the church, especially in the Western Hemisphere, makes this understandable. Countries where the gospel once had significant influence seem to be both rejecting the claims of biblical truth and embracing various forms of paganism. But when we view the work of God with a broader lens, we can notice that significant gospel advances are being made in parts of the world where the gospel did not previously have much influence. In the Southern Hemisphere and in parts of Asia, many remarkable stories can be told of the church being added to. God's church and her gathering work continue!

Being conscious of history's unfolding in the context of the divine plan not only encourages us to think in worldwide rather than provincial terms, but it also helps us understand difficult providences. The judgments of God against sin, sometimes reflected in the removal of His candlestick from unfaithful parts of His church, remind us that God is glorified in all of His attributes. Christ-centered living includes an awareness of the judgment of God on sin. God hates sin, and remembering that should foster a zeal for holiness in our own lives. It also reminds us again of our dependence on the active and passive obedience of Christ. It is an amazing truth that each day I can pray confessing my own sin, but also pleading God's covenant promises, boldly knowing that Christ as my Bridegroom takes my sin-filled life, wraps it up in the robes of His perfect righteousness, and presents my work to the Father as if it were a perfect work. He even takes my groanings and translates them into perfect prayers. How our heavenly Husband provides for us! How we ought to contemplate and remember His work always!

Christ-Centered Living Means to Take Comfort from His Gracious Attributes.

...the LORD is gracious and full of compassion. —Psalm 111:4b

As she contemplates the works of her Bridegroom, the bride becomes more aware of what she already knows—her Husband is most compassionate. That was already evident in Jesus' earthly ministry. We are told frequently that He was moved with compassion.

Two truths that may seem obvious and self-evident need to be mentioned here. Forgetting them or not knowing them is a cause, I fear, for much of our lack of Christ-centeredness in daily life. The first truth is this: Christ is a person. How often do we live with an image of God as a force or a power, but not a person with thoughts, emotions, and the capacity for relationship? True, our human understanding of personhood does not adequately capture what the divine personhood consists of. Nonetheless, when the Scriptures speak of the inter-Trinitarian relationship as well as when they describe God's relationship with His people, they give us insight into God's personality.

The second truth is this. Without diminishing any of God's other attributes, the predominant characteristic that shines through is His compassion and graciousness. How different would our lives be if we had a deeper impression of this? Instead of having a faint awareness of Him in the back of our minds as an aloof person in the heavens, we should be filled with a deep acquaintance with Him as a most compassionate and desirable person, someone whom we delight to be with, and whose characteristics earn our admiration and praise.

Christ-Centered Living Is Dependent Living

He hath given meat unto them that fear him: he will ever be mindful of his covenant. —Psalm 111:5

Many of us know a faithful husband whose example, whose provision for his wife, and whose faithfulness to his vows are exemplary. The care of our heavenly Bridegroom for His people far exceeds any human example. David could write, "I have been young, and now am old; yet have I not seen the righteous forsaken, nor his seed begging bread. He is ever merciful, and lendeth, and his seed is blessed" (Ps. 27:25–26). He provides for us and our every need, as a reliable husband and provider would. But His provision is also something that gives increase to His glory. "Whether therefore ye eat, or drink, or whatsoever ye do, do all to the glory of God" (1 Cor. 10:31).

The reliability of God is not simply a matter of practical consequence for His people, but is rooted in His eternal promise and plan. God is merciful, and His heart moves with compassion when He sees His people's need. But His care for His people does not come from a spontaneous response to their need; it is a matter of eternal promise and commitment. We must take care here, recognizing that we only have human and finite categories to describe and try to understand divine considerations. Still, we can say that all of God's works are efficient in accomplishing His purposes. There is an eternal plan that God is carrying out, and His care for His people is a matter of commitment. His people are His people as a matter of covenant promise. The writer to the Hebrews tells us that God swore an oath by the highest authority possible, Himself, which makes His promises most reliable and certain, with Jesus' ascension providing evidence of the integrity of His promise (Heb. 6:16–20). Having begun this work, God is not going to stop halfway. His care for His people is certain and reliable.

Christ-Centered Living Is Aware of His Victory over Sin

He hath shewed his people the power of his works, that he may give them the heritage of the heathen. —Psalm 111:6

The bride of Christ has confidence in Him not only because of what He does for her, but also because of what He does to His enemies. He is all-powerful and mighty, and His victory will be complete, such that every knee will bow and every tongue confess that He is Lord (Phil. 2:10–11). For many, translating this truth into lived, everyday experience is difficult. With Asaph in Psalm 73, it seems that the wicked prosper, and God's children suffer. It requires eyes of faith and entering into the sanctuary of God in order to see this truth as reality (Ps. 73:17). But does that mean that the believer should be praying imprecatory psalms of judgment against God's enemies? How does this square with our calling to evangelize and share the free offer of the gospel with those around us?

The need for balance here is crucially important. We do not see with divine eyes, nor is it our task to climb onto the judgment seat. The overwhelmingly clear message of the Scriptures is one of grace and gospel riches that are to be proclaimed. As long as someone is in the day of grace, proclaim the good news of Jesus Christ, pray the promises, and plead God's mercy. Like the Good Samaritan, we are to have compassion on those who might naturally be considered enemies. I need to recognize that when I seek the destruction of people, it almost always proceeds from a selfish and proud motivation rather than out of righteous and godly thinking. With good reason we should exercise caution and be extremely careful in making judgments regarding the eternal destiny of those around us, even of those who seem to be enemies of the gospel. How many Pauls and Manassehs are there yet to be gathered as part of the bride in God's glorious plan?

But this caution ought not to turn us to the opposite error of ignoring the reality of judgment. When we seek to translate biblical truths into practical worldview terms so that we can deal with the issues of everyday life, we can often ignore the judgment and second coming. This is understandable, given these are not pleasant topics to deal with, but that does not justify a lack of biblical balance. One of the practical ways we might rebalance our perspective on this is to go back to the fourfold distinction that Thomas Boston utilized a few centuries ago.[6] The reason for using the four categories of Creation-Fall-Redemption-Restoration is that it draws our attention to the lines between the categories and forces us to deal with the great event of Christ's separate coming and with the significant biblical data regarding judgment. It provides a reminder of the great change that is coming and helps us avoid the temptation of triumphalism, reminding us of the discontinuity between what we experience in time and what we will experience in eternity.

Christ-Centered Living Cultivates a Tender Conscience

His commandments are sure. They stand fast for ever and ever, and are done in truth and uprightness. —Psalm 111:7–8

The bride of Christ delights not only in His person but also in His ways. The kingdom of God is based on righteousness and truth, something that has been from eternity and will be through eternity. The delight of the three persons of the Trinity in this righteousness provides a basis for their communion. The psalmist speaks the Son's delight in the Father's will, words that the writer to the Hebrews repeats in reference to Christ's finished work. "Many, O LORD my God, are thy wonderful works which thou hast done, and thy thoughts which are to us-ward: they cannot be reckoned up in order unto thee: if I would declare and speak of them, they are more than can be numbered.... Sacrifice and offering thou didst not desire; mine

---

6. Thomas Boston, *Human Nature in Its Fourfold State* (Edinburgh: Banner of Truth, 1964). Boston wrote this book in 1720.

ears hast thou opened: burnt offering and sin offering hast thou not required. Then said I, Lo, I come: in the volume of the book it is written of me, I delight to do thy will, O my God: yea, thy law is within my heart" (Ps. 40:5–8; Heb. 10:5–9).

What a unity there is between the delight of the triune God and the bride of Christ! As the believer grows in grace and knowledge, he grows in love for God's law. There is not only protection and wisdom in the law, but the law also reveals to the believer more and more of the character of the Savior. Christ indeed is made unto us wisdom and righteousness and redemption and sanctification (1 Cor. 1:30).

Christ-Centered Living Is Eschatological in Focus

He sent redemption unto his people: he hath commanded his covenant for ever: holy and reverend is his name. —Psalm 111:9

We have been using the biblical metaphor of Christ as the Bridegroom and the church as His bride. As anyone who has been around a bride before a wedding can attest, a future-focus and optimism naturally accompany this time. The bride looks forward to the time when she will no longer be apart from her groom, and when they will always be together. The bride of Christ is likewise looking forward to living with her Husband forever. The time is coming when she will no longer see in part, but will be with her Groom "face to face" (1 Cor. 13:12). If we are to focus on the beauty and glory of Christ in everyday life, should we not view our present days and experience in an eschatological perspective? The bride of Christ is easily distracted by busy times and events requiring her attention and does not take the necessary time and focus to anticipate her future glory.

Christ-Centered Living Relies on Christ as Our Wisdom

The fear of the LORD is the beginning of wisdom: a good understanding have all they that do his commandments: his praise endureth for ever. —Psalm 111:10

All metaphors have their limitations. Focusing on the relationship between the church as the bride and Jesus Christ as the Groom highlights the intimate relationship of love that can animate our daily lives and help us live Christ-centeredly in our daily responsibilities. But the relationship between the church and her Groom is quite unlike any other marriage relationship that we know. For Christ is not only our Bridegroom; He is also our substitute. The challenge of daily Christ-centered living cannot be undertaken as a matter simply of human effort. Otherwise the preceding observations become a burdensome list of impossible standards that the bride can never live up to. But the psalm concludes with the wonderful comfort that Christ's coming to be wisdom for us provides a confidence both for the present and the future that is rooted outside of ourselves.

"The fear of the Lord is the beginning of wisdom." Our heavenly Husband provides all that we need. We began with Paul's confession of Galatians 2:20 that Christ lives in us, and we live by the faith of the Son of God. We live life in the flesh, but the flesh is so weak. But our heavenly Husband is also our substitute who has finished the work and is making preparations for the wedding; nothing relies on us. Human brides prepare for their wedding; the heavenly Bridegroom is preparing His bride. He has accomplished all, and when we by faith have eyes to see what He has done, we will glory in Him all the more. We read that those who observed Peter and John took note of the fact "that they had been with Jesus" (Acts 4:13). May we live with such an awareness of what Christ has done for us and who He is for us that those around cannot help but take note of Him who is our beloved Bridegroom.

CHRIST'S GLORIOUS EXALTATION

PART 4

CHAPTER 14

The Glory of Christ's Victorious Resurrection

Albert N. Martin

Consider the place of Christ's resurrection in our Lord Jesus' teaching and in apostolic preaching and teaching:

- "Then opened he their understanding, that they might understand the Scriptures, and said unto them, Thus it is written, and thus it behoved Christ to suffer, and to rise from the dead the third day: and that repentance and remission of sins should be preached in his name among all nations, beginning at Jerusalem. And ye are witnesses of these things" (Luke 24:45–48).

- "Wherefore of these men which have companied with us all the time that the Lord Jesus went in and out among us, beginning from the baptism of John, unto that same day that he was taken up from us, must one be ordained to be a witness with us of his resurrection" (Acts 1:21–22).

- "Moreover, brethren, I declare unto you the gospel which I preached unto you, which also ye have received, and wherein you stand; by which also you are saved, if ye keep in memory what I preached unto you, unless ye have believed in vain. For I delivered unto you first of all that which I also received, how that Christ died for our sins according to the scriptures; and that he was buried, and that he rose again the third day according to the scriptures" (1 Cor. 15:1–4).

- "Remember that Jesus Christ of the seed of David was raised from the dead according to my gospel" (2 Tim. 2:8).

- "Blessed be the God and Father of our Lord Jesus Christ, which according to his abundant mercy hath begotten us again unto a lively hope by the resurrection of Jesus Christ from the dead" (1 Peter 1:3).

These texts, set before the reader without any comment, clearly establish the truth that our Lord Jesus Christ's resurrection from the dead is nothing less than foundational. It is a fact woven into the very fabric of the biblical gospel and its doctrine of salvation from sin and its consequences. As we take up the subject of the glory of Christ's victorious resurrection, it is crucial at the outset of our study to identify the two massive presuppositions upon which the entire doctrine of Jesus Christ's resurrection rests.

Presupposition #1—The Fact of the Empty Tomb

All four gospels contain various details concerning the fact that after the Roman soldiers established with certainty that our Lord was truly dead, His body was taken down from the cross. Then, as recorded in John 19:40, it was "wound in the linen clothes with the spices, as the manner of the Jews is to bury." Joseph had that dead body, now bound in linen and spices, carried into a garden where there was a new sepulcher, one in which no man had ever been laid. After laying Jesus' lifeless form on a stone slab within the sepulcher, they rolled a large stone to the mouth of the sepulcher while several women carefully watched this burial procedure.

Matthew 27:62–66 informs us that the day after the burial of Jesus, Pilate capitulated to the Pharisees' request that the entombed body be made more secure by sealing the stone that blocked the sepulcher's entrance and assigning a group of Roman soldiers to stand guard at the tomb.

The gospel accounts, each supplying differing incidences, together affirm that on the first day of the week, various men and women came to the sepulcher, only to find that the large stone that had blocked its entrance was rolled to one side. The angels invited different people to step inside and see that the tomb was empty. When they did, they also saw the Lord Jesus' grave clothes, now lying there like a deflated balloon in the shape of a man's body, indicating that they no longer bound Jesus' body. They also saw the napkin that had been placed on His head,"wrapped together in a place by itself" (John 20:7). As has often been remarked, the stone at the mouth of the sepulcher was rolled to one side, not to let our Lord out of the sepulcher but to allow the witnesses to enter and behold that empty tomb. Some of these eyewitnesses of the empty tomb also heard the unequivocal assertion of the angel that said, "I know that ye seek Jesus, which was crucified. He is not here: for he is risen, as he said" (Matt. 28:5–6).

Presupposition # 2—The Fact of the Manifold Personal Eyewitness Interactions with a Live Jesus

Consider the clear message of the following texts of Scripture.

- "The former treatise have I made, O Theophilus, of all that Jesus began both to do and teach, until the day in which he was taken up, after that he through the Holy Ghost had given commandments unto the apostles whom he had chosen: to whom also he showed himself alive after his passion by many infallible proofs, being seen of them forty days, and speaking of the things pertaining to the kingdom of God" (Acts 1:1–3).

- "And as they thus spake, Jesus himself stood in the midst of them, and saith unto them, Peace be unto you. But they were terrified and affrighted, and supposed that they had seen a spirit. And he said unto them, Why are ye troubled? and why do thoughts arise in your hearts? Behold my hands and my feet, that it is I myself: handle me, and see; for a spirit hath not flesh and bones, as ye see me have. And when he had thus spoken, he showed them his hands and his feet. And while they yet believed not for joy, and wondered, he said unto them, Have ye here any meat? And they gave him a piece of a broiled fish, and of an honeycomb. And he took it, and did eat before them" (Luke 24:36–43).

- "And after eight days again his disciples were within, and Thomas with them: then came Jesus, the doors being shut, and stood in the midst, and said, Peace be unto you. Then saith he to Thomas, Reach hither thy finger, and behold my hands; and reach hither thy hand, and thrust it into my side: and be not faithless, but believing. And Thomas answered and said unto him, My Lord and my God" (John 20:26–28).

- "And that he was seen of Cephas, then of the twelve: after that, he was seen of above five hundred brethren at once; of whom the greater part remain unto this present, but some are fallen asleep. After that, he was seen of James; then of all the apostles. And last of all he was seen of me also, as of one born out of due time" (1 Cor. 15:5–8).

These many individuals and groups of people had images of the risen Christ indelibly stamped on their retinas. They knew they had seen Him alive. Living fingers had touched and handled the living hands and feet of this same Jesus. Sane, rational human beings heard Him speak and conversed with Him as one of their kind. Robert Reymond, commenting on this second presupposition of the convincing testimony of many eyewitnesses, writes,

> Viewed as evidence it is true, of course, that the fact of the empty tomb alone does not prove that Jesus rose from the dead, but it does indicate that something happened to his body. The numerous post-crucifixion appearances of Jesus act to explain what had happened to his body: he had risen from the dead. And the fact that the appearances occurred to individuals, to a pair of disciples, to small groups, and to large assemblies, to women, and to men, in public and in private, at different times of the day, and both in Jerusalem and in Galilee, removes any and all likelihood that these appearances were simply hallucinations. An individual may have a hallucination, but it is highly unlikely that entire groups and large companies of people would have the same hallucination at the same time.[1]

These two presuppositions—the fact of the empty tomb and the manifold eyewitnesses to a living Jesus—constitute the empirically grounded, historically rooted realities that form the foundation of our belief in the bodily resurrection of our Lord Jesus Christ from the dead. As we take up some of the biblical teaching concerning the significance and implications of our Lord's resurrection, we must do so conscious that the Scriptures constantly assume that the significance and implications of the resurrection rest upon a real, empty tomb and a real, living Jesus. All so-called spiritual blessings and experiences of a so-called resurrection that are detached from the historical facts connected with the empty tomb and a seen, touched, heard, once-dead, now-living Jesus, are delusionary. The empty tomb and multiple witnesses are the two foundational presuppositions that must condition all of our thinking of the resurrection.

---

1. Robert Reymond, *A New Systematic Theology of the Christian Faith* (Nashville: Thomas Nelson, 1998), 570.

Seven Aspects of the Glory of Christ's Victorious Resurrection

First of all, Christ's resurrection is glorious as the confirmation of the veracity of His personal claims. Prior to His death upon the cross, our Lord made some utterly stupendous and unique claims relative to His person and mission. He claimed to be God's unique Son. That is, He claimed to be one who shared in the very divine essence (John 5:17–18; 10:30–33). Our Lord also makes such a claim when He says that "no man knoweth the Son, but the Father; neither knoweth any man the Father, save the Son" (Matt. 11:27). Simply stated, our Lord here claims that only deity can comprehend deity.

Our Lord's resurrection from the dead confirms the veracity of this claim to deity. Only one who is essentially God can lay down His life and take it up again of His own volition (John 10:16–17). For this reason, it is His resurrection from the dead that constitutes the crowning "sign" that validates Christ's claims to His unique person as the God-man (see Matt. 12:38–40). John Gill perceptively remarks: "Hereby, [that is, in the resurrection of Christ], is given further proof of his proper deity, and divine Sonship; and, by this it appears, that he is the Lord God Almighty, who could and did raise himself from the dead! This declares him to be the Son of God with power; shows that he is the Lord of all, both of the dead and the living; that he has the keys of hell and death, and can and will unlock the graves of his people, and set them free as he has himself."[2]

The incident recorded in John 20:26–29 is a clear example of how the resurrection validates our Lord's claim to deity. When doubting Thomas confronts the tangible risen Lord, he exclaims, "My Lord, and my God." These were not words of nervous or careless profanity precipitated by a surprising event. Rather, they were the words of a man who came to see Jesus' true identity when Thomas beheld his Lord in His resurrection life and power.

Furthermore, while living and ministering among men prior to His crucifixion, our Lord claimed to be the appointed Judge of the world (John 5:22, 27–29; Matt. 7:21; 25:31). When Joseph of Arimathea and Nicodemus wrapped Jesus' body in grave cloths and placed Him in Joseph's tomb, He did not have much to persuade anyone that He was indeed the appointed Judge of the world who

---

2. John Gill, *A Body of Divinity* (Grand Rapids: Sovereign Grace Publishers, 1971), 414.

would one day sit upon the throne of glory, gathering the nations before Him to determine their eternal destinies. However, the apostle Paul tells us that God now commands "all men everywhere to repent: because he hath appointed a day, in which he will judge the world in righteousness by that man whom he hath ordained; whereof he hath given assurance unto all men, in that he hath raised him from the dead" (Acts 17:30–31). Our Lord Jesus' resurrection from the dead does indeed validate His claim that He is the appointed Judge of the world.

However, not only is our Lord's resurrection glorious in that it constitutes the validation of the veracity of His personal claims, but also, in the second place, Christ's resurrection is glorious as the termination of His state of humiliation. As the eternal Son, the uncreated Word of God who was Himself God, all of God's glory surrounded and attended Him in His pre-incarnate state. Subsequent to His incarnation, our Lord was not unmindful of that previous pre-incarnate glory that had been His. In the prayer recorded in John 17, He prayed, "O Father, glorify thou me with thine own self with the glory which I had with thee before the world was."

However, from the moment of His conception in the womb of the Virgin Mary, He entered upon His state of humiliation. That humiliation involved successively downward steps until it culminated in His death on the cross and burial in Joseph's borrowed tomb. Philippians 2:6–8 contains the record of those downward steps of humiliation; they reach their lowest point when His lifeless body, now bound with linen and spices, lies upon a stone slab in that tomb. Death has conquered. Jesus is dead. This, surely, was the nadir of His poverty and humiliation. The apostle Paul tells us that "he was crucified through weakness" (2 Cor. 13:4a). Yes, the weakness was patent. He was impaled upon that cruel instrument of execution, a cross, until He bowed His head and yielded up His spirit to His Father. However, the weakness is intensified when it issues in His lifeless body being placed in that borrowed tomb.

Mary's womb was the beginning of His humiliation. His exodus from Joseph's tomb marked the beginning of His exaltation. Question 46 of the Westminster Larger Catechism asks, "What was the estate of Christ's humiliation?" The answer, given with beautiful, biblical precision, is this: "The estate of Christ's humiliation was his low condition, wherein he for our sakes, emptying himself of his glory, took upon him the form of a servant, in his conception and birth, life, death, and after his death, till his resurrection." The resurrection constituted nothing less than a radical about-face in the events that constituted our Lord Jesus' redemptive activities. Mary's womb and Joseph's tomb bracket His humiliation. His resurrection was nothing less than the first installment of the Father's answer to our Lord's prayer in John 17:5.

Then, in the third place, Christ's resurrection is glorious as the first step to His formal installation as the messianic King and Lord. As certainly as the resurrection marks the end of His humiliation, that very same event can be viewed in a wholly positive way—it is the beginning of His exaltation. The resurrection is indeed humiliation ended, but exaltation begun. As Philippians 2:5–8 traces the downward steps of our Lord's humiliation, a passage such as Ephesians 1:19–23 traces the upward steps of His exaltation, from the empty tomb to the enthronement and the conferral upon Him of the highest place of power and honor. Breaking into the middle of Paul's prayer on behalf of the Ephesian Christians, we read, "And what is the exceeding greatness of his power to us-ward who believe, according to the working of his mighty power, which he wrought in Christ, when he raised him from the dead, and set him at his own right hand in the heavenly places, far above all principality, and power, and might, and dominion, and every name that is named, not only in this world, but also in that which is to come: and hath put all things under his feet, and gave him to be head over all things to the church."

Our Lord Jesus' resurrection as the first step to His ultimate and formal installation as the messianic King and Lord was a dominant note in the chord of truth sounded by Peter in his Pentecostal sermon. Luke records some of the details of that sermon with these words: "This Jesus hath God raised up, whereof we are all witnesses. Therefore being by the right hand of God exalted, and having received of the Father the promise of the Holy Ghost, he hath shed forth this which you now see and hear. For David is not ascended into the heavens: but he saith himself, the Lord said unto my Lord, sit thou on my right hand, until I make thy foes thy footstool. Therefore let all the house of Israel know assuredly, that God has made that same Jesus, whom ye have crucified, both Lord and Christ" (Acts 2:32–36). He is not made "Lord and Christ" in terms of the constitution of His person and offices. When He was born, the heavenly visitors announced to the shepherds, "Unto you is born this day in the city of David a Saviour, which is Christ the Lord" (Luke 2:11). Rather, Peter announces the fact that the resurrection has led to the formal installation of Jesus as the messianic King and Lord at the right hand of the Father.

It was in the anticipation of this formal installation that our Lord could say what He did concerning the fact that "all power [that is, all authority and the right to rule] is given unto me in heaven and in earth" (Matt. 28:18). This is the New Testament's uniform testimony. Paul writes, "For he must reign, till he hath put all enemies under his feet. The last enemy that shall be destroyed is death" (1 Cor. 15:25–26). The writer to the Hebrews is an additional confirming voice when, speaking of Jesus, he says that He "sat down on the right hand of God; from henceforth expecting till his enemies be made his footstool" (Heb. 10:12–13).

These three things—the confirmation, the termination, and the installation—have primary reference to what the resurrection meant to our Lord Jesus Christ Himself. However, that same mighty triumph over death has many and wonderful implications for us as the people of God, and to those who are outside the pale of God's saving grace. Consider with me then, in the fourth place, that Christ's resurrection is glorious as the divine affirmation of an accomplished redemption.

One of the seven words that our Lord uttered during the agonizing hours upon the cross was the penultimate cry, "It is finished." Most likely, this is the cry that Matthew describes as "when he had cried again with a loud voice..." (Matt. 27:50). This was not a muted cry of despair—"I am finished." Rather, it was the shout of a successful and conquering Savior. The word John uses to capture this cry is a perfect passive tense of the verb *teleo*, which means to bring to an end by completion. When our Lord uttered these words, He was loudly declaring that all that He went to the cross to accomplish was indeed accomplished and would remain accomplished.

But shortly after uttering this cry of triumph, He bowed his head and dismissed His spirit into His Father's hands. Within a short time, that dead and utterly lifeless body will be taken down from the cross, lovingly prepared for burial by Joseph of Arimathea and Nicodemus, and then laid in Joseph's tomb in a garden near the place of a skull where Jesus had been crucified. As they lay the body in that tomb, questions arise in our minds. Was the cry "It is finished" a valid cry? How can it be? The wages of sin is death, and death seems to have had the last word and still holds the upper hand over our Lord. As He was entombed, it appeared that the last enemy had his foot firmly planted on the neck of our Lord's now lifeless body.

Granted, there did seem to be some divine affirmations of the great cosmic implications of the success of His sufferings on the occasion of His death. Scripture informs us that the temple veil was rent from top to bottom, that the earth quaked, that rocks split open, and that local graves yielded up some of their dead. Could these supernatural events constitute the eloquent amen of God to the cry "It is finished"? Yes, they could, but Jesus was still dead, and the question clings to our minds, had the work really been accomplished? Was it really finished?

For several reasons, the Father had decreed that our Lord would lie under the power of death for part of three days. One of those reasons, no doubt, was to underscore the fact that Jesus truly did die. It was to make it evident that He did not swoon on the cross or experience a comatose state to be followed by resuscitation a few hours later.

Yes, death seemed to have spoken the last word. No doubt the fiendish powers of hell clapped their hands with demonic delight. Jesus of Nazareth was dead. Really dead. But, Easter morning comes. The first day of the week arrives, and with it a vacated tomb. And what does that vacated tomb say to us? The answer comes from a text such as Romans 4:25. Paul writes concerning our Lord Jesus that He "was delivered for our offenses, and was raised again for our justification." The words can legitimately be rendered, "and was raised again on account of our justification." In other words, our Lord's resurrection by the Father was the necessary affirmation of an accomplished redemption. All that was necessary to render full preceptual obedience to the law's demands, and to render complete satisfaction of the law's penal sanctions was accomplished in the life and death of Jesus, our representative, surety, and substitute. In other words, the resurrection was God's thundering amen to Jesus' loud cry, "It is finished." Calvin captured and expressed this truth beautifully:

He was put to death for our sins, and raised for our justification—Romans 4:25. This is as if he had said "Sin was taken away by his death, righteousness was revived and restored by his resurrection." For how could he by dying have freed us from death if he himself succumbed to death? How could he have acquired victory for us if he had failed in the struggle? Therefore, we divide the substance of our salvation between Christ's death and resurrection as follows: through his death, sin was wiped out and death extinguished; through his resurrection, righteousness was restored and life raised up, so that—thanks to his resurrection—his death manifested its power and efficacy in us.... So then, let us remember that whenever mention is made of his death alone, we are to understand at the same time what belongs to his resurrection.[3]

Dear child of God, when your conscience seems to be unable to shake off the haunting sense of guilt and condemnation for your sin, go by faith and stand by Joseph's empty tomb and hear your loving heavenly Father say to you, "He was raised again for your justification." Then say to yourself, "I will no longer dishonor the Savior by doubting that His resurrection is God's affirmation of my completed redemption." Has God not said, "That if thou shalt confess with thy mouth the Lord Jesus, and shalt believe in thine heart that God hath raised him from the dead, thou shalt be saved" (Rom. 10:9)?

My unconverted reader, do not complicate what God has made so clear and simple. Stop looking within for signs of grace, hoping that if you find them you will have a warrant to embrace the Savior. No, a living and resurrected Jesus stands before you in the gospel, offering you Himself and the complete salvation that is in Him. Joseph's empty tomb loudly declares that there is a completed and fully sufficient salvation in Christ. Do not look for anything in yourself as the warrant to embrace the Savior and the salvation that is in Him. As the hymn writer says, "All the fitness he requireth, is to feel your need of him."

Consider with me now, in the fifth place, the wonderful fact that Christ's resurrection is glorious as the certification of our future bodily resurrection. The Scriptures give to us as the people of God sufficient information concerning the intermediate state and what

---

3. Calvin, *Institutes*, 2.16.13.

awaits us the moment we die, so that no biblically instructed child of God need fear the approach of the last enemy. Rather, the child of God should face death with the confidence that "to be absent from the body is to be at home with the Lord" (2 Cor. 5:8), and that to die in the Lord is to "depart and to be with Christ, which is far better" (Phil. 1:21–23). It is perfectly legitimate to have fears and apprehensions concerning the act of dying, since it is a totally unfamiliar experience for us. However, to fear the result of dying is not a legitimate Christian fear.

However, nowhere does the Bible say that this blessed experience of being with Christ in the full consciousness of communion with Him in this intermediate state is the Christian's hope. Yes, this anticipation of being with Christ is a Christian's confidence, his longing, and his expectation. But, in biblical language, it is not his hope. Rather, the biblical doctrine of the Christian's hope is that when our Lord Jesus Christ returns bringing the perfected spirits of His own with Him, we shall at that time be given resurrected bodies, fashioned after the body of His glory. That glorification to which we have been predestined in God's loving choice and purpose (Rom. 8:29), that glorification secured by our Lord Jesus' redemptive work (Eph. 5:25–27), that glorification that will be actually effected in us by the Holy Spirit's mighty work (Rom. 8:11) involves our perfected spirits being joined once more to our perfected bodies. Negatively, they will be constituted bodies free from everything connected with the curse that came upon us because of Adam's sin. Positively, they will be bodies endowed with capacities and faculties that will suit us for life in the new heavens and the new earth.

It is this hope to which Paul refers when he writes, "For our conversation [better rendered, our citizenship] is in heaven; from whence also we look for the Saviour, the Lord Jesus Christ: who shall change our vile body [that is, the body of our humiliation] that it may be fashioned like unto his glorious body, according to the working whereby he is able even to subdue all things unto himself" (Phil. 3:20–21). First Corinthians 15:42–44, 51–54 make similar assertions.

Is all of this just wishful thinking on the part of the people of God? No, the Scriptures make it abundantly clear that our Lord Jesus' resurrection is, among other things, God's certification to us that we also shall rise from the dead, even as He rose. First Corinthians 15:20–26 is perhaps the clearest statement of this fact: "But now is Christ risen from the dead and become the first fruits of them that slept.... Christ the first fruits; afterward they that are Christ's at his coming." In His resurrection, Christ is the first fruits, that is, the initial bundle of the sheaves of the harvest of resurrected bodies. However, He is only the first fruits. We constitute the full harvest. As surely as the first fruits in the person of Christ have been gathered, we who remain as the full harvest shall also be gathered. It is for this reason that Paul uses the language of absolute necessity with respect to our resurrected bodies, asserting that "this corruptible must put on incorruption, and this mortal must put on immortality." Because the Head of the body rises and conquers death, all of us who constitute His mystical body must also share in that conquest by rising from the dead.

But there is even more. In the sixth place, Christ's resurrection is glorious because it leads to His initiation into a new phase of His high priestly ministry of intercession and advocacy for His people. This implication of the resurrection of Christ opens up a very rich vein of biblical truth.

The Shorter Catechism (Q. 23) asks, "What offices does Christ execute as our Redeemer?" The answer given is that "Christ, as our Redeemer, executes the offices of a prophet, of a priest, and of a king, both in his estate of humiliation and exaltation." However, subsequent to His resurrection, His ascension, and His session at God's right hand, our Lord enters upon a new phase of His function in all three of these offices. No aspect of this fact is more encouraging and comforting to the people of God than that which applies to His expanded ministry as the sympathetic High Priest, Intercessor, and Advocate of His people. Carefully ponder this truth as it is clearly expressed in Romans 8:34–35a; Hebrews 7:24–25; 1 John 2:1–2; and Hebrews 9:24. Consider the words of John Owen, who, referring to this high priestly ministry of our Lord Jesus, wrote these words:

> This is a continuance and carrying on of his oblation, for the making out of all the fruits and the effects thereof unto us. This is called his "appearing in the presence of God for us" (Hebrews 9:24); that is, as the [Aaronic] high priest, having offered the great offering for expiation of sin, carried in the blood thereof into the most holy Place, where was the representation of the presence of God, so to perfect the atonement he made for himself and the people; so the Lord Christ, having offered himself as

a sweet-smelling sacrifice to God, being sprinkled with his own blood, appears in the presence of God, as it were to mind [God] of the engagement made to him, for the redemption of sinners by his blood, and making out of the good things to them which were procured thereby. And so this appearance of his has an influence into purchased grace, inasmuch as thereby he puts in his claim for it in our behalf.[4]

The seventh and final aspect of the glory connected with Christ's resurrection is found in the fact that Christ's resurrection is glorious in establishing the configuration of all true and saving religion. There are certain foundational truths that the Scriptures clearly reveal. We who preach must seek to be as equally clear in our proclamation of those foundational truths as the Bible is in setting them before us. One such truth is that the salvation of guilty, spiritually dead, blind, impotent, self-absorbed, rebellious, hell-deserving sinners rests down upon the foundation of the completely objective, external, once-for-all redemptive activity of our Lord Jesus Christ as the representative, surety, and substitute for His people. We must thunder forth this glorious truth that salvation in all of its marvelous facets is to be found in Christ and in Christ alone. It is a salvation not of "do," but of "done." Furthermore, we must articulate with the greatest clarity that this salvation is to be received by faith and by faith alone. Yes, we must preach that saving faith will always be accompanied by true repentance and issue in a life of good works. But neither repentance nor our good works are the soul's appropriating acts. That is reserved for faith alone. Surely, this foundational truth is affirmed by the apostle with the words of 1 Corinthians 3:11: "For other foundation can no man lay than that which is laid, which is Jesus Christ."

However, the Scriptures are equally clear, and our preaching should make equally clear another foundational truth: in the application of this objectively provided salvation in Christ, His death as sin, for sin, and to sin and His subsequent resurrection to newness of life, established the configuration of all saving experience of the salvation procured in His redemptive activities. In other words, all

---

4. John Owen, *The Works of John Owen* (London: The Banner of Truth Trust, 1966), 168. If you desire to explore this truth further, I cannot recommend too highly the sermon by John Murray, found in volume 1 of his *Collected Writings*, entitled "The Heavenly, Priestly Activity of Christ." It is full of soul-ravishing truth. Also, if you have not done so already, read Joel Beeke's essay in chapter 10 of this book.

who receive salvation by faith alone, in virtue of their faith union with Christ, receive that salvation in a way that is configured precisely according to the pattern of its procurement in Christ. Did Jesus die for sin and to sin and rise from the dead to newness of life in order to secure our salvation? The Scriptures affirm that when we become partakers of that salvation by faith and union with Christ, we die with Him. We die both to sin's condemning power and to its tyrannical dominion and bondage. This is the explicit teaching of Romans 6:1–14. Furthermore, when we are personally united to Christ by faith and the indwelling of the Holy Spirit, we then rise with our Lord Jesus into newness of liberated life. This new life is a life no longer lived unto ourselves, but unto Him who for our sakes died and rose again (2 Cor. 5:15; Eph. 2:5–6; Col. 2:20).

In other words, a crucified and risen Christ who has procured our redemption by His death and resurrection through the ministry of the Holy Spirit produces a crucified and risen community of followers. In powerfully applying Christ's salvation to God's elect, the Holy Spirit unites men and women to Christ. In virtue of that union with Him, they die to sin's dominion and slavery, rising to newness of life lived unto God in loving and grateful response to the saving mercy received from the crucified and risen Christ.

If your professed experience of God's salvation in Jesus Christ is not configured by His death and resurrection, you have no biblical grounds to call yourself a true Christian. The scriptural witness is clear. "Therefore if any man be in Christ, he is a new creature: old things are passed away; behold, all things are become new" (2 Cor. 5:17). The crucifixion and resurrection shape that new life possessed in Jesus Christ. The apostle Paul's testimony is not unique. Every true child of God can say with Paul that "I am crucified with Christ: nevertheless I live; yet not I, but Christ liveth in me: and the life which I now live in the flesh I live by the faith of the Son of God, who loved me, and gave himself for me" (Gal. 2:20).

Conclusion

In seeking to set before you the glory of Christ's victorious resurrection, I have identified the two foundational presuppositions that undergird all the biblical teaching concerning the resurrection of our Lord Jesus Christ. Building upon the foundation of those two presuppositions, I have set before you seven propositions that capture some of the biblical teaching concerning those things that make our Lord's resurrection a most glorious reality. May the contemplation and believing grasp of these wonderful truths cause you to say, "Thanks be unto God for his unspeakable gift" (2 Cor. 9:15).

CHAPTER 15

The Investiture of the Lamb

James Grier

The book of Revelation is different from any other New Testament book. The first thing that is striking about the book is its amazing imagery and powerful, evocative effect on the reader. The second is that it is an apocalyptic book that is also prophetic. Chapter 1 says that a person who reads and retains this book's prophecy will be blessed (v. 3).

But the book of Revelation is also a circular letter. It is written to seven churches in Asia. If you travelled to each of these seven churches in geographical sequence, you would form a pretty even circle.

Revelation is not a book that answers a lot of questions. It seems to have mixed metaphors all through it and is a little difficult to read. Frankly, the best way to take it in is by beginning at chapter 1 and reading straight through chapter 22. Stopping to ask questions kills our understanding of this book. So does too much organizing. We sometimes think that because the book is prophetic, we should take a ruler and chart and lay out all the events in the book in order. John had no such intent with Revelation. He uses no predictable order, and the images he uses are very different from the ones to which we are accustomed.

I would recommend that you just sit down and read the entire book every day for thirty days. Do not ask questions: do not ask how a lamb can go to a throne and take a scroll (an interesting question because lambs do not have hands). But when you think about it, the purpose of Revelation is not to answer such questions. Rather, its purpose is to inundate us with the most powerful images imaginable. Its purpose is to overpower our imagination with the vision John received from God, through Christ, then passed on to the seven churches of Asia to encourage them, teach them, and warn them of the perils they faced.

The Condition of the Seven Churches

You cannot interpret Revelation without understanding the situation of the seven churches in Asia. These churches were going through some dramatic changes. The Roman Senate had appointed a new Caesar, Domitian, to rule over the Roman Empire. This new Caesar was very impressed with two of his predecessors, Julius Caesar and Caesar Augustus, who said Caesar was a god and should be worshiped. Domitian considered himself to be a god. He persuaded the Roman Senate to pass a piece of legislation that said, "You are free to worship whatever gods you wish to worship in the Roman Empire, but now you must add the worship of Caesar to the worship of your gods."

The apostle John said, "No, thank you." The seven churches of Asia said, "No, thank you." With that profession, their political situation dramatically changed. Up to this point, Christians had been well received; they had been part of the social and economic structure of the cities in which they existed. But now, because of the new Caesar, they would be disenfranchised economically and socially. They would suffer intense persecution because of their refusal to bow to Caesar as a god. In light of that, the Lord Jesus appeared to John on the Isle of Patmos, where the apostle was imprisoned, and gave him a message to pass on to the seven churches.

The First Vision

Revelation 4 shows us heaven's throne room. John begins this chapter by saying that he saw a door opening in heaven. An angel with a trumpet-like voice then said to John, "Come up hither, and I will shew thee things which must be hereafter." John, "in the spirit," saw a throne in the throne room, and on that throne a person.

John saw the throne of God, the *axis mundi*, the true center of the universe. He was so overwhelmed by what he saw that he was initially unable to describe it. He initially compared the seated sovereign to a jasper stone, which is so translucent that light may pass through it and be refracted into the full spectrum of the rainbow. But when John looked again, he said that He was like a carnelian